T0148911

Essays in French Colonial History:
Proceedings of the 21st Annual Meeting
of The French Colonial Historical Society

Essays in French Colonial History:
Proceedings of the 21st Annual Meeting
of The French Colonial Historical Society

A. J. B. JOHNSTON, EDITOR

MICHIGAN STATE UNIVERSITY PRESS

East Lansing

All Michigan State University Press books are produced on
paper which meets the requirements of American National
Standard of Information Sciences Permanence of paper for
printed materials ANSI Z39.48-1984.

Michigan State University Press
East Lansing, Michigan 48823-5202

02 01 00 99 98 97 1 2 3 4 5 6 7 8 9

Library of Congress Cataloging-in-Publication Data

French Colonial Historical Society. Meeting (21st: Sydney, N.S.W.
and Louisbourg, N.S.: 1995)
    Essays in French colonial history / A. J. B. Johnston, editor
    p.   cm.
    Includes bibliographical references.
    ISBN 0-87013-419-1 (alk. paper)
1. New Frnce—History—Congresses. 2. France—Colonies —
America—History—congresses. 3. French—North America —
History—Congresses. I. Johnston, A. J. B. (Andrew John Bayly)
II. Title.
F1030.F9   1995
970'.00441—dc21   97-9890

Contents

Preface

French Colonial history is a vast topic, or rather, topics. It covers the period from the first voyages of exploration through to the establishment of full-fledged colonies down to the era of de-colonization. It is a term that can refer to distinct time periods, and to areas around the world, wherever the French settled and administered, or tried to.

One of the best features of the annual meetings of the French Colonial Historical Society is that they attempt to cover this great range of topics. A mix of established experts and young scholars typically offer papers on a multitude of subjects that touch on several continents and cover a timespan of nearly five centuries.

The twenty-first annual meeting, held in Sydney and Louisbourg (Nova Scotia) was no exception. There were approximately sixty papers given in the twenty-five sessions, and the attendance topped 120 people. The social and cultural needs of the many French Colonial specialists were met in various ways: with Acadian music and cuisine, a visit to the eithteenth-century *ville fortifiée* of Louisbourg, wine and cheese receptions, and Cape Breton lobster.

Nearly half of the presenters at the 1995 FCHS meeting submitted their papers for consideration for publication. Of those, seventeen essays have made their way into print in this volume. Special thanks are due to the many readers and reviewers for their comments and assessments on the submitted articles.

Beginning with this volume, the *Proceedings of the French Colonial Historical Society* takes on a new look and a new life. This marks the first time that the publication of a selection of essays from an annual FCHS meeting is being handled by the Michigan State University Press. The move to the MSU

Press was welcomed by all FCHS members. It will mean that more potential readers than ever before will be made aware of the French Colonial Historical Society and of the scholarship produced by its members. Anyone interested in attending future conferences of the FCHS, or in receiving its newsletter, is invited to make inquiries through the MSU Press.

As for the collection of essays in your hands, all I can say is «bonne lecture».

A. J. B. JOHNSTON, EDITOR
Fortress of Louisbourg (Nova Scotia)

CHAPTER ONE

Military Outpost or Protestant Refuge: Villegagnon's Expedition to Brazil in 1555

Silvia Castro Shannon

En 1555, le roi de France finance l'établissement d'un avant-poste au Brésil afin de protéger les intérêts commerciaux français. Malheureusement, la colonie de Villegagnon à Rio de Janiero (1555–1560) a souvent été considérée, à tort, comme un simple refuge protestant raté. L'auteur prouve que, bien qu'un important conflit religieux opposait effectivement Villegagnon et les colons protestants envoyés par Calvin, ce bref incident a cependant éclipsé la vraie raison de la fondation de la colonie. Le présent article montre que cette déformation initiale de l'histoire remonte en fait au XVIᵉ siècle. A la lumière des opuscules politiques écrits tant par les Protestants que par les Catholiques, le présent document montre comment, à la veille des guerres de Religion, on a utilisé à des fins politiques en France les événements qui se sont produits au Brésil. Le mythe du refuge protestant est tellement enraciné dans les sources mêmes d'information, que les historiens ont minimisé l'important effort de colonisation entrepris par la France au Brésil.

In 1555, Nicolas Durand de Villegagnon, under the sponsorship of Henry II of France, set sail with 600 men to build a fort and establish a colony at what is today Rio de Janeiro, Brazil. The settlement was known as Fort Coligny. In 1557, Villegagnon was willing to allow the presence of religious dissenters and even welcomed two pastors sent by John Calvin from Geneva. A few months after the arrival of the Genevan contingent, Villegagnon turned on the Calvinists, expelling them from the colony in 1558. When five of the Calvinists returned, he executed three of them by tying their hands behind their backs and throwing them from a rock into the sea. After the seizure of Fort Coligny by the Portuguese in 1560, Villegagnon found little support at court for a new French expedition to the New World. Moreover, internal events in France had led him to become a partisan in the growing confessional dispute between the Catholics and the Calvinists. Villegagnon became a supporter of the House of Lorraine and the Catholic cause in the French Wars of Religion.

The events in Rio de Janeiro occurred during the period just prior to the outbreak of the French Wars of Religion. The colonial venture, the purpose of which was to establish a military presence in Brazil to protect French shipping interests, has been overshadowed by the French Wars of Religion. Historians' perceptions of the expedition to Brazil have been shaped and even distorted by the sixteenth-century writings published in France and Geneva. Influenced by the struggle in France, this literature did not offer any serious discussion of the intent of France in establishing Fort Coligny as a military outpost. Instead, the focus was on the idea that the colony was established as a Protestant refuge. This paper discusses how the historical record of Fort Coligny was shaped by internal events in France in the twenty years following the collapse of colony.

The distortion caused by the Wars of Religion has been an enduring one. Even modern scholars, because of the problem inherent in the sixteenth-century sources themselves, tend to look at the colony in Rio de Janeiro as an effort to establish a religious refuge.[1] Among the factors contributing to the shift in emphasis from military outpost to Protestant refuge are the following: the lack of any continuous record of the colony, the desire of the Calvinists to use the experience in Brazil in Protestant martyrologies, the focus of Villegagnon's writings directed only to the confessional dispute, and the outbreak of the brutal Wars of Religion in France.

Even though historians have persisted in discussing the French colony in Rio de Janeiro as a Protestant refuge or a *champs d'asile*, there can be no doubt that the colony was intended as a military outpost.[2] Villegagnon was chosen for the mission because of his extensive expertise in building military fortifications.[3] The building of the fort was the primary task given to Villegagnon by Henry II. The fort was to protect French ships and merchants and eventually led to a permanent settlement. The funding, the ships and the men were all provided by the Crown. Villegagnon's initial willingness to accept the Genevan workers and pastors was an effort to acquire hardworking, obedient workers to complete the fort. The establishment of a military outpost to help French traders was a royal project kept secret by Henry II to avoid a confrontation over Brazil because of the delicate relationship between France and Spain. For this reason, then, there are few sources in France that state the actual purpose of the colony and the active support Admiral Coligny and the Duke of Guise in the planning of the venture. All that remains are documents granting funds to Villegagnon and access to prisons for getting manpower with no explanation of purpose.[4]

Our understanding of the colony has been skewed by a lack of continuity in the primary sources. André Thevet and Nicolas Barré provide eyewitness accounts of the initial voyage of the French to Rio de Janeiro in late 1555. From February 1556 until the arrival of the Genevan contingent in March 1557, there are no existing sources. Most of the remaining information on the colony covers the period from the arrival of the Calvinists to their departure in 1558. These accounts, written later in France by Villegagnon and the Calvinists themselves, are focused on the confessional dispute that arose in the colony. Since the Calvinists were forced to leave the colony and to live with the Tupinamba Indians from late 1557 until their departure from Brazil in early 1558, they were unaware or uninterested in recording the events in the fort itself. From the time the Calvinists left in 1558 until the collapse of the fort in March 1560, there are no eyewitness accounts in French sources. The fall of the fort to the Portuguese elicited very little mention in French sources.[5]

The seizure of Fort Coligny in Brazil in March 1560, coincided with the conspiracy of Amboise in France. This conspiracy changed the dynamics of French politics as it was the first time French Calvinists used force against the Crown. While the French Calvinists, known from that time on as the Huguenots, would argue that their goal was an attack on the Duke of Guise and his brother, the Cardinal of Lorraine, the fact remained that the royal family was in the besieged castle of Amboise. This armed resistance, or attack, polarized the growing confessional dispute in France.

Returning to France to garner more funds and ships for the colony in Rio de Janeiro, Villegagnon found himself armed and fighting to protect the Crown at Amboise against the Huguenot conspirators. This meant that by the middle of 1560, Villegagnon, who had already incurred the wrath of the Calvinists for his actions in Brazil, had become an active partisan for the Catholic cause and the Guise family. Armed with the religious writings of the Calvinists he had questioned in Brazil, he became engaged in a propaganda campaign to discredit Calvin's religious views, offering even to debate Calvin himself.[6] The factions at court became increasingly divided along religious lines. Shortly after Amboise, Coligny himself openly became the protector of the Huguenots in France. Thus, by the time of the outbreak of the war in 1562, Villegagnon's two patrons at court, the men who had helped his early military career and the enterprise to Brazil, the Admiral Coligny and the Duke of Guise, were the identifiable leaders of the two opposing factions. They had become bitter enemies.

While to historians the two most significant sources on the colony have been the accounts written by Jean Crespin and Jean de Léry, these were not the first accounts to have circulated in France.[7] The first sources were a series of letters or remonstrances written by Calvinist writers to the Crown complaining of the treatment that they received from Villegagnon in Brazil and Villegagnon's own writings defending his actions. Many of these polemical writings, dated as early as 1560, have been preserved, setting the tone that would shift the focus of interest in the colony from a military or colonial expedition to a discussion of the Protestant refuge and Christian theology.[8]

While these records of the colony in Rio de Janeiro are not accurate, their significance needs to be acknowledged. They were printed and circulated both in France and in Geneva. Some were addressed to the Queen Mother, Catherine de Medici, in an effort by both parties to justify their actions in Brazil. Through these documents a reputation was established for Villegagnon and the myth of the Protestant refuge created. This legend became the enduring interpretation and explanation for the expedition to Brazil.

The writings of the Calvinists about their experiences in Brazil, published in 1560–61 had two interrelated objectives. The first was to complain about their treatment at the hands of Villegagnon, who had invited them to take part, then persecuted them, and finally executed three of their brethren. The second was to elicit from Catherine de Medici a sympathetic treatment for the Huguenots in France by defending their religious views from Villegagnon's "misrepresentations" and attacks.

For example, *La Response aux lettres de Nicolas Durand, dict le chevalier de Villegagnon addresée à la Royne mère du Roy (1561)* began with a lengthy ode in which Villegagnon was identified as a villain who invited and welcomed the Calvinists, feigning a desire to establish a Protestant refuge and then, like Polyphemus, martyred innocent guests. He was accused of being a man "who is not of any religion, not a true Christian, nor a papist." Villegagnon was portrayed as a threat to civil society. He was chided directly by the writer:

> You caused the death of those who left their country, their goods, their peace, to follow you, to a strange and barbarous place, to serve you. You took the lives of those who entrusted themselves to your protection. You were the executioner of those who chose you as their father.[9]

This became the prevalent characterization of Villegagnon in sixteenth-century Protestant sources. Modern historians still find themselves debating and responding to this interpretation.

Villegagnon's own writings also had identifiable objectives. First, he sought to establish his Catholic religious credentials by attacking Calvinist doctrines and disavowing responsibility for the offer of refuge to the delegation of fourteen members of the Reformed Church from Geneva. Second, he argued that Calvinist doctrine would undermine the French state by encouraging the same type of sedition he had witnessed in Brazil.[10]

These writings were not historical records, but polemics. In them, the only relevant period of the colony was that brief time in which the Calvinists were present in Brazil. The significance of the fort to French maritime and commercial interests faded even in Villegagnon's writings.[11] The debate about the expedition was of immediate personal relevance to both the Calvinist writers and Villegagnon. For the wider audience, the events in Brazil were part of a large debate on the confessional struggle in France.

After the fall of Fort Coligny, Villegagnon became even more important as a target and subject of Protestant polemics. He was held responsible for the shedding of the blood of three Protestant martyrs. There were also other reasons why Protestant writers might have wished to vilify him. Some Calvinist writers, the pastor Richer among them, tried to diminish Villegagnon by stating that he was not a true member of the French nobility and by refusing to use his title of *chevalier* de Villegagnon. Instead, Richer mocked Villegagnon for his pretensions.[12]

As much as contemporary writers denigrated his importance, we know that Villegagnon was closely connected to the Guise family, the leading Catholic noble family at court. Well received at court, Villegagnon returned to France in possession of documents which contained statements of Calvinist doctrine extracted from the pastor Richer in Brazil. In 1560–61, Huguenots were seeking a hearing from Catherine de Medici to argue their case for toleration. The conversion of France and even of the French Crown to the Reformed Church was still contemplated by them. Villegagnon used Richer's statements to demonstrate to Catherine de Medici and the court the heretical nature of Calvinism. Calvinists, in France and in Geneva, were sensitive about the use of theological assertions made in Brazil to repudiate Calvin. Realizing that he had the means to undermine the Reformed Church, Villegagnon wrote several discourses attacking and refuting the theological doctrines of Calvin by comparing them unfavorably with Catholic doctrine. These theological tracts were lengthy and detailed. The *Response du chevalier de Villegagnon aux Remonstrances faictes à la Royne mère du Roy* (1561) exceeded two hundred pages.[13]

Calvinist authors would protest vehemently that Villegagnon's theological knowledge was so insignificant that he did not merit a serious response. The anonymous author of *L'Estrille de Nicolas Durand, dict le chevalier de Villegagnon*, compared him to various uncultured beasts. Yet the same author who spent considerable time likening Villegagnon to a "*babouin*," nevertheless admitted that a response to his theological attacks on Calvin was needed because they might damage the Reformed Church. This harm might occur because Villegagnon's writings had not only been addressed to the Queen Mother and King, but were published and circulated throughout Europe.[14] Accordingly, Richer and other Protestants in 1560–61 carefully noted and refuted Villegagnon's theological arguments.

The threat Villegagnon posed was not just that he was interpreting Calvinist doctrine for Calvin, but that he was directly linking it to sedition. He accused the Calvinists of having undermined the Fort Coligny colony by refusing to obey him once he banned their preaching. At first, Villegagnon was content with just attacking their religious views and their disloyalty to him. But by 1561, Villegagnon was quite clearly using the example of sedition in Brazil as an indication of what could happen in France if Catherine de Medici allowed toleration.[15]

In the post-Amboise period, the charge of sedition was a great worry for the Calvinists. One of the ways they attempted to refute the charge was to portray Villegagnon as an inhumane monster from whom the Protestants were forced to defend themselves. Thus began the comparison of Villegagnon to Polyphemus. The pastor Richer began his work entitled *La refutation des folles resveries, execrables blasphemes, erreurs et mensonges de Nicolas Durand, qui se nomme Villegagnon* by comparing the military leader to a "cyclopian monster without the eye . . . who turned his wrath and all his weapons against a poor, innocent and helpless man."[16]

The author of *La Response aux lettres de Villegagnon* even wrote that God had sent Villegagnon to live in Brazil where "the most savage men who exist on the earth" could be found so that there could be no doubt that Ville-gagnon's cruelty made him "more barbarous than the barbarians."[17] While in the writings of the Calvinists in 1561, the *sauvages* are definitely seen as *sauvage*, they are already cast as being less so than Villegagnon. The contrast between the cannibals of the New World and the cruelty of Villegagnon is elaborated in *Bref recueil.* The anonymous author defended and excused the cannibals, but could not do the same for Villegagnon: "we have seen and read that the barbarians have killed, sacrificed, and eaten some Portugalois and French, but why? Because by their avarice and unmeasured ambition, they outraged and offended the same barbarians."[18] Villegagnon killed innocent men for their belief in God. This theme of contrasting the *sauvages* of the New World with the *sauvages* of the Old World would find its clearer expression in Lery's *Histoire d'un voyage* published in 1578.[19]

The charge of sedition was also confronted by one of the Calvinist writers who suggested that Isaiah, Jeremiah and Ezekiel would have been seen as seditious by Villegagnon. To further justify the refusal by the members of the Reformed Church to obey Villegagnon in Brazil, the accusation was made that the military leader was himself seditious. He was often called an Anabaptist.[20]

Another possible explanation for the obsession the Calvinist polemical writers had with Villegagnon may be that he provided a relatively safe target. He had been a ruler who had denied religious toleration. At the end of the *Reponse aux lettres de Villegagnon* the anonymous writer states that Ville-gagnon, due to his cruelty, will join the ranks of Nero, Domitian and

Diocletian, who persecuted the true Church.[21] What better way to chide the French Crown for past and present religious persecution than by doing so indirectly. Sixteenth-century pamphlets were extremely adept in making veiled attacks on the religious policy of the monarchy.

By the time Crespin's *Histoire des martyrs* began to circulate in France around 1564, the focus had shifted. Villegagnon and his charges were no longer an immediate threat to the Calvinists at court. Massacres and brutal warfare had become a reality in France. While Villegagnon was still portrayed as the man who had duped the faithful and shed the blood of the first Protestant martyrs in the New World, Protestant martyrologies began to expand. There were other lessons the Calvinists could learn from their experience in Brazil. In *Bref Recueil*, the writer explicitly stated that the tale of the three martyrs in Brazil and the persecution that they had endured was intended to "inspire and comfort the persecuted brethren whether in France or in Flanders or in any community."[22] The focus of the martyrologies became the martyrs and their actions, not the perpetrator. Villegagnon was then important only insofar as he had created the martyrs who were now examples for the faithful.

The Protestant version of the events was already established when Léry's *Histoire d'un voyage* was published in 1578. Léry's first-person narrative was so compelling that it would become the version adopted by the great historians de Thou, La Popelinière, Beza, Lescarbot.[23] The Protestant refuge foiled by Villegagnon would be the story told of the expedition to Brazil. Catholic apologists for Villegagnon would be forced to respond not to the issue of why the colony failed but how the Protestant refuge ended so disastrously.[24]

Villegagnon must bear some of the responsibility for the distortion of the record of the colony. By the time he arrived in France, he was concerned primarily with clearing his name and establishing his Catholic credentials. His writings, which were extensive, cast the events in Brazil exclusively in a religious context, while making no effort to explain the commercial nature of the colony in Rio de Janeiro.

In the late sixteenth century, historians read back into the events in Brazil the conflicts of their own times. Other inaccuracies then became part of the historical record. Since Coligny eventually became the head of the Protestant faction and lost his life in the massacre of St. Bartholomew's Day, sixteenth- and seventeenth-century writers accepted Léry's assertion that Coligny was responsible for the sponsorship of the Protestant refuge. In most of the writings of the polemicists of the first decade after the colony, Coligny's name was absent. Crespin, Richer and other pamphleteers did not mention Coligny's role. Villegagnon was given the credit, or the blame, for the idea. By the end of the century, historians like De Thou also gave Coligny primary responsibility for the colony in Brazil, which they maintained was not a military outpost but a religious colony for Huguenots.[25]

Historians since that time have all, in one fashion or another, given Coligny credit for the idea, or at least support of the concept, of establishing a Protestant refuge in 1555 or 1556. Even modern historians who know that for Coligny to have overtly deceived Henry II in 1555–6 would have been problematic since the extremely cautious Admiral had not yet converted will concede to Coligny an active role in the Protestant refuge.[26]

Just as Coligny's role was magnified as the sixteenth century progressed, so Protestant writers began to blame their bitter enemies, the Guises, for the change in Villegagnon's attitude towards Calvinists in Brazil. In the 1578 edition of *Histoire d'un voyage*, Léry charges that letters from the Guises warned Villegagnon in 1557 to cease giving shelter to the men from Geneva. In the 1580 edition, Léry added the rumor that some in France believed that the whole idea of a refuge was a trap by the Cardinal of Lorraine, Guise's brother, to find out who was sympathetic to the Reform. While most serious writers have dismissed Léry's rumors about the Cardinal of Lorraine, de Thous' accepting the scenario about the letters from the Guises being the turning point for the refuge has, in turn, led to its being accepted without further proof.[27]

Another distortion that emerged in late sixteenth-century sources was the assertion of the need for the refuge because of the imminent civil war in France. This necessity is problematic since no one could have known in 1555–56 that the religious problem in France would lead to a civil war. There was severe persecution, yet the Protestants were not armed and would have been incapable of mounting any serious resistance to the Crown. Still, modern historians, misled by sixteenth-century sources, have not questioned this scenario.[28]

In conclusion, the writings of the Protestant polemicists and of Ville-gagnon were centered on a short period in the life of the colony in Brazil. The first ships arrived in 1555, and for the next two years there were virtually no Protestants at Fort Coligny, which was far from being a Protestant refuge. The evidence suggests that the coming of the fourteen Calvinists from Geneva was an afterthought by Villegagnon, a response to a shortage of labor to build the fort. The colony survived the departure of the men from Geneva in 1558 until the fierce assault by the Portuguese in 1560. The colony was a failure for France and attracted little attention until recently. Renewed interest has emerged from the recent scholarship on André Thevet and Jean de Léry.[29] Yet, in revisiting the French colonial experience, historians must separate the distinct experience of the Calvinists in Brazil from the overall history of the colony, a history still to be written.

NOTES

1. Emphasis on the idea of a refuge can be seen in Frank Lestringant, *Le huguenot et le sauvage* (Paris: Aux Amateurs des Livres, 1990); Jules Delaborde, *Gaspard de Coligny, Amiral de France* (Paris: Sandoz & Fischbacher, 1879), 1:144–8; Junko Shimizu, *Conflict of Loyalties: Politics and Religion in the Career of Gaspard de Coligny, Admiral of France (1510–1572)* (Geneva: Droz, 1970), 25–7; Francisco de Varnhagen, *História Geral do Brasil* (São Paulo: Itatiaia, 1981), 285.

2. Nineteenth-century historian Paul Gaffarel wrote an overview of the French colonial effort in Brazil. The term *champs d'asile* is used in his *Histoire du Brésil français au seizième siècle* (Paris: Maisonneuve, 1878), 214.

3. For his early career, see Arthur Heulhard, *Villegaignon, Roi d'Amerique (1510–1572)* (Paris: 1897).

4. For the task assigned to Villegagnon, see, Jean Crespin, *Histoire des martyrs persecutez et mis à mort pour la verité de l'Evangile* (Paris: 1609), 433–433v; Nicolas Barré, *Copie des quelques lettres sur la navigation du chevalier de Villegaignon . . .* (Paris: 1557) in Henri Ternaux-Compans, *Archives des voyages ou collection d'ancienne relations* (Paris: 1840), 1:102–12. Documents pertaining to the first expedition can be found in Edouard Gosselin, ed., *Documents Authentiques et Inédits pour servir à l'histoire de la Marine Normande et du Commerce Rouennais pendant les XVI et XVII siècles* (Rouen: Boissel, 1876).

5. On the initial voyage to Brazil, see, André Thevet, *Singularitez de la France*

Antarctique, autrement nomme Amerique (Paris: 1557); Nicolas Barré, *Copie des quelques lettres sur la navigation du chevalier de Villegagnon . . . envoyées par un des gens du dict seigneur* (Paris: 1557); Jean de Léry's *Histoire d'un voyage faite au Brésil, outrement dit Amerique*, first published in 1578 (Paris), is the most complete account of the events in the colony for the Protestants. For the fall of the fort, the Portuguese provide the best accounts, for example, see Simao de Vasconcelos, *Chronica da Compania de Jesv no Estado do Rio . . .* (Lisbon: 1663).

6. Nicolas Durand de Villegagnon, *Lettres du chevalier de Villegaignon, sur les Remonstrances, à la Royne mère du Roy, sa souveraine Dame, 10 de Mai, 1561* (Paris: Weschel, 1561).

7. Léry, *Histoire d'un voyage faict en la terre du Brésil*; Jean Crespin, *Histoire des martyrs*. The two earliest accounts of the voyage, Barré's *Copie des quelques lettres* and Thevet's *Singularitez*, are not discussed in this paper since both men were in Brazil only during the initial months of the colony.

8. Among the Protestant writings: Augustin Marlorat, *Remonstrance à la Royne mère*; Pierre Richer, *La refutation des folles reseveries, execrables blasphemes, erreurs et mensonges de Nicolas Durand, qui se nomme Villegagnon, divisée en deux livres* (Paris: 1561); Jean Crespin (?), *Histoire des choses memorables souvenues en la terre du Brésil depuis l'an 1555 jusqu'à l'an 1558* (Geneva: 1561); Anonymous, *Bref recueil de l'affliction et dispersion de l'eglise des fidèles, partie de l'Amerique Australe, ou est contenue sommairement le voyage et navigation faictes par Nicolas de Villegagnon audict pays du Brésil et ce que est advenu* (Paris: 1564); Anonymous, *L'Estrille de Nicolas Durand, dict le chevalier de Villegagnon* (Paris: 1561); Anonymous, *La response aux lettres de Nicolas Durand de Villegagnon addressées à la Royne mère du Roy* (Paris: 1561); Léry, *Histoire d'un voyage*; Jean Crespin, *Histoire des martyrs*.

Villegagnon himself would write: *Les Propositions contensieuses entre le chevalier de Villegagnon et maistre Iehan Calvin concernant la verité de l'Evangile* (Paris: Weschel, 1561); *Lettres du chevalier de Villegagnon aux Remonstrances faites à la Royne mère du Roy, touchant la religion* (Paris: Weschel, 1561); *Response aux libelles d'injures publiez contre le chevalier de Villegagnon* (Paris: Weschel, 1561).

9. *La Response aux lettres de Villegagnon*, n.p. (The abbreviation n.p. will be used for works without pagination in these notes.) While no author claimed authorship of *La Response*, it was probably written by the pastor Pierre Richer.

10. For an example of Villegagnon's use of the events in Brazil to warn Catherine de Medici see, *La Response aux remonstrances*, 5–7; and *Response aux libelles d'injures*.

11. Villegagnon was attached to the memory of the fort. He was incensed when a Calvinist writer suggested that it was his *lascheté* that led to the loss of Fort Coligny. Villegagnon responded in his *Response aux libelles d'injures*, complaining that: "Puis il me reproche mon Fort, lequel dit que i'ay perdu laschement, comme si estant icy, ie le pouvois defendre là y garder des trahisons des faulx Chréstiens de leur secte."

12. Richer, *La refutation*, 3–21, provides a scathing sketch of Villegagnon's early career. He is portrayed as an incompetent whose career was an embarrassment at the French court.

13. Villegagnon studied theology in Paris before embarking on a military career. All of his writings cited in note 8 above contain elements of the theological debate which centered on the Eucharist and on baptism.

14. *L'Estrille*, n.p; *La Response aux lettres de Villegagnon*, n.p.

15. Villegagnon's *Lettres du chevalier* contains an explicit association between heresy and sedition: "qu'ils sont seditieux, apostatz pertubateurs de la paix et tranquilité publique, car le mot latin sedecere & apostat . . . signifie le mesme."

16. Richer, *La refutation*, 3–5. Richer felt especially betrayed by Villegagnon since it was his theological views in Brazil which were used by Villegagnon in France to discredit Calvin.

17. *La Response aux lettres de Villegagnon*, n.p.

18. *Bref recueil*, 11.

19. On the theme of the cannibals v. Europeans in Léry's work, see, Frank Lestringant, *Le huguenot et le sauvage* (Paris: Aux Amateurs des Livres, 1990).

20. *La Response aux lettres de Villegagnon*, n.p.

21. Ibid.

22. *Bref Recueil.*

23. Jacques Auguste de Thou, *Histoire universelle de Jacques Auguste de Thou* (London: 1734); Lancelot de Popelinière, *Les Trois Mondes de le seigneur de la Popelinière* (Paris: L'Huillier, 1582): Theodore de Beze (?), *Histoire écclesiastique des églises reformées au royaume de France* (Anvers, 1580), Marc Lescarbot, *Histoire de la nouvelle France . . .* (1602), (Paris: Tross, 1866).

24. Heulhard's *Villegagnon* is an example of a work dominated by the desire to restore Villegagnon's reputation.The two most recent biographies of Villegagnon, Chermont de Brito, *Villegagnon, rei do Brasil* (Rio de Janeiro: Livraria Francisco Alves, 1985) and Leonce Peillard, *Villegagnon, vice amiral de Bretagne, vice roi du Brésil* (Paris: Perrin, 1991) are still responding to this debate.

25. Jacques Auguste de Thou, *Histoire universelle* (London: 1734), 2:XVI, 648.
26. A number of Coligny's biographers subscribe to this view. Among them, Jules Delaborde, *Coligny*, 2:144–8; Junko Shimizu, *Conflict of Loyalties*, 25.
27. Compare Léry (1578), 87 with the 1580 edition, 77–8. For de Thou, see his *Histoire universelle*, 2:XIV, 651.
28. Paul Gaffarel in his *Histoire du Brésil français*, would write "à ce moment la guerre civile était imminente en France." The statement is not an accurate reflection of the situation in France in 1555 but is based on assertions made in 1561 when the need for refuge became more pressing for members of the Reformed Church.
29. See Frank Lestringant, *André Thevet, cosmographe des derniers Valois* (Geneva: Droz, 1991); *Le huguenot et le sauvage* (Paris: Aux Amateurs des Livres, 1990); and his "Calvinistes et cannibales. Les écrits protestants sur le Brésil (1555–60)" in *Bulletin de la Societé d' Histoire du Protestantisme français* (1980). Janet Whatley has edited an English translation of Léry under the title of *History of a Voyage to a Land known as Brazil, otherwise known as America* . . . (Berkeley: University of California, 1990).

CHAPTER TWO

A Massacre Revised:
Matanzas, 1565

John McGrath

La victoire des Espagnols sur les Français en Floride en 1565 est l'un des événements les moins bien compris de l'histoire coloniale française, en grande partie parce que les historiens se sont surtout fondés sur deux témoignages soi-disant oculaires, donnés par écrit après l'événement par Nicolas Le Challeux et Jacques Le Moyne de Morgues, et qui déforment gravement les faits. Toutes les autres sources d'information, et notamment les documents et les témoignages des vainqueurs espagnols, nous obligent à tirer des conclusions bien différentes, plus particulièrement au sujet du «massacre» des mille Français non armés. Une analyse comparative révèle que les récits des Espagnols se rapprochent davantage de la réalité des faits que les affirmations, dépourvues de tout fondement logistique, faites par Le Challeux et Le Moyne.

In early 1560, the Portuguese captured the French fortress in Brazil that had been established five years earlier. Despite the failure, Gaspard de Coligny, the Admiral of France, initiated a second major colonial enterprise two years later in North America. In September 1565, a Spanish offensive under the command of Pedro Menéndez de Avilés surprised and captured this outpost, known as Fort Caroline. Shortly afterwards, Spanish troops massacred hundreds of French soldiers and sailors who had been cast ashore at Matanzas Inlet by a hurricane. This bloody defeat ended the last major French attempt on the New World until the following century.

As with the case of Brazil, published French accounts of dubious accuracy have hindered our understanding of these events. Two purported eyewitness testimonies, written by Nicolas Le Challeux and Jacques Le Moyne de Morgues, respectively, presented an intentionally distorted version of the Matanzas Inlet massacres that ended this struggle. Their testimonies directly influenced numerous later French historical treatments that have confused writers—even modern scholars—about the final episode of this colonizing attempt.

Before looking at how and why a falsified history came to be accepted, it is necessary to give a brief background of the events that led up to the massacre. In 1562, Coligny had ordered the noted Norman captain Jean Ribault to conduct a reconnaissance of the southeast coast of North America. The small garrison that Ribault left in present-day South Carolina could not be reinforced due to the outbreak of the First War of Religion in France, and it was abandoned.[1] In 1564, a second and larger effort was made near present-day Jacksonville, under the command of René de Laudonnière, who established Fort Caroline. Hunger, Indian attacks, and mutiny threatened the settlement, while expected reinforcements failed to arrive. By the summer of 1565, Laudonnière had decided to evacuate his three hundred colonists.

Unknown to the French at Fort Caroline, two even larger expeditions—one French and one Spanish—were already preparing to sail to Florida. King Philip II of Spain had become concerned over the vulnerability of his returning silver fleets as they passed through the Bahama Channel. In March 1565, he had appointed his most experienced Indies captain, General Pedro Menéndez de Avilés, to lead a large settlement expedition and establish a permanent Spanish base on the east coast of Florida.[2] In the meantime, Coligny assigned Ribault, recently returned from captivity in England, to conduct an overdue relief mission to Fort Caroline. Each commander soon became aware of the other's preparations, and both expeditions were delayed to add armaments and soldiers.

By June, when his two dozen ships finally departed, Menéndez had more than a thousand troops and several hundred civilians under his command. He expected additional ships and soldiers to reinforce his fleet in the Indies. Ribault's seven ships, three of which were heavily armed galleasses, were also ready to sail by the end of June. At departure they carried close to a thousand individuals, probably three-quarters of whom were soldiers. By then the

Spanish had received the ominous news that the French expedition was composed of "all Protestants."[3]

Menéndez had followed the usual Spanish route to the south by way of the Canary Islands, where a severe storm caused him to lose contact with most of his fleet. He arrived in Puerto Rico with only five damaged ships during the second week of August. Meanwhile, Ribault had avoided the storm by sailing further north, and the French fleet reached the Florida coast, a hundred miles south of Fort Caroline, in the middle of August. However, after an inexplicably slow voyage north, Ribault arrived at his destination only on 28 August, literally within hours of the colonists' planned departure.

Menéndez had felt that his best chance of defeating the French was to surprise them by arriving at Fort Caroline ahead of Ribault. Delayed by the storm, he did not feel that he could afford to take extra time to repair his ships, procure supplies, and await the rest of the fleet. Instead, he immediately led four of his remaining ships, plus another vessel, directly to Florida through the uncharted Bahama Islands. They reached Fort Caroline on 4 September, and found that Ribault, because of a misunderstanding of Laudonnière's situation, had not yet unloaded his ships. A night attack on the French fleet failed, and the Spanish fled southwards to seek refuge in the harbor of St. Augustine, twenty-five miles away. Since the two largest Spanish ships had been unable to enter the harbor, they were dispatched toward Havana to avoid capture. This move effectively stranded Menéndez's forces until reinforcements could arrive with badly needed food and other supplies.[4]

Aware of the Spaniards' location, Ribault overruled Laudonnière's objections and took the offensive. With as many as eight hundred soldiers, almost his entire military contingent, aboard six ships, he arrived outside the harbor at St. Augustine on 10 September. After demanding that his outnumbered enemy surrender, Ribault waited an entire day for their reply. As he did so, a hurricane suddenly appeared that swept the entire French fleet away to the south.

Not only did this apparent miracle save the beleaguered Spaniards, but it led Menéndez to correctly conclude that, with Ribault's fleet unable to return north, Fort Caroline would be largely undefended against attack. Thus he ordered most of his soldiers on an overland march north, despite the storm. After a four-day trek through flooded swampland, Spanish troops entered the fort virtually unopposed at dawn on 21 September. According to most accounts, they executed the hundred or so men that they captured, but spared about fifty women and children.[5] A few dozen Frenchmen—including Jacques Le Moyne de Morgues, René Laudonnière, and Nicolas Le Challeux—managed to escape on the remaining French ships. They eventually made their way back to Europe. The later-published accounts of these three men provide ample detail—corroborated by the Spanish accounts—of the capture of Fort Caroline.[6]

Up to this point, the events are clear, since all of the surviving accounts agree on the essential issues surrounding the loss of the fort except for whether the women and children were also executed. What remains in dispute is the fate of the French fleet that Ribault had led to St. Augustine, and in particular, the fate of its sailors and soldiers. There are two separate sets of testimonies regarding what happened after Fort Caroline was captured by the Spaniards. The first is comprised of three Spanish testimonies composed by two officers and the company's chaplain, all of whom were present at, and took part in, the events that they described. Significantly, none of their testimonies was published until the nineteenth century.[7]

In contrast, the "French version" relies upon the published accounts of Le Challeux and Le Moyne, each of whom claimed to present the eyewitness testimony of a different survivor of these massacres. During the next fifty years French writers used first Le Challeux, and later Le Moyne, to publicize these bloody events as a prime example of Spanish savagery. Authors of such note as François de Belleforest, Lancelot Voisin de La Popelinière, and Jacques-August de Thou repeated and even expanded upon this tale well into the following century.[8] In the absence of any contrary published interpretation in Spain or elsewhere, this French account became the standard version of these events and its influence on historians is strong even today. This result is unfortunate, because the so-called "survivors' accounts" they rely upon are intentional fabrications of events, and the historical treatments they inspired are equally false.

Both the original French sources and the resultant narrative histories tell a similar story. They all agree that Menéndez, after enticing hundreds of shipwrecked Frenchmen to surrender by promising them safety, brutally executed almost all of them and then mutilated their bodies. There are three main reasons why this version of the massacres lacks credibility. First, it appears unlikely that the two original accounts were in fact based on the authentic testimonies of two different survivors, as claimed. Second, the French version of events, as it appeared in both the original and later treatments, is both internally inconsistent and logically impossible.

Finally, the unreliability of this French version of events becomes most obvious when one considers the overall European political and religious environment of the late sixteenth century. The conflagrations that typified this era were significantly fueled by an outpouring of printed material made possible by new economies in the publishing industry. For the first time, thousands of copies of books, pamphlets, and broadsides could reach much deeper into the literate sectors of the population, shaping their opinions and inflaming their hatreds. The writers and publishers who perpetuated this version of the French defeat in Florida played essential roles in the anti-Catholic and anti-Spanish propaganda campaigns of this period. While circumstantial, this last factor makes it impossible to consider their tale serious historical evidence.

Le Challeux, a Protestant Norman carpenter who had sailed with Ribault in 1565, was the original creator of the myth. His book *Discours de l'histoire de la Floride* first appeared in May 1566, less than half a year after his return to France. The first section, Book One, contains the author's personal observations of the events up to and including the fall of the fort. In most respects, aside from the question of the executions of women and children, this part of his account is compatible with the other first hand testimonies, both French and Spanish, and there seems no reason to doubt most of its gruesome details.

Le Challeux's second and third books deal with the massacre of unarmed sailors and soldiers, and it is here that fictitious elements have been added. The author asserted that he based Book Two upon what he had learned from a certain "Christofle le breton," who had miraculously escaped from Florida after having been left for dead.[9] It is hardly possible that such an individual could have returned to Europe in time to have his testimony published by the following May. Moreover, there is no corroboration of such a person's existence in any other source, French or Spanish, including Le Challeux's own Book One.

Laudonnière's cartographer, Le Moyne de Morgues, composed a second testimony, published twenty-five years later. Written to accompany a series of his woodcuts appearing in Theodore de Bry's series *America*, Le Moyne's

Brevis Narratio agrees in most respects with Le Challeux's account. It asserts the existence of a different survivor, spared at Menéndez's discretion, who had provided the author with details of the slaughter. Interestingly enough, while Le Challeux's earlier Book Two had listed and described each of the Frenchmen that had been spared, Le Moyne's informant was clearly not among these. Moreover, by way of explanation, Le Moyne provides us with a frankly incredible account of this informant's alleged odyssey through the Americas and Europe before eventually returning to France. As in the case of Le Challeux's supposed informant, the very existence of such a person—never mind the details of his story—must be regarded as unlikely.

Even assuming the existence of these two French "eyewitnesses," the story told by Le Challeux and repeated in its essentials by Le Moyne contains serious flaws. They report that Ribault's ships were all sunk offshore somewhere to the south of St. Augustine; yet, incredibly, all of the men save one, who had drowned, regrouped within a single day under Ribault's command. This entire contingent then marched north along the coast, and were within view of Fort Caroline on 21 September. In other words, in nine days this enormous group, which utterly lacked food and supplies, had marched close to a hundred miles, through a hurricane, without being detected by any of the Spanish and Indian patrols searching for them. Presumably by coincidence, they arrived at their destination the very day that the fort fell to the Spanish attack.

At this point, the Frenchmen supposedly encountered the Spaniards, who informed them that the fort had been captured. After negotiations led to an explicit promise that the French would be treated fairly if they surrendered, Ribault allowed his men to be bound. Almost immediately thereafter, the helpless captives were slaughtered in a single furious massacre, motivated purely by anti-Protestant religious zeal. The total number of French victims was reported by Le Moyne to have been more than eight hundred.

In contrast, the Spanish version is not only based upon more credible witnesses, but also makes considerably more sense. Perhaps our most important source is Menéndez himself, who composed a series of letters as official reports to King Philip. A second source is a more detailed account written by Menéndez's brother-in-law, Gonzalo Solís de Merás, who served as one of the senior Spanish officers in Florida and took a major role in most of the events. His testimony strongly reinforces that of Menéndez, even after discounting some minor exaggerations of the sizes of the respective forces. Also, the Spanish chaplain Mendoza de Grajales provided a third eyewitness testimony, from a different perspective, and his detailed descriptions of certain crucial events greatly substantiate the first two accounts.

Comparing the consistent version of these three witnesses to the French accounts, one finds some striking differences. According to the Spaniards, there were two different massacres, not one, which occurred about two weeks apart. Furthermore, both of these were reported to have taken place to the south of St. Augustine, instead of near Fort Caroline. Additionally, the Spanish accounts indicate that the victims were considerably fewer than the French writers claimed. They reported that there was a total of around two hundred executions in these two episodes. The rest of the Frenchmen, they believed, had either escaped or drowned. Finally, these sources uniformly deny that there were either promises of clemency or mutilations of the victims.

These Spanish accounts also give us a more reasonable explanation of why the executions took place. After capturing Fort Caroline, Menéndez had to divide his forces since he feared an attack against either of the positions he then held, and he remained unaware of the status or location of the French fleet. Returning to St. Augustine on 28 September, Indian scouts informed him that they had sighted a group of Frenchmen stranded on a sandbar a few miles to the south. Taking most of his available troops, who numbered only fifty, he confronted approximately 140 Frenchmen and demanded their surrender. Since the French were unarmed and without food or water, and reportedly in very poor condition, it appears they really had little choice if they were to survive.

Even so, Menéndez remained in a difficult position. His letters indicate that he feared attack by the remainder of the French fleet, which, as far as he could have known, was still at large. The surrendered Frenchmen out-numbered their captors by more than two to one, while Spanish food supplies were dangerously low. After considering his situation, Menéndez ordered his captives executed, with the exception of about two dozen Frenchmen who were either Catholic or who possessed valuable skills.

His report to Philip of 15 October carefully justified this decision. It explained that "to chastise them in this way would serve God Our Lord, as well as Your Majesty," and also emphasized that he had been following direct orders.[10] In fact, during 1562, Philip had told Menéndez that royal policy required him to "execute swift justice" on any Frenchmen encountered in the Indies. Additionally, in March of 1565, Philip had specifically instructed him to "cast out [any non-Spanish settlers] by the best means that seem to you possible."[11] While this order leaves little doubt that Menéndez had express royal permission to summarily execute any captured Frenchmen, one suspects that merely following orders was not a full explanation of his actions. It may well be that religious animosity made the decision easier. Yet it seems clear from both the account of Solís de Merás and the letter of Menéndez that even more important was a practical consideration: if the Spanish commander ordered the prisoners put to death, then his exhausted and undersupplied troops could avoid marching them back to St. Augustine. He was already concerned about having to provide for the women and children captured at Fort Caroline; having to feed and guard additional prisoners would have impossibly strained the capabilities of his still-threatened position.[12]

Both Menéndez and Solís de Merás reported a second encounter in the same area on 12 October.[13] On this occasion, Ribault, leading some two hundred survivors from his grounded flagship *Trinité*, offered to surrender if Menéndez would promise to spare his men. Menéndez refused. As a result, fewer than half of the Frenchmen surrendered while the rest fled into the woods. Though Menéndez then had 150 Spanish troops with him, there was virtually no food left at St. Augustine, since there still had been no reinforcement from Havana. Again, Menéndez chose to execute his prisoners, whose deaths at that point still accounted for only a fraction of the total forces of the French fleet. It is worth noting that on a later occasion, in early November, Menéndez encountered another hundred or so stranded Frenchmen who had regrouped even further south. This time the Spanish commander specifically promised to spare those who surrendered, and he kept his word. Eventually, all or most of these prisoners were repatriated. Additionally, Spanish records indicate that one of Ribault's ships had weathered the storm and was later captured near Puerto Rico. Those on board also avoided execution.[14]

What, then, did happen to Ribault's large attacking force? If we believe the Spanish witnesses, there were around two hundred Frenchmen executed or killed by Menéndez in two separate incidents near Matanzas Inlet. By the end of November, perhaps two hundred others had been captured at sea or on land. The fate of the rest—as many as five hundred men—remains imprecise. A few of them might have evaded capture and perhaps even returned to

Europe. Yet it is probable that the vast majority had been lost at sea before Spanish troops executed the first group of survivors on 28 September.

Le Challeux, however, asserted that only one Frenchman drowned, twenty were spared, and Menéndez's soldiers murdered the rest with fanatical glee in a single enormous blood bath. Quite understandably, he hesitated to publicize the fact that fewer were executed than drowned. For the French victims to become the heroic martyrs that the Calvinist cause required, Le Challeux magnified the extent of Spanish brutality and injected an element of treachery into his tale. His version deflects attention from the more relevant factors in the French defeat: a series of egregious errors in judgment by Ribault, compounded by the unexpected appearance of a hurricane. Later Calvinist and *politique* writers, including Le Moyne, followed Le Challeux's lead by deliberately misrepresenting these events to serve their own political and religious ends. They reduced the incidents at Matanzas Inlet to a moralistic fable, depicting the forces of Calvinist virtue against those of Spanish Catholic evil.

Le Challeux, Le Moyne, and Laudonnière had fortunately escaped the carnage at Fort Caroline, and each had returned to France by early 1566. At this time, although there was still official peace within the realm, there was considerable tension within the French Protestant community. The peace of Amboise, which had been dictated to them in 1563 following their defeat at Dreux, was considered unfairly restrictive. Additionally, French Protestants shared a growing suspicion that Queen Mother Catherine de Medici had entered into a secret agreement with King Philip, her son-in-law, to enforce religious uniformity within her realm. By 1566, the fear of Spanish military intervention in French affairs was appearing quite realistic, due to the threatening movements of Philip's troops along the French eastern frontier on their way to the Netherlands.[15]

In this unsettled environment, Le Challeux published his *Discours de l'histoire de la Floride* in Dieppe. It was republished four times in the same year. Similar writings appeared at about the same time, as Dieppe and other French Atlantic ports protested angrily over the French crown's lack of response to the Florida defeat.[16] In 1567, Gascon nobleman Dominique de Gourgues led a revenge mission to Florida without royal knowledge or approval. The campaign destroyed several newly built Spanish outposts and resulted in hundreds of Spanish deaths.

Following the St. Bartholmew's Day massacres in 1572, French writers, including Belleforest, Chauveton, and La Popelinière, published historical treatments of Florida that all relied exclusively on Le Challeux's testimony.[17] Over the next few years, the output of French literature that attacked Catholic persecution expanded enormously, with the appearance of such inflammatory works as the anonymously published *Le reveille-matin des François et leurs voisins* in 1573. One cannot help regarding these early treatments of the Florida defeat in light of the explosion of polemical publishing during this period of French history.

The later French accounts of this debacle can be placed in a slightly different context, but one that is equally damaging to their credibility. By the end of the 1570s, as the Netherlands conflict deepened and Elizabeth's relations with Philip deteriorated, Protestant publishers throughout Europe adopted a more specifically anti-Spanish focus. The contributions of Chauveton and La Popelinière in particular fit nicely alongside the other exaggerations and fabrications published by Protestants and *politiques* concerning Spanish atrocities in the Netherlands and the New World.[18] The polarization of Europe along religious lines hardened over the next decade, as England braced for war with Spain. In France, the Guise-led emergence of the French Catholic League changed the nature of that conflict. By 1591, when Le Moyne's account finally appeared in print in Frankfurt, France itself was being invaded by Spanish armies allied to the League, while Henri of Navarre, with *politique* support and English armies, battled for recognition as King of France. The European religious divisions of the last quarter of the century were exacerbated by wide-ranging propaganda campaigns from a variety of directions, resulting in both obvious and subtle distortions of contemporary events.

During this period most of the French treatments of the Florida debacle were written either by Protestants, such as Chauveton and La Popelinière, or else by *politique* Catholics such as Belleforest. Yet politico-religious considerations do not completely explain the misrepresentations of these incidents. For example, Thevet, though a staunch Leaguer, was also forced to rely on Le Challeux, simply because there were no other existing sources available for comparison. Thus, although Thevet minimized the religious motives behind the executions, it is not entirely surprising that he followed Le Challeux's other details quite precisely. Even as late as fifty years after the Florida defeat, when de Thou, d'Aubigné, and Lescarbot composed their respective works, evidence remained scarce and one-sided. Of these three later writers, only Lescarbot was even the least bit skeptical of his sources but he could offer no alternative interpretation besides speculation.

As noted, the Spanish sources remained unpublished for centuries. The accounts of Menéndez and Grajales—which were never intended for a wide audience—remained buried in Spanish archives until the nineteenth century. Neither Solís de Merás's chronicle nor a 1568 biography of Menéndez made it into print until relatively modern times.[19] This lack of easily accessible Spanish testimonies, combined with the apparent abundance of sixteenth-century French sources, resulted in unbalanced later historical treatments. However, even after most of the relevant Spanish material became accessible, writers such as Paul Gaffarel and Francis Parkman, among others, disparaged its veracity.[20] It may well be that Gaffarel, a Protestant himself, desired to emphasize the heroic aspects of this French initiative by minimizing Laudonnière's and Ribault's responsibility for the defeat. Parkman, a New England Yankee of distinctly Puritanical leanings, wrote during a period of strong anti-Catholic popular bias caused by the flood of Irish immigrants into America. The corpus of history Parkman left behind reveals a writer with little respect for Catholicism and even less understanding of the Spanish presence in the New World.

Perhaps unduly influenced by Gaffarel and Parkman, or perhaps simply wanting to present French history in as positive a light as possible, modern French and French-Canadian scholars have not significantly altered this basic interpretation. Charles de La Roncière, Charles-André Julien, Marcel Trudel, and Frank Lestringant have either regarded the sixteenth-century French historians as authoritative, or, equally naïvely, accepted Le Challeux's and Le Moyne's publications as genuine eyewitness testimony.[21] The Spanish sources have seldom been given proper attention, and the result is that even modern historical accounts of the final chapter of this colonial defeat have been uniformly vague and confusing.

In the case of the French defeat in Florida, it was not the victors but the victims who wrote the history. French contemporary writers have led succeeding generations to believe that their own countrymen were blameless and innocent, while the Spanish conquerors were barbaric and treacherous. A more accurate interpretation of the Matanzas incidents is both possible and necessary.

NOTES

1. Two accounts of this initial mission were published, by Ribault and his lieutenant René de Laudonnière. The first was entitled *The Whole and True Discoveriye of Terra Florida* (London: Thomas Hacket, 1563), and may have originally been composed in French as a report to Admiral Coligny. Laudonnière composed a three-part history of the entire French attempt between 1562 and 1565, *Histoire notable de la Floride* (Paris: Martin Basanier, 1586). The first part describes the 1562 mission. Both works were republished in English by Richard Hakluyt during the 1580s.

2. The definitive source in English on Menéndez's preparations is Eugene Lyon, *The Enterprise of Florida* (Gainesville Fla.: University Presses of Florida, 1976), especially pages 31–76. Lyon has researched Menéndez's role throughout this conflict and beyond, using the official records, letters, and other documents in Spanish archives, especially those at Seville and Salamanca. An invaluable Spanish source, which reprints many official Spanish documents and correspondence, is Eugenio Ruidiaz y Caravia, *La Florida: Su Conquista y Colonizacíon por Pedro Ménendez de Avilés*, 2 vols. (Madrid: 1843). One can also trace the altered scope of the expedition during that spring in volume 7 of *Archivo Documental Español*, compiled by the Royal Academy of Madrid (reprint Madrid: Real Academia de la Historia, 1960). See especially nos. 1028, 1046, 1047, and 1088, on pages 235–37, 313–14, 315, and 421–23 respectively.

3. There are three main sources of information regarding Ribault's preparations for the 1565 mission. The most detailed is a June 1565 intelligence report, by the Spanish doctor Gabriel de Enveja, that has been reprinted by Antonio Tibesar as "A Spy's Report on the Expedition of Jean Ribault to Florida, 1565," *The Americas* 11, no. 4 (April 1955): 589–92. The information it contains is substantiated by the first book of Nicolas Le Challeux's *Discours de l'histoire de la Floride*, first published in Dieppe by J. LeSellier in May 1566, especially pages 9–14; and detailed weapons manifests for the fleet, "Inventories de l'artillerie de laMarine," April–May 1566, Bibliothèque Nationale, Fonds français 21544, fols. 31–57.

4. On Menéndez's difficult voyage to Florida, there are three detailed accounts:

Menéndez's letters of August 13 and September 11; the chronicle of Gonzalo Solís de Merás, and a memoir by the Spanish chaplain Mendoza de Grajales. Menéndez's letters have been compiled by Martin Navarrete as "Correspondencia de Pedro Menéndez de Avilés," in vol. 2 of *Colección de Diarios y Relations para la Historia de los Viajes et Descubrimientos* (Madrid: Instituto Histórico de Marina, 1943). They have also been translated into English in Horace Ware, ed., "Letters of Pedro Menéndez de Avilés, *Proceedings of the Massachusetts Historical Society,* no. 8, 2d ser. (1894). Solís de Merás's account was originally written in 1567 as *Memorial que hizo Doctor Gonzalo Solís de Merás, de todas las jornadas y sucesos del adelantado Pedro Menéndez de Avilés, su cuñado, y de la conquista de la Florida,* published in Spain for the first time in 1893. It is available in English as *Pedro Menéndez de Avilés, Adelantado, Governor, and Captain-General of Florida,* ed. Jeannette Thurber Connor (Deland, Fla: Florida State Historical Society, 1923; reprint Gainesville Fla: University Presses of Florida, 1964). The testimony of Grajales appears in English translation as "Memoire of a Happy Result," in Charles E. Bennett, *Laudonnière and Fort Caroline* (Gainesville Fla. : University Presses of Florida,1975), 141–63.

5. In comparing the French and Spanish versions of the capture of Fort Caroline, only Le Challeux claimed that the Spanish executed the women and children. Spanish testimonies and records, though, clearly indicate the later logistical problems created by the possession of these prisoners, and we must accept that most and probably all of these most defenseless French settlers were in fact spared, as even Le Moyne's account acknowledges. See Lyon, "Captives of Florida," *Florida Historical Quarterly,* 50, no. 1 (1971): 1–24, as well as the Menéndez and Solís de Merás accounts.

6. In addition to Le Challeux's Book One, these include Laudonnière's third and final section and Le Moyne's *Brevis Narratio eorumquae in Florida Americae provincia Gallis acciderunt . . . quae est Secunda Pars Americae* (Frankfurt: Theodore de Bry, 1591).

7. Menéndez's letter of October 15, 1565 describes the capture of Ft. Caroline, his return to St. Augustine, and the two Matanzas incidents. It stresses throughout the commander's continuing fear of French attack even after the executions. Among this and Solís de Merás's and Grajales's accounts there is significant consistency, especially regarding the timing and location of the executions and the negotiations leading to the French surrender.

8. These accounts include, in chronological order, Belleforest's French edition of

Sebastian Münster's 1555 *La cosmographie universelle* (1575); Andre Thevet's *La cosmographie universelle* (also 1575); Urbain Chauveton's introduction to his translation of Girolamo Benzoni's *Histoire nouvelle du Nouveau Monde* (1578); La Popelinière's *Les trois mondes* (1582); de Thou's *Histoire universelle*, (1609); Marc Lescarbot's *Histoire de la Nouvelle France* (1609); and Agrippa d'Aubigne's *Histoire universelle* (1616).

9. Le Challeux, Book Two, 52.

10. Navarrete, *Viajes et Descubrimientos*, 2:57; Ware, "Letters of Pedro Menéndez," 428.

11. The earlier orders of 1562 reflected the new Spanish policy formulated after the Peace of Cateau-Cambrésis; Menéndez had been directed by Philip to "punish as corsairs" any Frenchmen captured in Florida; see Lyon, *Enterprise of Florida*, 22 n.6. Philip's later instructions are cited in "Capitulations and Asiento between Philip II and Pedro Menéndez de Avilés," 20 March 1565, in David B. Quinn, ed., *New American World: A Documentary History of North America to 1612* (New York: Arno Press and Hector Bye, 1979), no. 308, 2:384.

12. Menéndez's concerns about his ability to handle a large contingent of prisoners are evident from Solís de Merás (Connor edition), 102, and Lyon, *Enterprise of Florida*, 123. In early 1566, Philip himself cited Menéndez's logistical and supply problems to Catherine as the major reason why the commander had acted "a little more rudely and cruelly than his master would have liked." Catherine to Fourquevaux, 17 March 1566, in Hector de La Ferrière, ed. *Lettres de Catherine de Medicis* (Paris: 1885), 2:354.

13. Grajales was not present at this time, and did not report it.

14. Spanish records provide an accounting of the French who were captured between September and November. See Lyon, "Captives of Florida," 1-24; and Lyon, *Enterprise of Florida*, 124 n.41.

15. On the political and diplomatic currents in France at the time, and especially regarding Protestant feelings of betrayal and French fears of Spanish intervention, see J. A. de Thou, *Histoire universelle*, vol. 5, book 37, 33–37; Jules Delaborde, *Gaspard de Coligny, Amiral de France* (Paris, 1882), 2:388–95; James Westfall Thompson, *The Wars of Religion in France, 1559–1576: The Huguenots, Catherine de Medici, Philip II* (New York: Frederick Ungar, 1958), 299–301; Junko Shimizu, *Conflict of Loyalties: Politics and Religion in the Career of Gaspard de Coligny, Admiral of France* (Geneva: Droz, 1970), especially 121–27.

16. These included *Remonstrances très humble en forme d'advertissement des capitaines*

de la marine (La Rochelle, n.p., 1566), which complained about the failure of the crown to react to the earlier defeat in Brazil, and the independent publication of *Une requeste presentée au Roy Charles neufiesme, en forme de complainte* (Dieppe, 1566). The latter was purportedly written by "les femmes vevfes et enfans orphelins" of those who had died in Florida, and this comprised Book Three of Le Challeux's work. See also Louis Vitet, *Histoire de Dieppe* (Paris, 1844), 284–85; Gaffarel, *Floride française au seizième siècle* (Paris, 1875), 242–43.

17. This conclusion is not difficult—indeed it is obvious—for anyone who compares these accounts. Aside from the details of the mutilations of the French bodies, which are reported with variations of artistic license, the sequence and timing of events reported is identical, and often the later authors excerpt (most commonly without citation) phrases and even entire passages from Le Challeux's Books Two and Three.

18. Perhaps the best known of these are William of Orange's *Apologia* (1581) and the re-editions in various languages of Bartolomeo de Las Casas's *Very Brief Account of the Destruction of the Indies*, (usually titled *Tyrannies and Cruelties of the Spaniards Committed in the West Indies*) beginning in 1579.

19. Solís de Merás's account was written in 1567; the following year Bartolomé Barrientos, a professor at the University of Salamanca, composed *Vida y hechos de Pero Menéndez de Avilés*, which relied heavily on the former work.

20. For example, Gaffarel directly rebuts the work of the Spanish writer Andrés Gonzalez de Barcia Carballido y Zuñiga, whose *Ensayo Chronologico para la Historia General de Florida*, published in 1723, is a gross exaggeration of these events from the opposite perspective. Though Gaffarel consulted Menéndez, Grajales, and Solís de Merás about other events, he largely dismisses their contrary descriptions of the massacres. Parkman, in his 1865 *Pioneers of New France*, simply misrepresents the Spanish testimony, such as claiming that Solís de Merás had admitted that Menéndez broke a promise of clemency, when in fact that author had specifically stated the contrary.

21. These treatments include La Roncière's *Histoire de la marine française*, vol. 4 (Paris: Librairie Plon, 1909–1932); Julien's *Les voyages de découverte et les premiers établissements* (Paris: Gérard Montfort, 1948); Volume 1 of Trudel, *Histoire de la Nouvelle France*, entitled *Les vaines tentatives* (Montréal: Fides, 1963); and Lestringant, *Le huguenot et le sauvage* (Paris: Aux Amateurs des Livres, 1990).

CHAPTER THREE

Victor Hugues and the Reign of Terror on Guadeloupe, 1794–1798

William S. Cormack

Victor Hugues fut agent de la France révolutionnaire en Guadeloupe de 1794 à 1798, et l'ambiguïté même de sa carrière reflète la dynamique idéologique de la Terreur jacobine. Envoyé pour faire appliquer le décret de la Convention nationale abolissant l'esclavage, Hugues reprit la Guadeloupe aux Anglais et s'attaqua aux colonies et aux activités commerciales de l'ennemi dans la mer des Antilles. Propagande et subversion accompagnèrent ses tentatives militaires, et son régime se caractérisa par la répression brutale des ennemis politiques; les colons l'accusèrent même de corruption et dénoncèrent son comportement de dictateur. Hugues, qui avait pourtant affranchi les esclaves, refusa de faire appliquer la nouvelle constitution de 1795 en Guadeloupe, estimant que donner aux Noirs l'égalité totale entraînerait la disparition de la colonie. Cette restriction de la liberté des Noirs, qui semble aller à l'encontre des principes mêmes de la Révolution, est cependant conforme, comme d'ailleurs le recours à la répression, à l'idéologie de la Terreur: l'identification de l'autorité absolue avec le gouvernement révolutionnaire et avec ses agents.

In the spring of 1794 the French National Convention sent Victor Hugues as civil commissioner to the Windward Islands where he was to implement the decree of 16 Pluviôse Year II abolishing black slavery. In command of a small expedition, Hugues reconquered Guadeloupe from British occupation, freed its slaves, and turned the colony into a bastion of the Republic from which he launched attacks on British islands and a naval campaign against enemy commerce. Yet if Victor Hugues came to the West Indies brandishing the decree of Revolutionary emancipation, he also brought the guillotine of Revolutionary Terror. His treatment of enemies was ruthless and brutal. He and his colleagues forced the blacks to continue working the fields in order to maintain economy of the island. After 1795 he refused to implement France's new constitution. Throughout his tenure as agent of metropolitan government, colonists denounced him as a "cruel despot" and "execrable monster," as "the most vulgar, boorish, and foul-mouthed man," "the most skilled of squanderers and rogues," and "the most perfect pupil of Robespierre."[2] Thus the man and his achievements seem paradoxical, and suggest various interpretations.

The contexts of war and plantation agriculture certainly shaped developments on Guadeloupe between 1794 and 1798, as did Hugues's enigmatic personality. The ideological dynamic of the French Revolution, however, was vital. Both emancipation and authoritarianism flowed from Jacobin principles. The same Revolutionary government which abolished slavery in the colonies also justified dictatorship in France through the logic of popular sovereignty and crushed all opposition in the name of the nation's will. Even after Thermidor, Hugues continued to govern Guadeloupe according to these maxims. Therefore, rather than emphasizing the unique colonial situation, this discussion will suggest that Victor Hugues's regime represented the extension of the Jacobin Terror to the Caribbean.

Victor Hugues was born in Marseilles, but moved as a young man to Saint-Domingue where he became involved in the early stages of the Revolution. Although an ardent patriot, he returned to Europe in 1792 after losing his brother and most of his property to the slave revolt and civil war which ravaged that colony.[3] In 1793 he became prosecutor for the Revolutionary Tribunal at Rochefort and earned a reputation for ferocity: in September his indictment caused the execution of ten naval officers accused of complicity with the English occupation of Toulon.[4] Given these credentials, the Revolutionary government appointed Victor Hugues, along with Pierre Chrétien, as civil commissioner to the Windward Islands in April 1794. The two agents sailed in a squadron which included two frigates and transports carrying fewer than 1,500 troops. The government intended this meagre force to strengthen defences of Guadeloupe, unaware that the colony had already fallen to the British.

The Revolution of 1789 inspired black hopes of liberation and white fears for the slave economy in the sugar islands of the Caribbean. Within the free population, news from France exposed fundamental tensions between the *petits blancs*, including merchants, artisans, and commercial seamen, the *grands blancs*, or large plantation owners, and the *gens de couleur*, a heterogeneous class of mulattos and free blacks whose ownership of property made them potential defenders of slavery but whose demands for civil equality undermined principles of racial superiority.[5] On Guadeloupe, as elsewhere in the French West Indies, the Revolution undermined existing authority and provoked a struggle for power. *Petits blancs* proclaimed themselves to be "patriots" and referred to their planter opponents as "aristocrats." While patriotic enthusiasm ran high in 1790–91, in 1792 the planter-dominated Colonial Assembly led a counter-revolutionary rebellion against metropolitan government. Early in 1793 patriots, with the crucial support of the mulattos, regained Guadeloupe for the Republic. The French declaration of war against Spain and Great Britain, however, made the Republican regimes in the Windward Islands highly vulnerable. After failing in 1793, British forces captured Martinique in March 1794 and Guadeloupe the following month.[6]

Thus Victor Hugues's expedition reached Guadeloupe on 2 June to find it in British hands. The commissioners were undeterred and decided to attack the town of Point-à-Pitre. Chrétien led a night assault on fort Fleur-d'Epée which took its defenders by surprise and caused the British to evacuate not only Point-à-Pitre, but all of Grande-Terre, the north-east of the two linked islands making up Guadeloupe. Heavy French casualties, from yellow fever as well as from enemy action, accompanied this initial success, with Chrétien and the expedition's three generals among the dead. These losses appeared critical when a British fleet under the command of Admiral Jervis arrived on 11 June and laid siege to Point-à-Pitre. Victor Hugues rose to the occasion and inspired the French troops to endure bombardment and to repel assault.[7] In July the British retreated across the Rivière Sallée to fortified positions on Basse-Terre, Guadeloupe's south-west component. Despite the costly siege, however, Hugues was able to go on the offensive because he had raised a new army. He promoted junior officers to replace generals who had fallen. Moreover he followed the announcement of the decree of 16 Pluviôse with a proclamation ordering citizens of all colours to enlist as national volunteers.[8] Abolition of slavery thus provided the Republic with abundant black troops.

In September Victor Hugues ordered an attack on Camp Berville, forcing General Graham to capitulate the following month, and by mid-December his army had driven the remaining British forces from Basse-Terre.[9]

Terror was an integral part of this campaign. The terms of Graham's surrender allowed British troops to re-embark on Jervis's fleet, but Hugues demanded that French colonists of all colours who had supported them must remain behind. Cooper Willyams, chaplain aboard Jervis's flagship, described the fate of these prisoners:

> . . . three hundred, . . . were doomed to suffer death by the hands of their republican countrymen in cold blood, in a manner hitherto, I believe, unheard of, . . . Humanity must shudder at the idea; the republicans errected a guillotine, with which they struck off the heads of fifty of them. Thinking, however, this made of proceeding too tedious, they invented a more summary plan; they tied the remainder of these unhappy men fast together, and placed them on the brink of the trenches which they had so gallantly defended; they then drew up some of their undisciplined recruits in front, who firing an irregular volley at their miserable victims, killed some, wounded others, and some, in all probability, were untouched; the weight however of the former dragged the rest into the ditch, where the living, the wounded, and the dead, shared the same grave, the soil being instantly thrown upon them.[10]

Willyams was incorrect that no precedents existed for such action. In Revolutionary France similar mass executions occurred following the sieges of the rebel cities of Lyons and Toulon, and in the Vendée. Victor Hugues had signalled his intention to deal ruthlessly with traitors in June when he informed the Committee of Public Safety that he had formed a military commission to judge "aristocrats" captured under arms, and that several had already been guillotined.[11] Propaganda reinforced such severity. His proclamation of 17 July informed the citizens of Guadeloupe that it was not sufficient to retake the territory of the Republic or carry the fight to that of the enemy: "the one and the other must be purged of the monsters who sullied them and the vices they inflicted."[12] When his troops overran Basse-Terre, Hugues ordered the remains of British General Dundas, who had died of yellow fever in June, to be dug up and scattered to the winds. As Lebas, one of two other commissioners sent to Guadeloupe in 1795, put it, "Hugues has spread Terror among the English."[13]

Having regained Guadeloupe, Victor Hugues began operations to extend French influence in the Windward Islands. In April 1795 he sent troops under Goyrand, the commissioner who arrived with Lebas, to attack the island of Sainte-Lucie and fight alongside colonists resisting British occupation.[14] The British abandoned Sainte-Lucie in June, although they returned to retake the island in 1796. Hugues's primary objective was to recapture Martinique, but its defenses were formidable and the need to garrison Guadeloupe made a full-scale invasion impossible. Therefore he launched smaller raids against enemy colonies, in particular Saint-Vincent and Dominica, where French forces operated in alliance with the few remaining Carib indians who were confined there.[15] The incitement of Carib revolt, although disastrous, was part of a strategy of subversion: as in Europe, the Terror demanded an ideological struggle which paralleled the military effort against the enemies of the Revolution. Hugues hoped, and British governors feared, that French-inspired slave rebellions would conquer enemy colonies for the Republic.[16] In fact this uprising did not happen, and the small raiding parties achieved little. Nevertheless, Republican forces at Guadeloupe posed a constant threat.

Victor Hugues's major weapons against British power in the West Indies proved to be corsairs. Early in 1795 he ordered the French navy's few warships at his disposal to intercept enemy shipping en route from Europe. These patrols were highly successful, but privateers inflicted even more damage on British commerce. Between 1794 and 1798 corsairs from Guadeloupe took over 800 prizes.[17] This naval campaign was not without controversy, however. Crews of the navy warships did not receive their normal share of prize money. When sailors protested, Hugues imprisoned their representatives, dismissed their officers, and confined two frigates to fever-ridden backwaters as punishment for defiance.[18] The agent also exercised complete control over privateering. Outfitters of corsairs had to purchase letters of marque from Hugues, who also demanded a considerable share in their enterprise. Since he also dominated the prize court, he accumulated a personal fortune from the war on enemy trade.[19]

Victor Hugues's control of corsairs and his treatment of the naval station reflect two major accusations repeated throughout the denunciations of his conduct submitted to metropolitan authority: financial corruption and personal tyranny. Like agents of the Revolutionary government in France, Hugues sequestered *émigré* property on Guadeloupe in the name of the nation. Many colonists charged him with profiting from the administration of such property, and complained that he also requisitioned the goods of inhabitants who had remained loyal to the Republic. Thouluyre Mahé, a planter he imprisoned for failing to deliver his produce to national warehouses, claimed that Hugues and his colleagues regarded colonial wealth as the booty of conquest. He also accused the agent of ruling Guadeloupe as a despot: "His will is the supreme law in the colony."[20] Hapel de la Channie, a chemist who returned to France, condemned Hugues for requisitioning the women of the colony along with its wealth, shamelessly forcing many of them to become his concubines.[21] Another denunciation also characterized Hugues's regime as corrupt and arbitrary, and described the appointment of villains as spies and henchmen to maintain the "new Robespierre" in power.[22] General Pelardy, whom Hugues had dismissed and deported to France, told the Minister of Marine and Colonies that there had been "no Thermidor on Guadeloupe."[23]

The references to Thermidor and the new Robespierre demonstrate that colonists were aware of the new political climate in France since the summer of 1794, and that they hoped to rid themselves of Victor Hugues by linking him to the now-discredited Terror. Some of these denunciations also suggest resentment of the abolition of slavery and of the black troops, and support Hugues's claim that he faced continual opposition from former slave owners.[24] Although the evidence of financial corruption is inconclusive, it would seem that Hugues did not distinguish between the interest of the state and his own profit.[25] The accusation that cannot be denied, however, is that of dictatorship. Even a report submitted by Hugues's own envoys admitted the provisional nature of government on Guadeloupe, and recommended that laws of the Convention replace the Commissioners' *arrêtés*.[26] Yet Hugues ignored metropolitan legislation, as critics of his regime pointed out, and he would not publish the Consitution of the Year III which replaced the Convention with new legislative bodies and created the executive Directory. Indeed, Victor Hugues was forthright in his refusal to implement it on Guadeloupe: "The Constitution which offers such advantages in France, presents only difficulties in these countries; to promulgate it, to put it into action today, would mean the next day that the colonies would no longer exist."[27]

This refusal related directly to Hugues's attitude towards black liberation. It was noted earlier that his recruitment of the newly freed slaves made possible the conquest of Guadeloupe. These "*sans-culottes noirs*" within the colony's armed forces were the chief beneficiaries of the abolition of slavery. In a revealing letter to the Committee of Public Safety of July 1794 Hugues declared that, although he had always doubted negroes could be given liberty, he had to admit that they had conducted themselves well since their emancipation.[28] Nevertheless, he was adamant in later correspondence that the colony would be destroyed if blacks were granted full equality under the Constitution. Accompanying the decree of 16 Pluviose on Guadeloupe was a proclamation which announced that black citizens must continue to work. Hugues's proclamation of 18 June repeated this message more vigorously: "The Republic, in recognizing the rights you hold according to nature, had not intended to remove your obligation to earn your living by work."[29] It went on to state that blacks who were not in the army must return to the plantation; those who did not would be considered traitors and delivered to the rigour of the law. Hugues reinforced this general order with specific measures of coercion to keep the black labour gangs working the fields to maintain Guadeloupe's economic base.[30] "Nothing is more painful than agricultural labour in the colonies," Hugues informed the Minister in 1796, "a convict condemned to irons would not exchange his punishment for one year growing sugar."[31] Therefore constraint was necessary to preserve the agricultural workforce, constraint which contradicted the spirit of the constitution. Beyond the requirements of agriculture, Hugues also insisted that granting blacks full citizenship would plunge Guadeloupe into anarchy and civil war:

> . . . who could contain 90,000 strong and robust individuals, embittered by years of misery, by horrible torments and atrocious tortures; who could contain the Africans' natural ferocity strengthened by the desire for vengeance? . . . I have not believed it my duty to assemble the black people to name deputies, and I never will: honour and my conscience forbid it.[32]

While his repression of political opposition is clearly in keeping with the Terror, Victor Hugues's attitude towards blacks seems at odds with the Jacobin emphasis on equality. The colonial context, including his own experience on Saint-Domingue, was certainly important. When the Directory renewed its powers as agents of executive authority in 1796, it informed Hugues, Lebas and Goyrand that they must govern according to the Constitution, but must also maintain plantation agriculture:[33] there is some justice in Hugues's claim that the two were mutually exclusive. Yet the limitation of black liberty was not incompatible with the logic of the Terror. Claiming that they alone represented the nation's will, the Jacobins established the Revolutionary government in 1793 and exercised absolute authority in the name of the sovereign people. Robespierre defined Revolutionary government, which he saw as vital to defeat the enemies of democracy, as the despotism of liberty against tyranny. The decree of 16 Pluviôse freed the slaves of Guadeloupe: but just as the Jacobins in France restricted direct democracy and local freedom in the name of popular sovereignty, Victor Hugues could force blacks to work the fields and deny their right of primary assemblies on the grounds that his authority alone represented the nation's will on Guadeloupe. To keep up the struggle against the nation's enemies, agriculture had to continue and no resistance to his authority could be tolerated.

By late 1795, Victor Hugues's language in official correspondence reflected news of Thermidor: he and his colleagues were loyal only to the Convention, and they struggled against both extreme revolutionaries and reactionaries.[34] The Directory's decision to keep him on Guadeloupe, however, had less to do with his efforts to counter denunciations than with his undeniable success in preserving the colony for the Republic and in harassing the enemy. This success allowed his regime to continue until metropolitan government finally replaced him in 1798. The nature of this regime remains controversial and enigmatic. Having abolished slavery, Hugues confined blacks to the plantations and resisted granting them full rights. In part these actions reflected ingrained racism and in part the reality of colonial agriculture. Similarly, the war with Britain, and the resulting peril for Guadeloupe, helps to explain his authoritarian rule and ruthlessness towards enemies. There is also little doubt that he used Revolutionary rhetoric to disguise personal tyranny and corruption.

Yet in a more fundamental sense, Victor Hugues's regime was an authentic extension of the Terror to the West Indies. He came to the colonies as a committed agent of Revolutionary government, and his brutal treatment of traitors fit with that government's definition of Terror as swift and inflexible justice. His use of propaganda and subversion also conformed to Jacobin ideology. Above all, the Terror represented the identification of absolute Revolutionary authority with the state: Victor Hugues's domination of naval crews, white colonists, former slaves, and even of his own colleagues, should be seen in light of this identification. This view points to a wider conclusion. The complex struggles in the French sugar islands during the 1790s reflected the social and racial antagonisms inherent in the slave economy. Yet these struggles were also driven by developments in Europe, which included the colonial policies of successive national assemblies and the war with Great Britain. Moreover, the changing political climate in France provided the context in which the demands of colonial groups, and the response of metropolitan government and its agents were made. Therefore, despite the unique colonial situation, upheaval in the West Indies cannot be separated from the political and ideological dynamic of the French Revolution.

NOTES

1. I wish to acknowledge the financial support of the Social Sciences and Humanities Research Council of Canada, in the form of a postdoctoral fellowship, which made my research possible.

2. See Hapel de la Channie to Fourcroy, 3 Messidor an III (21 June 1795) and "Notes particulières sur la conduite et l'administration des agents particulières du directoire Exécutif aux isles du vent;" Archives des Colonies, Paris (hereafter Colonies), C 7A \ 48, ff. 69, 243.

3. See "Le citoyen Hugues au ministre du département maritime," in *Réimpression de l'Ancien Moniteur*, 31 vols. (Paris: Imp. d'A. René et cie., 1840–1854) (hereafter *Moniteur*), 14:299 (27 octobre 1792). See also Henri Bangou, *La Révolution et l'esclavage à la Guadeloupe 1789–1802: Epopée noire et génocide* (Paris: Messidor/ Éditions sociales, 1989), 69-70.

4. Victor Hugues, *Acte d'accusation contre les complices de la trahison de Toulon* (Rochefort: R. D. Jousseront, Imprimeur du Tribunal révolutionnaire, 29 Brumaire an II).

5. See for example Jacques Adélaïde-Merlande, *La Caraïbe et la Guyane au temps de la Révolution et de l'Empire* (Paris: Éditions Karthala, 1992), 15–29, and Lucien Abenon, Jacques Cauna, and Liliane Chauleau, *Antilles 1789: La Révolution aux Caraïbes* (Paris: Éditions Nathan, 1989), 34–68.

6. Anne Pérotin-Dumon, *Etre Patriote sous les Tropiques. La Guadeloupe, la colonisation et la Révolution (1789–1794)* (Basse-Terre: Société d'Histoire de la Guadeloupe, 1985), 140–220. See also A. Lacour, *Histoire de la Guadeloupe*, 4 vols. (Basse-Terre, 1857; reprint Paris: Edition et Diffusion de la Culture Antillaise, 1976), 2:1–270.

7. Hugues to Committee of Public Safety, 29 Prairial and 4 Thermidor an II (17 June and 22 July 1794); Colonies C 7A \ 47, ff. 12–13, 20–25.

8. "Proclamation . . . à tous les citoyens de la Pointe-à-Pitre et autres communes adjacentes, 20 Prairial an II (8 June 1794);" Colonies C 7A \ 47, f.9.

9. Contre-Amiral Leissègues, "Conquête de la Guadeloupe sur les Anglais;" Colonies C 7A\ 47, ff. 107–110, esp. f. 109. See also Lacour, 2:323–41. For the text of Graham's capitulation, see *Moniteur*, 23:225 (18 janvier 1795).

10. Cooper Willyams, *An Account of the Campaign in the West Indies in the Year 1794* (London, 1796; reprint Basse-Terre: Société d'Histoire de la Guadeloupe, 1990), 137–38.

11. Victor Hugues to Committee of Public Safety, 29 Prairial an II (17 June 1794); Colonies C 7A \ 47, f.13.

12. "Proclamation. Victor Hugues . . . au citoyens de l'Ile Guadeloupe, 29 Messidor an II (17 July 1794);" Colonies C 7A \ 47, f. 16.

13. Lebas to Committee of Public Safety, 20 Fructidor an III (6 September 1795); Colonies C 7A \ 47, f. 06. Regarding the exhumation of General Dundas, see *Arrêté* of 20 Frimaire an III (10 December 1794), reproduced in French and English; f. 38.

14. Hugues and Lebas to Committee of Public Safety, 20 Messidor an III (8 July 1795); Colonies C 7A \ 48, ff. 22-24. See also *Moniteur*, 25:604–5 (31 août 1795).

15. *Arrêté* of 11 Germinal an III (31 March 1795); Colonies C 7A \ 48, f. 10. See also J. Saintoyant, *La Colonisation française pendant la Révolution (1789–1799)*, 2 vols. (Paris: La Renaissance du Livre, 1930), 2:241–42.

16. See for example Hugues and Lebas to Lavaux on Saint-Domingue, 19 Messidor an III (7 July 1795); Colonies C 7A \ 48, ff. 14, 17–18. See also H. J. K. Jenkins, "Guadeloupe, savagery and emancipation: British comment of 1794–1796," *Revue française d'Histoire d'Outre-Mer* 65, no. 240 (1978): 325–31.

17. "Jugemens du tribunal de commerce sur les prises, . . . depuis le 23 Vendémiaire an 3ème . . . jusqu'au 7 Brumaire an 7ème;" Colonies C 7A \ 48, ff. 79–157. See also H.J.K. Jenkins, "The Heyday of French Privateering from Guadeloupe, 1796–98," *Mariner's Mirror* 64 (1978): 245–50.

18. Thouluyre Mahé, "Coup d'oeil sur la Guadeloupe et dépendances en 1797 (v.s.), l'an 5 de la République;" Colonies C 7A \ 49, f.139. See also Saintoyant, 2:253.

19. See his *Arrêté* of 23 Fructidor an III (9 September 1795); Colonies C 7A \ 48, f. 33. See also Lacour, 2:414–15.

20. Thoulurye Mahé, "Coup d'oeil sur la Guadeloupe;" Colonies C 7A \ 49, f. 139. See also "Extrait d'une lettre du citoyen Thouluyre Mahé, datée du port de la liberté, le 5 frimaire 5 année (25 November 1796);" ff. 135–136.

21. Hapel de la Channie to Representative Fourcroy, 3 Messidor an III (21 June 1795); Colonies C 7A \ 48, ff. 69–70.

22. "Notes particulières . . . ;" Colonies C 7A \ 48, ff. 243-250, esp. ff. 245–46.

23. Pelardy to Minister of Marine, 15 Fructidor an III (1 September 1795); Archives de la Marine, Paris, BB 4 \ 85, ff. 84–85.

24. See for example Hugues and Lebas to Committee of Public Safety, 27 Brumaire an IV (18 November 1795); Colonies C 7A \ 48, ff. 35–36.

25. Bangou, 106.

26. "Observations presentées au Comité de salut public sur la situation de la Guadeloupe, 22 Thermidor an III (9 August 1795);" Colonies C 7A \ 48, ff. 73–76.

27. Hugues and Lebas to Minister of Marine and Colonies, 22 Thermidor an IV (9 August 1796); Colonies C 7A \ 49, f. 43.

28. Hugues to Committee of Public Safety, 4 Thermidor an II (22 July 1794); Colonies C 7A\ 47, f. 24.

29. "Proclamation . . . 30 Prairial an II (18 June 1794);" Colonies C 7A \ 47, f. 14. See also "Proclamation . . . 19 Prairial an II (7 June 1794);" f. 08.

30. See for example the Arrêté of 2 Frimaire an IV (23 November 1795); Colonies C 7A \ 48, f. 41.

31. Hugues and Lebas to Minister of Marine and Colonies, 22 Thermidor an IV (9 August 1796); Colonies C 7A \ 49, f. 44.

32. Colonies C 7A \ 49, ff. 43, 65.

33. Minister of Marine and Colonies to Hugues, Lebas and Goyrand, 12 Nivose an IV (2 January 1796); Colonies C 7A \ 49, ff. 155–56.

34. See, for example, Hugues and Lebas to Committee of Public Safety or to the President of the Directory, 4 Nivose an IV (25 December 1795); Colonies C 7A \ 48, ff. 42–43.

CHAPTER FOUR

Ile Royale:
The Other New France

Peter Moogk

En 1950, Marcel Giraud montre que c'est le climat religieux et politique qui régnait en France au début des années 1700, au moment de la colonisation de la Louisiane, qui a donné à ce territoire son caractère particulier. La monarchie était appauvrie et l'Église découragée, ce qui explique pourquoi la colonie était administrée par le privé et connue pour son laxisme moral. L'île Royale, autre colonie française établie en même temps, nous permet de vérifier cette hypothèse de l'influence marquante de l'époque.

Les deux colonies possédaient en effet une structure politique et juridique semblable, et la même hiérarchie sociale. En ce qui concerne l'île Royale cependant, l'ampleur des dépenses de construction des fortifications et des immeubles publics ne cadre pas tout à fait avec l'image de pauvreté de l'État que donne Giraud. L'utilité stratégique de l'île et la valeur de son poisson séché aux yeux de la France pouvaient toutefois justifier l'appui du roi, dont ne bénéficiait pas la colonie du sud. De par sa vocation purement commerciale, axée sur la pêche de la morue, la colonie du Cap-Breton se distinguait des autres sociétés coloniales françaises, fondées sur l'agriculture et la traite des fourrures. En conséquence, la géographie et le commerce ont été des éléments tout aussi déterminants dans la formation du caractère particulier de l'île Royale que l'époque à laquelle cette formation a eu lieu.

THE MARCEL GIRAUD THESIS

In 1950, Marcel Giraud published an article in which he argued that much of Louisiana's distinctiveness, when compared to seventeenth-century Canada, was due to the political and religious situation in France when the southern colony was founded.[1] In the early eighteenth century, the French Crown was impoverished and the Roman Catholic Church was no longer animated by Counter-Reformation zeal. Thus, according to Giraud, the development of Louisiana was entrusted to private companies from 1712 until 1731. For Marcel Giraud, the time of colonization was as important to the character of the colony as was its geographic setting. Louisbourg on Ile Royale [Cape Breton Island], founded in the same decade as New Orleans, provides an opportunity for testing the Giraud hypothesis about the imprint of the times. How much of Ile Royale's distinctiveness, compared with that of Canada, was due to the fact that it, too, was an early eighteenth-century settlement? Thanks to the historical research undertaken since 1961, stimulated by the partial reconstruction of the fortress, it is possible to sketch out an answer to that question.

PARALLELS WITH LOUISIANA

Although the first settlers of Louisbourg were transplanted from the old French settlement of Plaisance [f.1622] on Newfoundland and they were joined by a small number of Acadians, the fortified seaport on Cape Breton was really an extension of eighteenth-century France, as was Louisiana. Its administrative structure was the same as that of the royal government of Louisiana: governor, commissaire-ordonnateur, and superior council. The Coutume de Paris was the rule for settling civil disputes as it was in other French colonies. Just as the laws and administration followed the same pattern, so the state of the Roman Catholic church and of religion on Cape Breton were similar too.

The most remarkable feature of religious life in the two colonies was the toleration which their governments showed for large numbers of Protestant Christians in their midsts, described as those "of the so-called reformed religion." Officially, the Roman Catholic Church's monopoly of religious functions was upheld and the exclusion of Jews and Protestants from the

French colonies was not rescinded. In practice, civil governments ignored members of the prohibited faiths as long as they conformed outwardly to Roman Catholic ascendancy and made no show of their own beliefs. This indulgence went farthest on Ile Royale and in Louisiana. The presence of a few Protestant bachelor merchants at Quebec was of great concern to the bishop of the colony in the 1750s; the presence of heretics was not an issue on Ile Royale or in Louisiana. The Swiss Karrer Regiment, which contained Lutherans and Calvinists, was stationed at Louisbourg from 1722 until 1745 and in Louisiana in the 1750s.[2] Although denied the freedom to worship publicly, the Swiss Protestants were exempted from participation in religious processions at Louisbourg. Puritan New Englanders, whose ships delivered provisions and building materials, were politely received in this Atlantic seaport. Just as the military and commercial needs of the Cape Breton colony overcame bureaucrats' religious scruples, so the need for European settlers in Louisiana caused the formal exclusion of heretics to be put aside. A few thousand German-speaking Protestants were invited to settle in Louisiana in the 1720s.[3] These immigrants came in family groups and retained a separate cultural identity for two generations.

In the St. Lawrence Valley there were no minority communities within the European population; outside the French-speaking population, there were villages of Christian Indians. Amerindian and black slaves lived as individuals within white households, but did not gather together to maintain a separate culture. European newcomers were quickly absorbed by the French-speaking, Roman Catholic Canadiens. Individual Irishmen, Englishmen, Portuguese and Italians arrived, married into established families, and were soon part of the French-speaking population. Even their surnames were assimilated, as in the case of Farnsworth, which became "Phaneuf," and the memory of their origins faded. Among Canadiens, religious and linguistic homogeneity was the rule.

Ile Royale, like Louisiana, was not nearly so culturally uniform. In addition to the Swiss soldiers who spoke German, there were several hundred Basques from southwestern France on Ile Royale.[4] Louisbourg had strong trading connections with the southwestern ports of Bayonne and St-Jean de Luz. Most Basques were transient fishermen and sailors. The Basques [Euzkadi] were a quarter of Ile Royale's summertime population during the 1740s and they remained a separate people. Even after the decline of the migratory fishery in the 1750s, several Basque families remained on the island. Joannis Etchegeray might answer to "Jean d'Etcheverry" but the Basques preferred their own names and language when speaking among themselves and when writing letters to their families. They shared advice on how to survive within the French empire. A Basque relative of the Louisbourg port captain, Joannis Galand d'Olabaratz, wrote of his apprehension about letting a son go to Martinique whose "climate is hardest on Basques."[5] Another Basque was advised to write in French when seeking a favour from an influential Louisbourgeois, Joannis Borda called "Jean Laborde," though he too was a native Basque.[6] Conformity to the dominant culture was the way to advance socially.

Quite apart from the numerous Protestants, there were similarities in the structure and discipline of the Roman Catholic Church on Ile Royale and in Louisiana. In both colonies, vicars general represented the Bishop of Québec without having much disciplinary authority; otherwise, there was no religious hierarchy. Friars, army chaplains, missionaries, hospital brothers, nuns, and teaching sisters operated without close ecclesiastical supervision. The Récollet friars of Ile Royale sometimes defied the Bishop of Québec's Vicar-General in France, the Abbé de l'Isle-Dieu. Missionaries from adjacent Nova Scotia visiting Louisbourg reported to civil officials and willingly acted as French political agents. The Micmacs [Mi'kmaq] served by the missionaries occasionally came to Louisbourg. Unlike Canada, where the Aboriginal peoples had an important economic role in the fur trade, the Micmacs were marginal to the Ile Royale economy. Their principal value was as military allies of the French. In Louisiana, trade with the native Indians was subsidized to maintain their military support for the French.

Charles Edwards O'Neill has argued that the royal government deliberately withheld a bishop from Louisiana to make the leaderless clergy more manageable. "In Louisiana the clergy never obtained the influence that prelate and priest had (or were reputed to have) in Canada. [. . .] if any individual representative of the temporal authority contended with a cleric, the latter habitually lost."[7] On the other hand, some central authority would have aided indirect governmental control. As a consequence of structural decentralization, the relaxation of church discipline in the 1700s was most pronounced in these peripheral settlements. At Louisbourg, the untithed population worshipped in the King's Bastion chapel and expected the Crown to bear the expenses of a religious establishment. Archaeologists at Louisbourg have found few of the brass crucifixes, holy medals, and religious rings that are commonplace finds at older, mainland sites. This fact may reflect both a decline in lay devotion as well as the rarity of Amerindians, to whom such pious tokens were given. Religious apathy among the laity matched indiscipline among church personnel.

In Louisiana and on Ile Royale the priests, friars, and brothers lacked the self-sacrificing asceticism of their seventeenth-century predecessors. In both colonies, priests were accused of moral laxity and an indifference to canonical rules more frequently than in Canada.[8] The six Franciscan friars who performed pastoral duties on Cape Breton, wrote A. J. B. Johnston, were accused of "failing to visit the sick, listen to confessions, [. . .] they allowed young children to act as godparents, generally allowed marriages to go ahead with only one or no bann having been read, and they did not insist on a formal betrothal."[9] The Franciscans' superior was recalled to France in 1727 for ignoring church requirements for marriages and for frequent public drunkenness. Clerical indiscipline was due to the leaderless and fragmented nature of the Church on Cape Breton.

In Louisiana, where Capuchin friars served the population, the clergy were sometimes no better than the laity, who lacked spiritual instruction. In 1727, the Ursulines arrived to instruct young girls and to run a hospital. One nun at New Orleans reported to her father that "the devil here possesses a large empire [. . .] not only do debauchery, lack of faith and all other vices reign here more than elsewhere, but they reign with an immeasurable abundance!"[10] As Charles O'Neill once remarked, calling a priest "father" in Louisiana could be more than a respectful form of address; it could be a statement of fact.

In the political and legal framework as well as in the nature of the church, there are strong parallels between Ile Royale and Louisiana. This evidence seems to sustain Marcel Giraud's argument that the early eighteenth century produced a different type of French colony in the Americas. There were, however, contrasts.

THE DISTINCTIVENESS OF ILE ROYALE

Giraud's emphasis on the poverty of the royal government to explain company rule in Louisiana in 1712–1731, however, is challenged by the generous royal expenditures on Louisbourg in the same era. In 1719–1723 the Conseil de la Marine spent 374,063 *livres* on Ile Royale's public works, principally on the defences of Louisbourg. This expense was more than twice the amount spent on public works in Canada in the same period. The sum is not immense, but it does raise doubt about the reputed poverty of the government during the regency (1715–1723). In 1724, the annual allocation for government construction on Ile Royale was raised from 80,000 to 130,000 *livres*.[11] After the fishery and maritime trade, government building contracts were a third major industry in Louisbourg.

Government expenditures on Ile Royale, made at a time when Louisiana was entrusted to private companies to save public funds, require a comment. The poverty of the monarchy, evidently, was not absolute; the government could still direct money to vital projects, such as the protection of Ile Royale. The retention of royal control over Ile Royale might have something to do with the difficulty of farming out its one resource to a chartered company. The idea of leasing the island to a monopoly company was considered and discarded, for the cod fishery involved too many powerful, private interests in France to permit the establishment of a monopoly. Those private interests had to be heeded. The government expenditures on fortifications at Louisbourg were a measure of the importance of the cod fishery to the ports of western France before the 1750s. The dry fishery, which produced long-lasting cod fillets with little salt, needed a land base for drying the fish. After 1713, northeastern Cape Breton was the piece of French territory closest to the Newfoundland fishing banks and its inshore waters were equally productive. An anonymous memorialist described Cape Breton as "assise au milieu des mers les plus poissonneuses."[12] Thus, Ile Royale became the centre of France's dry fishery in North America.

Louisbourg, in particular, had a roomy, ice-free harbour. The decision in 1719 to make this fishing community the administrative centre for the Gulf of St. Lawrence region and to fortify it was affected by strategic as well as commercial considerations. This haven could accommodate naval vessels for the protection of the seasonal fishing fleet and the sea lane into Canada. In war, privateers used the port as a base to harass enemy shipping. In 1706 Antoine-Denis Raudot, co-intendant of New France, had seen the value of the harbour as a place where homebound French merchant vessels from the Americas and Asia might stop to take on water and provisions and to repair damage. He and other memorialists of the time did not anticipate the full potential of the port as a goods-transhipment point between Canada, France, the West Indies, and New England. Eventually, about 150 merchantmen would stop at Louisbourg each year, dwarfing the maritime traffic between France and Canada or between France and Louisiana.[13] Commerce with New England violated imperial laws against direct trade between the French colonies and foreign territories, but did, however, supply the foodstuffs and building materials that the rest of New France could not furnish and was a good outlet for West Indian products. Accordingly, local officials granted extraordinary permits and concealed the full extent of this trade in their correspondence with superiors. Open, illegal trade also existed between Louisiana and the Spanish settlement at Pensacola.

Concentration on the fishery and overseas trade made civilian society on Isle Royale thoroughly commercial. Louisbourg and its outports had an inadequate agricultural hinterland at a time when farming was the foundation for European and colonial economies. The terrain on the east coast of the Royale is rocky; the soil, acidic and poorly drained, and the climate, cold and damp. Louisbourg was chosen to be the regional capital because of its value to the fishery and in spite of its unsuitability for agriculture. Only a fifth of the resident population of the island was engaged in farming. Apart from a scattering of farms along the road to the Mira Valley and in the valley itself, the nearest agricultural region was Ile St-Jean, [Prince Edward Island], an island dependency of Louisbourg. Acadians had begun to migrate to Ile St-Jean after 1720 and it might have become Cape Breton's granary with time. Louisbourg, however, depended on imported foodstuffs throughout its history.[14]

In the system of land tenure, the island resembled Louisiana. Freehold land grants were expected to attract settlers and the seignorial system was not established in either colony. Yet, in both colonies, land concessions gave recipients water frontage and the holdings extended inland at right angles to the coast or river shoreline.

The urban layout of the principal towns was also alike. At New Orleans and Louisbourg, military engineers imposed on the towns a rectilinear grid of streets which expressed the official values of order, symmetry, and hierarchy. Along the Mississippi River, under chief engineer Pierre Le Blond de La Tour, Adrien de Pauger laid out the street alignments to which existing structures had to conform or be removed. De Pauger struck one recalcitrant building owner over the head with a stick when the householder refused to relocate.[15] Nature intervened in 1722 when a hurricane levelled the older structures; then the orderly development of New Orleans proceeded. At Louisbourg, military engineers tolerated the eccentric Presqu'Ile du Quay area established by migrants from Placentia, but they ordered the demolition of private dwellings along the quayside to accommodate public buildings and a broad landing. Homes in the new "Quartier du Roi"—in southwest Louisbourg—had a certain social cachet, yet merchants, officers and tavern-keepers lived as neighbours in the port. In New Orleans, the allocation of town lots was made according to social rank and occupation; rank was measured by proximity to the Place d'Armes and the parish church facing it. The layout of that southern city expressed the hierarchical and symmetrical ideal that Louisbourg's designers had in mind before they compromised with geography and private interests.[16]

Ile Royale was notable for its thoroughly mercantile outlook. The island depended on the export of dried cod fish, supplemented with timber and coal. In value, cod fillets and oil accounted for over three-quarters of the island's exports. Apart from trades that served the fishery, such as shipbuilding, French Cape Breton lacked a diversified economy. Food imports and finished goods had to be paid for by fish products or re-exported West Indian goods. The market for cod was more reliable than the European demand for furs, but the precarious dependence on one export commodity does remind one of Canada's reliance on fur exports to France. When fish prices fell or the catch declined, as it did after 1738, Isle Royale had an immediate balance-of-payments problem.

Despite the absence of *seigneurs, voyageurs,* and fur-traders—stock figures in New France's history—Ile Royale's social structure resembled the hierarchy of the St. Lawrence Valley settlement, give or take a few occupational groups. Replace Montreal's *marchands-équippeurs* who signed up canoemen with Cape Breton's *habitants pêcheurs* [fishing concessionaires or proprietors] who employed migrant fishermen to man their shallops and schooners, and we have a close approximation in social rank. At the top there was a privileged elite made up of government administrators, military officers and wholesale merchants. Without seigneuries, these social leaders could not imitate France's landed aristocracy. Officials and officers invested discreetly in trade and the fishery. The blurring of the boundary between merchants and those worthies who served the king with pen and sword permitted intermarriage between these groups. At the bottom of society, the paucity of farmers meant that there was a sharp drop from the level of craftsmen, innkeepers and retail shop-keepers to the mobile proletariat of private soldiers, indentured workers, servants and slaves, who were in the lowest rank.

Canada and Ile Royale adhered to the values of old-regime France, despite modifications in social structure. Ken Donovan observed the same assumption that rank demanded an appropriate lifestyle, whatever one's real wealth was. "In this regard," he concluded, "the people of Louisbourg were no different from those of Canada where status symbols and physical trappings were most important."[17] On Ile Royale the commercial spirit was more apparent than in Canada and it touched all ranks.

CONCLUSION: THE IMPRINT OF THE TIMES AS AN HISTORICAL EXPLANATION

The imprint of metropolitan values should have been strongest on Ile Royale because of its continuous, large-scale trade with France and the yearly influx of fishermen from Europe. The people of Ile Royale had insufficient time to develop a regional identity like that of the Acadiens and Canadiens. The first thirty-two years of Louisbourg's existence ended with the 1745 siege and the removal of the population. The return of many of these people to the island in 1749, after the restoration of French rule, indicates that some had developed an attachment for Cape Breton. Their second sojourn ended after nine years with a second conquest and evacuation. Combine this disrupted history with the continuous exchanges with France and one can understand why Ile Royale remained an overseas extension of the parent state.

French Cape Breton reminds us that there was not just one New France, in cultural and social terms. Different societies co-existed within the colony's political boundaries. What the eighteenth-century settlements of Ile Royale and Louisiana illustrate, as Marcel Giraud observed, was how the date of foundation and settlement could profoundly affect a settlement's character. Ile Royale, with its strong eighteenth-century imprint, reminds us of the stamp of seventeenth-century France upon the St. Lawrence Valley settlement called Canada. Time of colonization is a key consideration for understanding the differences in French settlements, but the contrasts between Louisiana and Ile Royale show that timing is not the sole consideration. Cape Breton's strategic and commercial importance to the French government entitled it to preferential treatment, in comparison with that other eighteenth-century French colony in North America: Louisiana.

NOTES

1. Marcel Giraud, "France and Louisiana in the Early Eighteenth Century," *Mississippi Valley Historical Review* 36, no.4 (March 1950): 657–74.

2. Allan R. Greer, "The Soldiers of Isle Royale, 1720–1745," *History and Archaeology*, no.28 (Ottawa: National Historic Parks and Sites Branch, 1979) provides more information on the Karrer Regiment.

3. Glen R. Conrad, ed., *Immigration and War, Louisiana: 1718–1721* (Lafayette: University of Southwestern Louisiana, 1970).

4. A. J. B. Johnston, "The People of Eighteenth-Century Louisbourg," *Nova Scotia Historical Review* 11, no.2 (December 1991): 75–86, reveals the wide range of cultural origins within the community's population. The article has been reprinted in Eric Krause, Carol Corbin, and William O'Shea, eds., *Aspects of Louisbourg* (Sydney: University College of Cape Breton Press, 1995), 150–61.

5. Public Record Office [PRO], High Court of Admiralty Series 30 [HCA 30], Box 264, Bundle 2, Letter 21: 8 mars 1757 - Dolabarats de Piaube at St-Jean de Luz to M. Dolabarats "captaine du port de louisbourg."

6. PRO, HCA 30, Box 261, #113: 15 mars 1757.

7. C. E. O'Neill, *Church and State in French Colonial Louisiana* (New Haven: Yale University Press, 1966), 286. In 1752, Ile Royale's governor lamented the absence of a strong, central authority among the island's clergy, so that government officials did not always favor the fragmented nature of the church. See Archives de l'Armée, série 1A, vol.312, art 3393, pièce 38: Mémoire du Comte de Raymond, janvier 1752, quoted in Robert J. Morgan and Terrence D. MacLean, "Social Structure and Life in Louisbourg," *Canada: An Historical Magazine* 1, no.4 (June 1974): 62.

8. Cornelius J. Jaenen, *The Role of the Church in New France* (Toronto: McGraw-

Hill Ryerson, 1976), 120–22, acknowledges a few cases of moral laxity among Canada's clergy, which, on the whole, "was singularly well behaved and disciplined, dedicated and devout."

9. A. J. B. Johnston, *Religion and Life at Louisbourg, 1713–1758* (Montreal/Kingston: McGill-Queen's University Press, 1984), 153.

10. M. M. Costa, ed., *The Letters of Marie Madeleine Hachard, 1727–28* (New Orleans: Laborde Printing Co., 1974), 55, 58.

11. Frederick J. Thorpe, *Remparts lointains: La politique française des travaux publics à Terre-Neuve et à l'Ile Royale, 1695–1758* (Ottawa: Éditions de l'Université d'Ottawa, 1980), 170. See also B. A. Balcom, *The Cod Fishery of Isle Royale, 1713–58* (Ottawa: Parks Canada, 1984), 5, for annual budgets for all of the colony's expenses in 1721–1757.

12. "Anonymous Memoirs of 1706" from the Archives des Colonies reprinted as an appendix to chapter 1 in J. S. McLennan, *Louisbourg from its Foundation to its Fall, 1713–1758* (Sydney: Fortress Press, 1969), 23.

13. Terry Crowley, *Louisbourg: Atlantic Fortress and Seaport* (Ottawa: The Canadian Historical Association, 1990), 17. Christopher Moore, "The Other Louisbourg: Trade and Merchant Enterprise in Ile Royale, 1713–58," *Histoire sociale / Social History* 12, no. 23 (May 1979): 79–96, deals with the evolution of the island's overseas commerce and the growth of a local mercantile group. This fine article has been reprinted in Krause, et al, eds., *Aspects of Louisbourg*, 228–49.

14. For differing perspectives on the significance of agriculture in Ile Royale's economy, see Andrew Hill Clark, "New England's Role in the Underdevelopment of Cape Breton Island During the French Regime, 1713–1758", *The Canadian Geographer / Le géographe canadien* 9 (1965): 1–12; and Christopher Moore, "Cape Breton and the North Atlantic World in the Eighteenth Century," in Kenneth Donovan, ed., *The Island: New Perspectives on Cape Breton History, 1713–1990* (Fredericton & Sydney: Acadiensis Press and UCCB Press, 1990), 30–48.

15. Leonard V. Huber, *New Orleans: A Pictorial History* (New York: Bonanza Books, 1971), 1–2, 24.

16. Sieur Chevillot's 1711 plan for Mobile followed the same gridiron plan centred on Fort Louis and parallel to the river bank. French military engineers' devotion to the military architecture of Sébastien Le Prestre de Vauban cultivated a taste for geometric orderliness.

17. Kenneth Donovan, "Tattered Clothes and Powdered Wigs: Case Studies of the Poor and Well-to-Do in Eighteenth-Century Louisbourg," in K. Donovan, ed.,

Cape Breton at 200: Essays in Honour of the Island's Bicentennial (Sydney: University College of Cape Breton Press, 1985), 2. Accusations of past misconduct in France, which reveal the mutual suspicion among immigrants, appeared at Louisbourg. See the exchange of insults between Angélique Butel and Servanne Bonnier in 1744 cited in A. J. B. Johnston, *The Summer of 1744: A Portrait of Life in 18th-Century Louisbourg* (Ottawa: Parks Canada, 1983), 59–60. Such recrimination occurred between seventeenth-century settlers in Canada. See Peter N. Moogk, "Thieving Buggers and Stupid Sluts: Insults and Popular Culture in New France," *William and Mary Quarterly*, 3d ser. 36 (October 1979):, 544–45.

CHAPTER FIVE

L'activité commerciale des femmes de familles marchandes à Louisbourg au XVIIIᵉ siècle

Josette Brun

Between 1713 and 1758 in Louisbourg's merchant community, it was common for wives to participate in running the family business. While the husbands most often took care of the formal aspects of managing the business, the wives did play a role. The wives whose business activities are documented in the notarial archives seem to have been actively involved, judging by the responsibilities they took on. Continuing to run the family business was a strategy used by 36% of the widows. For a large number of widows, this was only a temporary measure because they remarried quite quickly; others seemed to make it their veritable occupation and take advantage of the independence conferred upon them by their marital status. Solitude, poverty and insecurity were, however, the lot of many widows who had to support their family financially as well as handle their domestic responsibilities. Therefore, it is not surprising that remarriage occurred so frequently, especially since women were scarce and a merchant's widow was considered to be a good catch.

Ce travail a comme objectif de répondre à quelques questions soulevées au terme de notre recherche sur les femmes d'affaires¹ de la colonie française de l'île Royale au XVIIIᵉ siècle.² Dans une thèse de maîtrise, nous avons montré que les affaires font partie intégrante de la vie d'un bon nombre de femmes de la colonie. Elles ont laissé des traces de leurs activités dans les recensements et les archives notariales de l'île Royale. Les recensements nominaux, avares d'informations sur les occupations des femmes mariées, révèlent néanmoins que de 3 à 7% de la population féminine adulte prend part aux activités commerciales de la colonie en 1724, 1726 et 1734 et que ces femmes représentent pendant ces deux dernières années le dixième de la communauté d'affaires de l'île Royale. Les conceptions sociales dominantes de l'époque en ce qui a trait aux rôles masculin et féminin de même qu'un cadre juridique contraignant pour les femmes mariées expliquent qu'elles soient minoritaires dans ce domaine. Le contexte familial est le facteur primordial expliquant leur participation en affaires. C'est en effet en tant qu'épouses et surtout comme veuves d'hommes d'affaires qu'elles sont actives dans ce domaine, collaborant à l'entreprise familiale du vivant de leur mari ou menant elles-mêmes cette entreprise après la mort de celui-ci.

Plusieurs questions demeurent en suspens en ce qui concerne la nature et l'ampleur du phénomène. Quelle forme prend la collaboration des épouses? Prennent-elles une part active à la gestion de l'entreprise? Quel pourcentage des veuves d'hommes d'affaires poursuivent l'entreprise familiale? Privilégient-elles d'autres stratégies de survie, tel le remariage, après la mort de leur conjoint? Nous suggérons en conclusion de notre thèse de maîtrise que la collaboration des épouses est nécessaire au bon fonctionnement de l'entreprise familiale et que leur participation témoigne d'un véritable partenariat dans le couple. De même, tout indique que le maintien de l'entreprise familiale est une stratégie privilégiée par les veuves d'hommes d'affaires, mais que le remariage constitue aussi un choix évident pour un bon nombre d'entre elles.

LES SOURCES

Nous avons choisi les familles marchandes de la ville de Louisbourg comme laboratoire d'étude pour la vérification de ces hypothèses. Ce choix s'explique par la disponibilité d'une liste de marchands de cette ville établie par Christopher Moore dans le cadre de sa thèse de maîtrise réalisée en 1977.[3] Trois autres sources nous permettront de compléter l'analyse qui sera à la fois quantitative et qualitative : une liste des femmes d'affaires de Louisbourg tirée de notre thèse sur l'île Royale;[4] des sources généalogiques portant sur cette colonie française[5] de même que l'inventaire analytique des archives notariales de Louisbourg.[6]

Moore a identifié, à partir des recensements et des archives notariales et judiciaires, 147 hommes formant le «noyau» de la communauté marchande de Louisbourg, c'est-à-dire constituant les cas les plus sûrs. La principale limite de cette source tient au manque de précision des critères de sélection des marchands. En observant les fiches constituées par l'auteur, on remarque que certains marchands sur lesquels de maigres informations étaient disponibles ont été retenus tandis que d'autres ont été rejetés. Par exemple, Antoine Peré, habitant-pêcheur[7] de Louisbourg que l'on dit marchand à plusieurs reprises dans les archives notariales, n'y figure pas, contrairement à Michel Lagoanere, dont le «statut de marchand est douteux».[8] De plus, s'il note au passage l'activité de certaines épouses ou veuves de marchands en affaires, cette question ne semble pas avoir fait l'objet d'une recherche systématique de sa part. Ces femmes (même la marchande publique Julienne Minet) ne figurent pas dans le groupe des 147 marchands.

L'identification des marchandes de Louisbourg comporte évidemment des difficultés particulières.[9] Les recensements ne tiennent pas compte de l'occupation des femmes mariées et n'indiquent pas toujours l'occupation des veuves chefs de famille. Les archives notariales ne révèlent quant à elles qu'une partie de l'activité commerciale des habitants de la colonie puisque de nombreux actes ne sont pas ratifiés devant notaire. De plus, l'activité notariale des gens d'affaires ne nous informe que sur l'aspect formel de la gestion d'une entreprise et ne nous dit rien sur la répartition quotidienne du travail. Il convient de préciser que nous intégrons à l'analyse les veuves de marchands qui mènent une entreprise de pêche ou un établissement (auberge ou cabaret) qui existait avant le décès du mari marchand.

L'inventaire analytique des archives notariales de Louisbourg nous a permis d'identifier les actes liés à la gestion de l'entreprise familiale signés par les marchands ou leurs épouses. Tous les actes notariés «faits et passés» à Louisbourg ne se sont pas rendus jusqu'à nous, mais les greffes conservés (13 volumes) en constituent sûrement une bonne partie. Ils couvrent d'ailleurs toute la période d'existence de la colonie, soit de 1713 à 1758 (sauf la période d'occupation britannique de 1745 à 1748). Le statut matrimonial des marchands identifiés par Moore de même que les dates de décès des deux membres du couple et celles de remariage des veuves ont été obtenues dans le dictionnaire généalogique compilé par S. White à partir des registres paroissiaux, des contrats de mariage et des recensements de l'île Royale.

Ce travail compte trois parties. Nous situerons d'abord l'importance socio-économique de la ville de Louisbourg et brosserons un bref portrait de sa communauté marchande masculine et féminine. Les parties sub-séquentes porteront l'une sur l'activité commerciale des femmes mariées et l'autre sur les stratégies utilisées par les veuves de marchands pour assurer leur survie et celle de leur famille.

La colonie française de l'île Royale, située au Cap-Breton, a été créée en 1713, au lendemain du traité d'Utrecht qui a fait passer l'Acadie et Terre-Neuve aux mains des Britanniques.[10] La France veut en faire une nouvelle base pour la pêche de la morue dans l'Atlantique Nord-Ouest et pour la protection de cette industrie lucrative, tout en faisant de l'île Royale un lieu de transit pour le commerce entre la métropole et ses colonies. Louisbourg, avantagé par son havre pouvant accueillir une centaine de bateaux et par sa situation privilégiée pour la pêche, est choisie comme centre administratif et militaire de la colonie en 1718; sa fortification débute deux ans plus tard. La ville forteresse devient vite le centre commercial, le port de pêche le plus actif et la ville la plus populeuse de la colonie. Pendant la première occupation française, 40% de la population totale et le tiers de la population civile habite à Louisbourg; pendant les années 1750, la ville abrite 70% de la population totale et 60% de la population civile de l'île Royale. Louisbourg compte 890 habitants en 1720, 1 633 en 1734 et 4 000 en 1752. Cette population comprend une bonne proportion de soldats et de pêcheurs saisonniers. La forte immigration de main-d'oeuvre masculine provoque d'ailleurs un déséquilibre démo-graphique prononcé dans la colonie. La plupart des femmes de l'île Royale vivent à Louisbourg où elles ne forment que 12% de la population en 1734.[11] La plupart de ces femmes sont originaires des colonies d'Amérique du Nord (c'est-à-dire du Canada, de l'Acadie et de l'île Royale), contrairement aux hommes qui proviennent pour la plupart du continent européen.

C'est l'industrie des pêches qui a créé la communauté marchande de Louisbourg. La morue séchée est le seul produit de la colonie qui dépend des produits alimentaires et matériels importés pour survivre. Louisbourg devient la plaque tournante du commerce entre la France et ses colonies d'Amérique du Nord et des Antilles en plus d'être le pivot des échanges commerciaux à l'intérieur de la colonie. Tout cela crée un espace commercial important dont s'emparent les habitants de la capitale où sont établis presque tous les marchands de l'île Royale; peu d'agents de firmes françaises se sont établis à Louisbourg comme c'est le cas à Québec.[12] La petitesse de la population civile limite les possibilités pour la vente au détail, mais les habitants-pêcheurs, les aubergistes et cabaretiers, les capitaines de navires, l'administration locale et les détaillants doivent être approvisionnés en marchandises diverses. La réexportation des produits importés,[13] la vente et l'achat de bateaux ainsi que les activités de cabotage entre la capitale et les autres établissements occupent aussi les marchands de la colonie. Ces derniers forment environ 1 pour cent de la population de l'île Royale de 1720 à 1752.[14] En 1734, près de la moitié (49,2%) des hommes d'affaires de la ville sont actifs dans le commerce, certains s'y consacrant et d'autres cumulant deux occupations.[15]

La plupart des femmes d'affaires de la colonie (56,3%) se trouvent à Louisbourg.[16] Elles sont marchandes, habitantes-pêcheurs, cabaretières ou aubergistes. C'est d'ailleurs dans la capitale que l'on trouve 19 des 23 marchandes[17] de l'île Royale. Elles sont presque toutes épouses ou veuves de marchands. Ces femmes représentent 52,8% des femmes d'affaires de la ville tandis qu'elles sont minoritaires (35,9%) chez celles de la colonie.[18] Elles y sont surtout nombreuses pendant les années 1730, période commerciale particulièrement intense; 12 d'entre elles sont actives pendant ces années. En 1734, si l'on se fie au recensement, 13,8% des marchands de Louisbourg sont des femmes.[19]

DES COLLABORATRICES

Si l'économie de Louisbourg est propice au développement d'une communauté marchande importante, la part que peuvent y prendre les femmes y est toutefois limitée par les conceptions sociales dominantes qui présentent le mariage comme étant la destinée naturelle de la femme et la sphère domestique comme sa principale sphère d'activité; les fonctions publiques, la gestion des biens et les affaires sont en effet perçues comme des tâches masculines. Cependant, la survie de la famille dépend du travail de tous ses membres et la femme est appelée à collaborer au travail de production qui varie selon l'occupation du mari.[20] À Louisbourg comme ailleurs en Nouvelle-France, le mariage est le statut normal d'une femme adulte.[21] En vertu du droit privé, qui relève de la Coutume de Paris,[22] une femme qui prend mari perd la pleine capacité juridique dont bénéficie la célibataire majeure. Elle vit en communauté de biens, à moins de stipulations contraires dans son contrat de mariage, et n'a plus le droit d'administrer ses biens, de s'engager par contrat, de soutenir une action en justice ou de devenir marchande publique (c'est-à-dire mener une entreprise autonome) sans l'autorisation de son mari. Les femmes ne conservent de pouvoir que sur leurs «propres», ou biens hérités, dont le mari a la gestion mais dont il ne peut disposer sans l'autorisation de son épouse.

Dans ce contexte, que nous apprennent les documents sur la collaboration des épouses de marchands à l'entreprise familiale?[23] Sur les 147 marchands identifiés par C. Moore, 100 ont une épouse à Louisbourg.[24] Les activités commerciales de 14 d'entre elles ont laissé des traces dans les archives (voir le tableau 1). Une minorité significative des épouses de marchands contribuent au fonctionnement de l'entreprise familiale. De plus, si l'on tient pour acquis que les veuves marchandes qui font l'objet de la prochaine section ont été mêlées de près à la gestion de l'entreprise familiale du vivant de leur mari, c'est 22% des conjointes de marchands qui y participent.[25] Ce total peut lui-même être qualifié de conservateur en raison des limites des sources.

TABLEAU 1

Épouses de marchands de Louisbourg actives en affaires, 1713–1758.

CATÉGORIE	NOMBRE
Épouses de marchands en affaires*	14
Marchands mariés	100
Marchands de Louisbourg	147

Sources : Moore, «Merchant Trade; White, Dictionnaire généalogique; Brun, «Les femmes d'affaires».

Il y a ainsi, comme le souligne France Parent pour la ville de Québec en 1686,[26] un écart entre le prescrit légal et la réalité des femmes dans cette ville coloniale française. La marge de manoeuvre accordée par la Coutume de Paris aux femmes mariées (ou plutôt, à leurs maris) pour ce qui est de leur partici-

---

* Onze d'entre elles font partie de la liste de femmes d'affaires tirée de notre thèse de maîtrise et l'activité commerciale des trois autres a été notée par C. Moore.

pation dans le monde des affaires est donc exploitée par les membres de la communauté marchande de Louisbourg.

C'est dans les archives notariales que les épouses ont laissé des traces de leurs activités commerciales. Si l'on se fie à la nature des documents, ces femmes semblent prendre une part active à la gestion de l'entreprise familiale (voir le tableau 2). Onze épouses de marchands font l'objet d'un acte notarié ou signent elles-mêmes un document lié aux activités commerciales de la famille.[27] L'un de ces actes concerne la nomination de Julienne Minet comme marchande publique par son mari Claude Mullot. Ce dernier l'autorise a acheter et vendre toutes sorte de marchandises concernant la profession qu'ils font d'aubergiste et marchand en cette dite ville comme les marchandes publiques ont pouvoir de faire conformement aux ordres du Roy.[28]

La Coutume de Paris précise qu'une femme «n'est réputée marchande publique pour débiter la marchandise dont son mary se mesle : mais est reputée marchande publique, quand elle fait marchandise séparée, & autre que celle de son mary».[29] Elle peut alors, de façon autonome, «accomplir tous les actes juridiques nécessaires à son commerce, et ces actes engagent la communauté, de même qu'ils lui profitent, le cas échéant»[30]

TABLEAU 2

Actes notariés de nature commerciale concernant les épouses de marchands de Louisbourg, 1713–1758.

NATURE DU DOCUMENT	NOMBRE D'ACTES
• nomination de marchande publique	1
• procuratrices	6
-trois nominations de procuratrices	
-trois femmes agissant à titre de procuratrices	
• femmes accompagnant leur mari	4
ENSEMBLE	11

Source : Col., Instrument de recherche no 396, Série G3,
Notariat, volumes 2037–2039, 2041-2047, 2056–2058.

Six autres actes fournissent un indice de la participation active des épouses à la gestion de l'entreprise familiale. Il s'agit de trois actes signés par des épouses agissant à titre de procuratrices de leur mari et de trois nominations de procuratrices. Les trois femmes qui agissent à titre de procuratrices de leur mari se présentent devant notaire pour réaliser des transactions entourant l'achat ou la vente de bateaux.[31] L'une d'elles, Anne Guyon Després, sera marchande pendant une dizaine d'années après la mort de son mari, Jean Chevalier. Nous n'avons pu retracer les procurations accordées par ces marchands à leur épouse, documents qui auraient pu nous fournir un meilleur indice du degré de responsabilité qui leur est confié. Ne font-elles qu'apposer leur signature au bas d'un acte qui reprend fidèlement les termes d'une procuration? Les trois exemples de procurations que nous avons sous les yeux accordent plutôt une grande liberté d'action aux épouses. Le marchand Joannis Galand Dolhabarats confie à sa femme, Catherine Despraube, la tâche de choisir des arbitres en France pour la révision de son compte avec le négociant François Duperié de Saint-Jean-de-Luz.[32] Pour sa part, le marchand Georges Rosse permet à son épouse, Barbe Thesson dit Laflourie, de

> regir, gouverner et administrer toutes les affaires que le dit Sieur Rosse pourra avoir en cette Isle pendant son absence, regler et arreter tous comptes qu'il pourra avoir de quelle nature qu'ils soyent avec toute sorte de personnes, en recevoir le reliquat, en donner quittances et decharge, faire tous actes requis et necessaires, se presenter en justice tant en demandant que deffendant pardevant tous juges qu'il appartiendra, faire les achats dont elle aura besoin, s'obliger au payement et generallement negocier toutes les affaires que le dit Sieur constituant aura en cette isle pendant son absence.[33]

Il promet de ne rien révoquer de ce qu'elle aura accompli. En novembre 1732, François Chevallier accorde la même responsabilité à son épouse de moins d'un an, Marguerite Doyon, soit de «gérer, régler, et arrêter toutes les affaires (qu'il) peut avoir en cette isle pendant son absence de quelle nature et espèce que ce soit . . . et génerallement faire tout ce (qu'il) feroit s'il étoit sur les lieux.»[34] Le Sieur Chevallier semble avoir laissé son épouse avec bien peu de ressources puisqu'un an après son départ, devant le tribunal de Louisbourg, elle dit ne rien savoir d'une dette contractée par son mari deux ans avant son mariage et affirme que ce dernier «ne luy a rien laissé pour s'abriter et bien moins pour acquitter les debtes».[35] La Cour donnera tout de même raison au créancier.

Les procurations ne sont pas des actes que l'on fait à la légère puisqu'elles sont fort coûteuses et lient les maris aux décisions que prendront leur femme. La confiance dont font preuve ces marchands à l'égard de leur épouse témoigne du savoir-faire de ces dernières dans ce domaine d'activité et de leur participation active à la gestion de l'entreprise familiale, notamment en cas d'absence du mari.

De même, la formulation de l'acte par lequel les nouveaux époux Barbe Le Neuf de La Vallière et Louis Delors reçoivent du père de ce dernier un don de 5 000 livres «pour le commerce qu'ils font»[36] présage des années de collaboration à venir. En effet, Louis Delors précisera dans son testament, 13 ans plus tard, «qu'il nomme pour tutrice generalle et administreresse de ses biens Barbe Leneuf de la Vallière . . . attendu qu'elle est instruite de ses affaires».[37]

Les trois autres actes signés par les deux membres du couple montrent qu'il est de l'intérêt des épouses de veiller au bon fonctionnement de l'entreprise familiale puisqu'elles s'engagent aux côtés de leur mari face à d'éventuels créanciers. Dans ces quelques cas, leur signature semble requise «pour la scurette [sûreté] du payement» d'une somme pour laquelle le couple hypothèque tous ses biens.[38] Le mari ne peut hypothéquer le propre héritage de sa femme sans son consentement, ni obliger cette dernière «plus avant que jusques à la concurrence de ce qu'elle ou ses heritiers amendent de la communauté» sans son autorisation.[39] Pour sa part, Jeanne Peré s'engage avec son mari Martin Benoît à rembourser 1 796 livres au négociant Pierre Martissans, et accepte, en plus d'hypothéquer tous les biens meubles et immeubles du couple, de mettre en gages «tous les droits [qu'elle a] dans sa communauté».[40] L'on peut, dans ce cas, parler d'un véritable partenariat.

Ces épouses de marchands se font cependant rares devant notaire lorsqu'il s'agit de questions commerciales, ne s'y présentant jamais à plus d'une reprise, et les archives notariales ne comptent aucun acte ratifié par les trois procuratrices[41] et la marchande publique. Cela laisse croire qu'elles participent peu, sur le plan formel bien sûr, à la gestion de l'entreprise familiale. Ce n'est évidemment pas le cas de la marchande publique, Julienne Minet. C. Moore nous apprend que la boutique est connue comme la «boutique de la Mullot, marchande», et que c'est elle qui est nommée dans pratiquement tous les actes de l'entreprise.[42] Pour ce qui est des autres femmes, il convient de vérifier, pour les années de vie commune du couple, le nombre d'actes notariés signés par leur mari pour des questions de même nature. L'inventaire analytique des greffes de notaires de Louisbourg permet d'identifier les parties en cause de même que le contenu de chaque acte. Il arrive cependant que les documents manquent de précision sur la nature de la transaction; les cas où il pourrait s'agir de questions financières qui touchent à autre chose qu'au commerce n'ont pas été retenus.

Les marchands de Louisbourg dont les épouses signent ou font l'objet d'un acte notarié se présentent devant notaire plus souvent que leurs épouses, mais le nombre d'actes ratifiés n'est pas très élevé : 90 % ne s'y présentent pas plus de six fois pendant la période étudiée (voir le tableau 3). Il serait donc risqué de conclure que les rares présences de ces épouses de marchands devant notaire reflètent leur faible participation à l'entreprise familiale puisqu'on n'y voit guère plus souvent le chef de famille. C'est peut-être le cas de Marguerite Coeffé, qui n'accompagne son mari François Lessenne qu'une fois devant notaire pendant que ce dernier signe 28 actes notariés alors que leurs années de vie commune.[43]

TABLEAU 3

Nombre d'actes notariés de nature commerciale passés par les marchands de Louisbourg pendant leurs années de mariage. *

NOMBRE D'ACTES FAITS DEVANT NOTAIRE	NOMBRE DE MARCHANDS
0 à 2	2
4 à 6	7
28	1
ENSEMBLE	10

Source : Col., *Instrument de recherche no 396, Série G3, Notariat, volumes 2037-2039, 2041–2047, 2056–2058.*

En somme, la collaboration des épouses à l'entreprise familiale est chose commune à Louisbourg de 1713 à 1758. La plupart de celles dont l'activité commerciale a laissé des traces collaborent activement à la gestion de

* Il s'agit bien sûr des marchands dont les épouses ont été nommées procuratrices, marchande publique ou qui les ont accompagnés devant notaire.

** Nous avons éliminé le cas de François Chevallier, parti en «voyage d'affaires» l'année même de son mariage (en 1732) et disparu en mer : de 1716 à 1731, il a signé 9 actes devant notaire.

l'entreprise, quoique les maris semblent s'occuper plus activement de son aspect formel, sans doute en bonne partie à cause du coût des procurations.

Devenue veuve, une femme recouvre sa capacité juridique et jouit des mêmes droits que la célibataire majeure. Plusieurs options s'offrent à elle au décès de son conjoint. Elle peut renoncer à la communauté de biens (si celle-ci est grevée de dettes, par exemple) et en retirer ses effets personnels (préciput) ou son douaire, pension viagère portant habituellement sur la moitié des biens propres du mari; la partager avec ses enfants et bénéficier ainsi de la moitié des biens tout en assumant la moitié des dettes; ou la poursuivre avec l'accord de ceux-ci. La veuve peut ainsi continuer l'entreprise du mari. En cas de remariage, le partage doit être fait : la veuve, ses enfants et son nouveau mari en obtiennent chacun le tiers.[44]

A la lumière de nos résultats sur la participation active des épouses à l'entreprise familiale, l'on pourrait s'attendre à ce qu'un bon nombre de veuves décident de poursuivre ces activités. Est-ce le cas? Sur 100 familles de marchands à Louisbourg de 1713 à 1758, 25 ont été rompues par le décès du mari avant la dernière conquête de Louisbourg.[45] Les stratégies utilisées par les veuves prennent plusieurs formes. Certaines veuves se remarient rapidement sans qu'on ait d'indications qu'elles aient touché aux affaires, d'autres mènent l'entreprise un certain nombre d'années avant de se remarier et d'autres sont actives en affaires jusqu'à leur décès sans jamais convoler en secondes noces.

La majorité des veuves de marchands (64%) ne semblent pas avoir touché aux affaires : la moitié de ces femmes se sont remariées, assez rapidement semble-t-il, et on ne connaît pas le sort des autres (voir le tableau 4). Le maintien de l'entreprise familiale est tout de même une stratégie privilégiée par une bonne partie des veuves de marchands pour subvenir à leurs besoins et à ceux de leur famille. C'est ce que font 36% d'entre elles. La plupart sont marchandes, mais certaines se consacrent plutôt (ou aussi) à une autre activité à laquelle s'adonnait le couple avant le décès du mari, soit la pêche ou la tenue d'auberge et de cabaret. Trois des neuf femmes seront en affaires pendant une dizaine d'années et ne se remarieront pas (voir le tableau 4.1). Du décès de son mari vers 1720 jusqu'à sa propre mort en 1732,

Marie Charlotte Brouillet s'occupe de commerce tout en menant l'une des plus importantes entreprises de pêche de Louisbourg, fournissant notamment de l'équipement aux habitants-pêcheurs et diverses marchandises à l'administration locale.[46] Anne Guyon Després fait d'abord le métier de couturière après la mort de son mari en 1720,[47] mais c'est comme marchande qu'on l'identifie de 1726 à 1734,[48] donc pendant près de dix ans. Catherine de Beaujour perd son mari Pierre Lelarge en 1733 et on la trouve active en tant que marchande et aubergiste pendant les dix années qui suivent. Elle mène une entreprise de cabotage qui lui permet de fournir des matériaux de construction et autres marchandises aux habitants des autres établissements ainsi qu'à l'administration locale.[49]

TABLEAU 4

Stratégies de survie des veuves de marchands à Louisbourg de 1713 à 1758.

STRATÉGIE	NOMBRE	POURCENTAGE
En affaires	9	36%
N'ont pas touché aux affaires	16	64%
• 7 femmes qui se remarient		
• 9 femmes au sort inconnu		
ENSEMBLE	25	100%

TABLEAU 4.1

Stratégies de survie des veuves dont le sort est connu.

STRATÉGIE	NOMBRE
Ne se remarient pas, actives en affaires pendant une moyenne de 10 ans	3
Active en affaires pendant une moyenne de cinq ans avant de se remarier	4
Active en affaires, décède au bout de trois ans	1
Active en affaires, durée inconnue	1
Se remarient rapidement (en général, au bout d'un or de deux ans)	7
ENSEMBLE: veuves dont le sort est connu	16

Sources : Moore, «Merchant Trade»; White, «Dictionnaire généalogique»; Brun, «Les femmes d'affaires».

Simone Jeanne Million, veuve de Elie Thesson dit Laflourie, dirige une entreprise de pêche de la mort de son mari en 1741 jusqu'à son propre décès en 1744. Avant sa mort, Élie Thesson avait nommé son épouse «tutrisse et administreresse des personnes et biens de leurs enfants», reconnaissant dans son testament que

> sa dite epouse a une parfaitte connoissance des affaires de leur communauté, quelle a au surplus tous les menagements et la conduite qu'une femme peut avoir, et que par consequant qu'il est de l'interet de leurs enfants que eux et leurs biens soient regis et gouvernés par elle.[50]

Trois autres femmes seront en affaires pendant plusieurs années avant de se remarier. Jeanne Bausché, veuve de Jean Gaillon dit Préville, est aubergiste de 1734 à 1741, année de son remariage avec Thibeau Plasanet dit Lépine. Après la mort de son mari Jean Rodrigue, en 1733, la marchande d'origine acadienne Anne LeBorgne de Bellisle mène avec ses fils une entreprise commerciale jusqu'à son remariage en 1738 avec le Sieur Jean Duperié. Barbe Vincent, qui se trouve à la tête d'une entreprise de pêche après le décès de son mari Benjamin Lemanquet, se remarie avec Louis LeBon au bout d'un ou de quatre ans.

Ces veuves assurent pendant un certain temps un moyen de subsistance à leur famille en maintenant une entreprise qui pourra être léguée aux enfants, qui bénéficient du même coup de l'expérience qu'elles ont dans ce domaine. Le veuvage est peut-être un état avantageux pour certaines d'entre elles. Libérées de l'autorité d'un père ou d'un mari, elles profitent des privilèges que leur confère leur statut matrimonial pour voir elles-mêmes à la survie financière de la famille en mettant leur expérience et leurs compétences à l'épreuve. C'est peut-être ce qui explique qu'elles ne se soient pas remariées malgré le déséquilibre démographique[51] de la colonie et le bon parti que constituent les veuves de marchands. D'autres facteurs, tels l'âge au veuvage et la charge familiale (le nombre d'enfants) pourraient cependant avoir limité leurs possibilités de remariage. Pour d'autres, le maintien de l'entreprise familiale est une stratégie temporaire. Un bon nombre de veuves préfèrent partager la lourde responsabilité de subvenir aux besoins financiers de la famille avec un nouveau mari. En tout, 40% des veuves de marchands se remarient tôt ou tard. Ce pourcentage se rapproche mais est plus élevé que celui noté par D. Gauvreau pour Québec, qui est de 35%.[52] L'auteure ne fournit cependant pas de données sur la période de déséquilibre démographique que connaît la ville au XVIIe siècle.

Le veuvage est loin d'être un état avantageux pour la plupart des femmes; plusieurs se trouvent en effet dans une situation précaire après la mort de leur mari et font face à la pauvreté et à la solitude. Le cas de Marguerite Doyon illustre bien ce fait. Près de deux ans après le départ du Sieur Chevallier pour un «voyage d'affaires» aux Antilles, on le croit perdu en mer. Réduite à un «Etat bien affligant», «seulle en cette ville sans ses parents de son coté» et «sans assistance», Marguerite Doyon informe les autorités judiciaires de son intention de renoncer à la communauté de biens entre elle et son mari et d'aller retrouver sa famille à Québec.[53]

CONCLUSION

La collaboration des épouses à l'entreprise familiale est un phénomène répandu dans la communauté marchande de Louisbourg de 1713 à 1758. Si les maris s'occupent le plus souvent de l'aspect formel de la gestion de l'entreprise, les épouses n'en sont toutefois pas écartées. La plupart de celles dont les activités commerciales ont laissé des traces dans les archives semblent y participer activement. La marchande publique est un cas exceptionnel, mais les épouses qui agissent en tant que procuratrices de leur mari bénéficient elles aussi de la confiance de ce dernier qui leur accorde parfois une grande liberté d'action pour la gestion de l'entreprise familiale, notamment lorsqu'il doit s'absenter de la ville ou de la colonie. Les épouses ont intérêt à veiller à la bonne marche des affaires puisque certaines d'entre elles acceptent d'hypothéquer leurs biens et de mettre en jeu les avantages dont elles pourraient bénéficier une fois devenues veuves.

La preuve la plus concluante de la participation active des femmes mariées à l'entreprise familiale est certes le pourcentage élevé de femmes de marchands qui sont actives en affaires après la mort de leur mari. Le maintien de l'entreprise familiale est une stratégie favorisée par 36% des veuves. Ces femmes assurent ainsi un moyen de subsistance à leur famille tout en maintenant une entreprise qui pourra être léguée aux enfants. Certaines paraissent en faire une véritable occupation et profiter de l'indépendance que leur confère leur statut matrimonial tandis que d'autres se remarient au bout de quelques années. Solitude, pauvreté et insécurité sont le lot de bien des femmes après la mort de leur mari. La lourde tâche de subvenir seule aux besoins financiers de la famille s'ajoute aux responsabilités domestiques pour la plupart d'entre elles. Il n'est donc pas surprenant que les remariages soient aussi fréquents, la rareté des femmes et le bon parti que constituent les veuves de marchands aidant.

Il serait intéressant d'explorer les sources d'assistance possibles pour les veuves dans le besoin, par exemple, en provenance de la congrégation religieuse de Louisbourg ou de l'administration locale. Le don de vivres que fait le commissaire-ordonnateur à quatre veuves sans ressources au cours des années 1720[54] est-il un cas isolé ou une pratique courante dans la colonie? Combien de veuves concluent des ententes avec leurs enfants pour s'assurer un gîte et la nourriture? Il faudrait aussi s'interroger sur les stratégies utilisées par les veuves de divers groupes sociaux, la situation d'une veuve d'officier et celle d'une veuve d'artisan, par exemple, n'étant sans doute pas comparables. Les problèmes particuliers auxquels font face les hommes qui perdent leur conjointe mériteraient aussi d'être étudiés.

NOTES

1. Le terme (femme, homme ou gens) «d'affaires» est utilisé dans ce travail même s'il ne fait son apparition, selon le *Robert*, qu'au cours de la deuxième partie du XVIIIe siècle. Il fait référence aux marchands, aux habitants-pêcheurs, aux aubergistes et aux cabaretiers.

2. Josette Brun, «Les femmes d'affaires dans la société coloniale nord-américaine : le cas de l'île Royale, 1713–1758», thèse de maîtrise, Université de Moncton, 1994.

3. Christopher Moore, «Merchant Trade in Louisbourg, Ile Royale», thèse de maîtrise, Université d'Ottawa, 1977. Cette liste m'a été gracieusement prêtée par l'auteur.

4. Brun, «Les femmes d'affaires». Nous avons ajouté à cette liste les trois épouses dont C. Moore a relevé la participation en affaires et Simone Jeanne Million, identifiée comme habitante-pêcheur dans les archives judiciaires. Archives nationales du Canada, MG1, Archives des Colonies (désormais Col.), Série G2,

Greffes des tribunaux de Louisbourg et du Canada (désormais Série G2), vol. 188, no 1–287, novembre 1744 à février 1745.

5. Stephen White, *Dictionnaire généalogique des familles acadiennes* (en préparation), Centre d'études acadiennes, Université de Moncton.

6. France, Archive Nationales [AN], Col., Instrument de recherche no 396, Série G3, Notariat (désormais Série G3), volumes 2037–39, 2041–47, 2056–58.

7. Habitant-pêcheur : habitant qui dirige une entreprise de pêche.

8. L'auteur note sur la fiche biographique de Michel Lagoanere : «merchant status doubtful».

9. Brun, «Les femmes d'affaires», 47–51 et 79–88.

10. Les informations qui suivent sont tirées du premier chapitre de notre thèse, 11–36.

11. Elles sont proportionnellement plus nombreuses à Louisbourg que dans les autres établissements de la colonie, où elles ne représentent que 7 pour cent de la population en 1734.

12. Moore, «The Other Louisbourg : Trade and Merchant Enterprise in Ile Royale 1713–58», *Histoire sociale/Social History* 12, no 23 (mai 1979), 87.

13. Ces produits proviennent principalement de la France, des Antilles et de la Nouvelle-Angleterre.

14. Moore, «Merchant Trade», 40.

15. AN Col., Série G1, Registres de l'état civil, Recensements et documents divers (désormais Série G1), vol. 466, no 69, Recensement de 1734.

16. Brun, «Les femmes d'affaires», 94.

17. Sont marchandes toutes celles qui tiennent des activités commerciales, qu'elles se consacrent ou non à cette occupation. Deux marchandes sont aussi (ou d'abord) aubergistes et deux autres mènent une entreprise de pêche.

18. Brun, «Les femmes d'affaires», Annexe E. On note une différence marquée entre les femmes d'affaires de la ville et celles des autres établissements; 16 femmes d'affaires sur 27 qui habitent à l'extérieur de la capitale (60 per cent) sont des veuves menant des entreprises de pêche qui ont pu être identifiées grâce aux recensements nominaux; à Louisbourg, la réalité est plus complexe : c'est là que se trouvent presque toutes les marchandes, les aubergistes et les cabaretières, et les femmes mariées y sont plus nombreuses (ou plus visibles à cause de l'accessibilité des notaires).

19. Quatre femmes (toutes des veuves) sont identifiées comme marchandes en 1734 sur un total de 29 marchands.

20. Olwen Hufton, «Le travail et la famille», dans *Histoire des femmes XVIᵉ–XVIIIᵉ*

siècles, sous la direction de Georges Duby et Michelle Perrot (Paris: Plon, 1991), 27–46 passim.

21. Catherine Rubinger, «Marriage and the Women of Louisbourg», *Dalhousie Review* 60, no 3 (automne 1980): 446.

22. Voir la section sur la condition juridique des femmes dans Brun, «Les femmes d'affaires», 40–45.

23. Pour d'autres études portant sur les femmes d'affaires en Nouvelle-France, voir: France Parent, «Entre le juridique et le social : le pouvoir des femmes à Québec au XVIIe siècle», thèse de maîtrise, Québec, Université Laval, Les cahiers de recherche du GREMF, 1991, 94; Jan Noel, «New France : Les femmes favorisées», dans *Rethinking Canada, The promise of Women's History*, sous la direction de Veronica Strong-Boag et Anita Clair Fellman, 2e édition (Toronto: Copp Clark Pitman, 1991), 28–50; Kathryn Young, «Kin, Commerce and Community, Merchants in the Port of Quebec from 1717 to 1745», thèse de doctorat, Université du Manitoba, Winnipeg, 1991; J. F. Bosher, *The Canada Merchants, 1713–1763* (Oxford, Clarendon Press, 1987).

24. Nous avons éliminé les marchands qui ont une épouse en France et le couple qui s'est installé à Québec pendant l'année suivant leur mariage.

25. Il y a en fait neuf veuves, mais l'une fait déjà partie du groupe des épouses actives en affaires.

26. Parent, «Entre le juridique», 220.

27. Les trois autres épouses en affaires ont été identifiées par C. Moore dans des sources autres que les recensements et les archives notariales.

28. AN Série G3, vol. 2039 (2e partie), no 21, 22 novembre 1736.

29. Coutume de Paris, articles 234–236. Dans Bourdot de Richebourg, *Grand Coutumier général*, vol. 3 (Paris, 1724), 29–55. Nous nous référerons désormais aux articles de la Coutume.

30. François Cugnet, *Traité abrégé des anciennes Loix, Coutumes et usages de la colonie du Canada, aujourd'huy Province de Québec* (Québec, Guillaume Brown, 1775), 109. D'autres femmes ont peut-être mené des entreprises de façon autonome à Louisbourg, mais les documents ne nous permettent pas de le confirmer.

31. Marie Josephe Petit de Boismorel, épouse de Joseph Brisson : AN Série G3, vol. 2046, no 88, le 4 nov. 1738; Marie Reine Paris, épouse de Jean-Baptiste Morel : Ibid, vol. 2047, no 22, 4 juillet 1743; Anne Guyon Després, épouse de Jean Chevalier : Ibid, vol. 2057, no 38, le 30 septembre 1717.

32. Ibid, vol. 2046, no 37, 9 décembre 1737.

33. Ibid, vol. 2039, no 108, 30 octobre 1735.

34. Ibid, vol. 2038, no 60, 28 novembre 1732.

35. AN Série G2, vol. 191, 1er registre, «Audiance du lundi 11 janvier 1734 entre Jean Dupré, demandeur, et l'épouse du Sieur Chevalier, déffenderesse».

36. AN Série G3, vol. 2046, no 151, 20 septembre 1739.

37. Ibid, vol. 2047 (2e partie), no 16, 1er décembre 1752.

38. Marie Josephe Godeau et Claude Perin : Ibid, vol. 2046, no 135, le 15 avril 1739; Marguerite Coeffé et François Lessenne : Ibid, vol. 2046, no 59, le 26 septembre 1738; Jeanne Peré et Martin Benoît, Ibid, no 71, le 1er février 1738.

39. Coutume de Paris, articles 225 et 228.

40. AN Série G3, vol. 2046, no 71, le 1er février 1738.

41. Catherine Despraube devait cependant agir «en France».

42. Moore, «Merchant Trade», 78. L'auteur n'indique pas la source de cette information, mais fait peut-être référence à Col., Série C11B, Correspondance générale, Île Royale (désormais Série C11B), vol. 26, 1744, qui comprend des listes d'habitants qui ont fourni des vivres ou des marchandises aux autorités pour armer des bateaux.

43. On ne connaît pas la date de décès des époux. Un seul acte est ratifié après la première conquête de Louisbourg (le 4 novembre 1752). Les 27 autres actes sont faits de 1724 à 1743.

44. Les choses se compliquent lorsqu'il y a des enfants d'un premier lit, la communauté devant être subdivisée à nouveau.

45. La date de décès de 40 marchands n'a pu être identifiée (certains ont sans doute quitté Louisbourg); les 35 autres sont décédés après la conquête (ou peu avant, c'est-à-dire en 1756 ou 1757). Note : Les maris de deux veuves marchandes (Mariane Ponce et Marguerite Richard) à Louisbourg ne font pas partie de la liste de C. Moore : Antoine Peré, identifié comme marchand à plusieurs reprises dans les archives notariales (AN Série G3, vol. 2058, 1724, no 6); et Joseph Dugas, caboteur à Port Toulouse avant son décès en 1733.

46. Brun, «Les femmes d'affaires», 110. AN Série G2, vol. 476, «Papiers concernant Nicolas Berrichon et Marie Brouillé, veuve Berrichon ainsi que leurs cinq enfants. 1721, 1732–1733».

47. Ibid, Série G1, vol. 466, no 67, Recensement de 1724.

48. Ibid, no 68 et 69, Recensements de 1726 et 1734. Série G3, vol. 2037, no 20, le 30 juin 1728; et no 54, le 1er septembre 1729.

49. Christopher Moore, «The Sea and Jean Lelarge», *Louisbourg Portraits* (Toronto:

Macmillan of Canada, 1988), 170; Série G2, vol. 191, 2e registre, 31 juillet 1738; Série C11B, vol. 26, 1744.

50. AN Série G3, vol. 2046 (2e partie), no 69, 27 février 1741.

51. Sur la plus grande propension au remariage chez les veuves dans un tel contexte démographique, voir Danielle Gauvreau, *Québec. Une ville et sa population au temps de la Nouvelle-France* (Sillery, Presses de l'Université du Québec, 1991), 128–29; et Raymond Roy et Hubert Charbonneau, «La nuptialité en situation de déséquilibre des sexes : le Canada du XVIIe siècle», *Annales de démographie historique*, 1978, 285–94.

52. Gauvreau, *Québec. Une ville*, 133.

53. AN Série G2, vol. 191, 1er registre, «Audience du 24 may 1734, Arrest sur la requeste de Marie Doyon, épouse de François Chevalier (. . .)».

54. J. S. McLennan, *Louisbourg from Its Foundation to Its Fall, 1713–1758* (London, Macmillan, 1918; reprint Halifax, The Book Room, 1979), 80.

CHAPTER SIX

Compagnonnage in Eighteenth-Century New France

Leslie Choquette

Dans la France du XVIIIᵉ siècle, beaucoup de jeunes ouvriers appartenaient à des organisations semi-clandestines d'aide mutuelle, appelées compagnonnages, qui s'occupaient de leur formation professionnelle, de leur migration, de leur placement et des barèmes de salaires imposés, et qui favorisaient la convivialité. Le présent document pose les deux questions suivantes : L'itinéraire généralement suivi par le compagnon pouvait-il conduire ce dernier jusqu'en Nouvelle-France? Certains aspects de l'organisation ou de la culture du compagnon ont-ils été apportés outre-mer?

Nous pouvons répondre par l'affirmative à la première question. En effet, les mécanismes de recrutement et d'immigration qui existaient à l'époque permettaient à des ouvriers et à des soldats canadiens de venir de ces milieux de travail français. Il est plus difficile cependant de répondre à la seconde question. On trouve bien, dans le centre urbain qu'était Louisbourg, des traces du turbulent, regroupement de compagnons qui se rencontraient à l'auberge, et de leur refus agressif de se laisser exploiter, mais si le compagnonnage a pu contribuer à la culture de la classe ouvrière de Louisbourg, il ne s'est jamais implanté en tant qu'organisation en Nouvelle-France. En Amérique du Nord, l'absolutisme royal a réussi à empêcher l'établissement de compagnonnages structurés.

Many recent studies of New France have focused on the issue of social reproduction, or the ways in which an Old World society was transplanted to North America. As both France and New France were primarily rural societies, the emphasis has understandably been on the reproduction of rural institutions. However, a large proportion of emigrants to New France came from urban backgrounds, and the colony of Ile Royale (Cape Breton Island) was urban in character almost from its founding. It therefore makes sense to extend our investigation to urban institutions. This essay considers the North American fate of one such institution, the journeymen's *compagnonnage*. Specifically, it poses two questions: First, could the habitual itinerary of the *compagnon*, or journeyman artisan, be extended to include New France? Second, were aspects of journeyman organization or culture transferred overseas?

To begin, we offer a brief explanation of the custom or practice of compagnonnage. The term "compagnonnage" refers to three inter-regional confraternities of artisans, known variously as the *Enfants de Maître Jacques (Dévorants)*, the *Enfants du Père Soubise (Bons Drilles)*, and the *Enfants de Salomon (Gavots)*. Young men joined these societies in their late teens, after completing an apprenticeship. Provided they did not marry, they could remain active members until their mid-twenties. During that time, they participated in regular rituals, some of them akin to the carnivalesque antics of local *Abbayes de la Jeunesse*, or bachelor societies.[1]

To the chagrin of the authorities, who regarded the organizations of footloose young men as dangerous, compagnons adopted surnames that they used among themselves, virtually to the exclusion of their given names. These surnames always included a geographical component and were meant to convey to each compagnon a secure, regional identity as he prepared to set out on his travels. Among the Gavots, the surname consisted of a place name joined to that of a quality or flower: "Parisien le Bienvenu" or "Bourguignon la Rose." Dévorants preferred to couple a baptismal name with a place name, as in "Pierre le Nantais."[2] All compagnons wore "colors," in the form of cockades of multicolored ribbon, which they defended jealously. The five accepted colors were white, red, blue, yellow, and green.[3]

At the center of compagnonnage was the *Tour de France*, a voyage that enabled the young artisan to perfect his skills, see the world, and sow his wild oats. Studying and working would be typically accompanied by brawling with compagnons from other societies (for the three groups were bitter rivals), by drinking, and by sexual exploits. As the condition of compagnonnage was defined by constant mobility, most of the conviviality was focused on inns and taverns.

The Tour de France had no fixed duration, but generally lasted between three and seven years. While on the Tour, compagnons would move from town to town at irregular intervals, travelling by foot, stagecoach, or ferry as their budgets allowed. Upon arrival in a new town, they would go to an inn affiliated with their society, accept the hospitality of a *mère des compagnons*, and seek out a *rouleur*, or compagnon in charge of job placement. Thanks to the rouleurs, compagnonnage "dominated the labor market, perhaps in the seventeenth, certainly in the eighteenth century."[4] The different societies conveniently forgot their rivalries where labor relations were concerned, and they cooperated frequently to boycott workshops or even entire towns.[5] The militancy of compagnons, particularly in trades such as joiner, carpenter, locksmith, shoemaker, and baker, was a thorn in the side of officials throughout the Ancien Régime.[6]

The length of a compagnon's stay in any one town could vary from a few days to several months, depending on the state of the labor market in his trade and on his personal whims. In choosing his next destination, he would generally respect a traditional itinerary that led him from town to town according to a recognizable pattern. The itinerary, however, was "variable depending on the society, and also changed depending on the location of work."[7] The situation was particularly fluid for stonemasons, whose work took them to building sites anywhere and everywhere, earning them the nicknames of *étrangers* and *passants*, strangers and passersby.[8]

By its flexibility, the Tour de France was highly subject to short-cuts, and could end elsewhere than at the point of departure, sometimes prematurely, sometimes after prolonging the period of mobility. An offer of marriage, an enlistment in the military, even a colonial indenture could break the normal circuit of the Tour, and alter the loosely structured itinerary of the compagnon.

There is some evidence that compagnons maintained an organized presence outside of France during the Ancien Régime. For example, Protestant compagnons emigrated to the Thirteen Colonies, where they established a society, the *Compagnons de Philadelphie*, in 1724.[9] Compagnons also crossed the Atlantic as individuals. Records from the 1770s list journeymen tailors and wigmakers arriving in Rouen and Nantes from "l'Amérique," most likely the West Indies.[10]

Nevertheless, colonial officials charged with recruiting artisans for the naval yards, the mines, forges, and construction sites rarely mentioned compagnons. Recruiters made particular reference to them only four times in the course of the French Regime: seven cordwainers in 1732, several ship's carpenters in 1740, seven bakers and a cooper in 1751, six or eight gunsmiths in 1759.[11]

Thirty-odd compagnons among the hundreds of artisans mentioned in the official colonial correspondance hardly seem noteworthy. Indeed, if journeymen were conspicuous in New France, it was perhaps by their absence. Another category of document, however, those drawn up in the presence of the artisans themselves, reveals a different picture.

Contracts of indentured servitude, for example, sometimes included the designation "compagnon."[12] Those drawn up in La Flèche (Sarthe) in 1653, at the instigation of Jérôme Le Royer de la Dauversière, the *procureur* of the *Société Notre-Dame pour la conversion des sauvages en Nouvelle-France*, are a case in point. Most of the individuals La Dauversière recruited to go to the new settlement of Ville-Marie (Montréal) were peasants from the vicinity of La Flèche. Only ten people had arrived there from a considerable distance. Nonetheless, the first men to indenture themselves, a week before any of the peasants, were "Pierre Godin *compagnon charpentier* de la ville de Chastillon sur Seine, Paul Benoist *aussy compagnon charpentier* de la ville de Nevers, René Bondy *aussy compagnon charpentier* de la ville de Dijon, René Truffaut *aussy compagnon charpentier* de la ville de Laval & Fiacre Ducharme *compagnon menuisier* de la ville de Paris."[13] All in all, 10 compagnons contracted to emigrate from La Flèche: five natives of Maine and Touraine, two Parisians, and three from Burgundy and Nivernais.[14] These formal affiliates of the Tour de France made up about a quarter of the artisans recruited in La Flèche, including eight of the eighteen from the building and woodworking trades, one of the six from the garment trades, and one of the seven metalworkers.

A century later, in the form of the *témoignages de liberté au mariage*, documents required by the Canadian clergy between 1757 and 1820 in order to prevent bigamous marriages, we find another source which confirms the presence of compagnons in North America. In these cases we can almost hear them speak.[15] Antoine Boudin, who arrived in Canada in 1757 with reinforcements for the Régiment de Berry, described his personal odyssey while testifying for a friend:

> came before us [wrote the priest] antoine Boudin *dit* St-Germain native of Paris St Sulpice parish aged 26 years or thereabouts in the troops for 2 and a half years and in Canada for 7 months with the Regt of berry Who . . . assured us that pierre d'arnonville whom he calls Bourninville is not married in france and this through knowing Him since Childhood, having lived with his father for five years to learn there The trade of mason after which having done his tour de france for nearly 3 years he enlisted in Bordeaux From whence he returned to paris to say farewell to his father, and from there went to Brest where he embarked for Canada where he found The said Bourninville.[16]

Boudin's story reveals the interdependence of theoretically distinct migratory options: the Tour de France, military service, and emigration to the colonies. In the eighteenth century, compagnons' itineraries were at best loosely defined, and as such, served easily as springboards from which to tap into other migratory networks. The most common alternative network was that provided by the army, a veritable "school of mobility"[17] widely attended by young men of the popular classes.[18] Other points worthy of mention are Boudin's confusion about his friend's last name and the seeming unlikelihood of their coincidental reunion in Canada.

Since compagnons commonly referred to each other by surnames alone, family names could be unfamiliar to them. Boudin's mistake was in no way exceptional; he knew his friend not as d'Arnonville, but by his sobriquet of Bellehumeur.[19] As for the apparent coincidence of two childhood friends turning up independently in Canada, such things occurred all the time, not only among emigrants to the colonies, but along the tortuous routes of the Tour de France. In spite of the vast distances involved, the social world of the compagnon, soldier, or compagnon turned soldier was restricted. It was defined by far-flung but tightly knit networks of social relations. The inns and other gathering places frequented by the compagnons gave them access to a store of information about migratory and employment possibilities. This information circulated in writing as well as through conversation. The glazier Ménétra's account of his Tour de France conveys the importance of letters in determining his movements. We lack similar evidence for emigrants to New France, yet their relatively high rate of literacy suggests that letters must have affected their decisions as well.[20] It thus seems appropriate to take such "chance" encounters as those of the Parisians d'Arnonville dit Bellehumeur and Boudin dit Saint-Germain in our stride.

If compagnons could extend their itineraries to North America, what explains the reluctance of administrators to discuss their recruitment? A look at the documents reveals part of the answer, though part only, to be semantic. In the official correspondence between France and New France, workers are often described as "ouvriers" or as "gens de métier" without further qualification. The writers, it seems, cared little for the niceties of juridical rank, and based their classification scheme simply on skill. Provided a worker had learned his trade, his place in the traditional hierarchy was largely irrelevant.[21]

In addition to this tendency to view artisanal competence in non-corporatist terms, however, there was a strong official distrust of compagnons. That distrust is better understood in the context of the general hostility of the Ancien Régime to organized compagnonnage.

Throughout the early modern period, the influence of compagnonnage in the economic and cultural spheres prompted a vigorous counter-offensive on the part of French authorities. As early as 1539, François I prohibited the societies in the aftermath of a printers' strike in Lyon and Paris.[22] A royal edict of 1571 outlawed them in perpetuity.[23] Fifty years later, the authors of the *Code Michaud* anticipated the French revolutionaries in ordering the dissolution of all workers' associations.[24] The Church, meanwhile, pursued a purification program of its own, accusing the compagnons of heterodoxy in 1639. They were eventually condemned by both the *Officialité* of Paris and the Faculty of Theology of the Sorbonne.

The campaign against compagnonnage continued, indeed intensified, in the eighteenth century. The state took the lead in introducing repressive measures aimed at both dissolving the associations and controlling the mobility of individual compagnons. A system of written passports existed as early as the first half of the seventeenth century, and the *Conseil du Roi* broadened its application in 1749. Subsequent direction reminded local officials to be vigilant in their surveillance of migrant compagnons.[25]

Officials in New France adopted the policies of their French counterparts, with the difference that they were able to implement them more effectively.

Rightly or wrongly, compagnons were equated with domestics, and their movements out of the colony were strictly controlled through a system of *congés*. The Church also kept a close watch on the situation. Several religious figures who were prominent in colonization ventures were leaders of the fight against compagnonnage.[26]

The apparently aimless wandering of young male workers was a source of worry and frustration for colonial administrators. In 1731 Governor Saint-Ovide of Ile Royale complained of "an infinite number of young people who come here without hope of being able to work for the *habitant* or the works of the King, who not finding what they had hoped for, go back just as they came." More was the pity, he continued, for "they were almost all tradesmen, masons or carpenters, all people useful . . . to the colony."[27] Whether or not these young men were in fact compagnons is not known. Yet it is plausible. Why else, in chronically labor-starved Louisbourg, could useful artisans not find employment? An explanation is that the authorities, desperate as they were for manpower, refused to provide short-term work to footloose compagnons. Saint-Ovide's solution to the dilemma was to induct them into the army, and he was quite irritated when the *commissaire-ordonnateur* made him desist for lack of a royal order permitting him to do so.

We can therefore answer our question about journeyman organization squarely in the negative. Compagnons did not perpetuate their associations in New France. Royal officials and churchmen alike prevented the implantation there of structured compagnonnage. Did aspects of journeyman culture survive nevertheless?

As far as the colony along the St. Lawrence River is concerned, there is little evidence that they did. The organization of work was such that artisans were either isolated helpers in small-scale enterprises, often with the status of indentured servant, or else independent masters. Since access to independent status was unrestricted, compagnons were free to set up shop upon arrival or, if indentured, upon expiration of their term of service. It was common for them to assume the title of master as soon as they received their first Canadian contract.[28]

But if conditions along the St. Lawrence worked against the maintenance of journeyman militancy and conviviality, the same thing cannot be said of Louisbourg. The town's elaborate fortifications required huge infusions of regimented labor, skilled as well as unskilled, with an emphasis on the building trades. Coincidentally, the artisans who were most sought after for Louisbourg were those who traditionally held pride of place in the compagnonnages: stonecutters, joiners, locksmiths, carpenters, plasterers, and roofers.[29]

The militancy of Louisbourg's workers did scandalize administrators from the first to the final days of the settlement (1713–58). Already in 1714, they were striking over pay, much to the disgust of the major of the garrison. "When it was a question of working no one appeared," he wrote indignantly. "What is very sure is that these are very bad workers."[30]

Strikes and insubordination continued in subsequent years, prompting the engineer to complain in 1720 that the workers, through "tumultuous contestations," had raised the daily rate in some ateliers from twenty to thirty or even thirty-five *sous*.[31] In 1722, the entrepreneur himself seized his quill to demand redress. Without it, he warned, "the mutiny of the soldiers shall increase and ruin me with false expenditures without advancing the work."[32]

In the 1730s and 1740s, strike activity abated, probably due to more effective repression, but the "spirit of licentiousness and revolt" did not.[33] Desertion became a chronic problem,[34] and a full-fledged mutiny broke out among the troops in 1744.[35] By the 1750s, wages were again an issue, with workers, according to the engineer, "making the law."[36] Soldiers working in the private sector were earning thirty and even forty *sous* per day, while in the royal ateliers, the going rate was thirty for day labor and forty to fifty for piece work.[37] Civilian artisans also were costing too much. In 1754, the engineer observed that twenty-nine recently arrived masons and carpenters were pocketing 2,060 *livres* of the king's money each month, an average daily wage of over fifty *sous* per person.[38]

Nor was that all. For these workers, drinking rivalled striking as a favorite pastime; they were not only mutinous, but drunk.[39] Time after time, the taverns emptied out the workshops, to the prejudice of the *ouvrages du Roi*. On "Saint Monday," rainy days, even ordinary work days, workers seemed intent on pursuing what authorities could only term "a continuous disorder and debauchery."[40] A royal scribe wrote angrily in 1717, "It is impossible to have them for service, or even the most pressing needs without dragging them from the taverns which are in no greater number than there are houses."[41] Laments about working-class drunkenness, coupled with wholly ineffectual attempts to regulate the spirits trade, were an omnipresent feature of the colonial regime.[42]

Of course, there is no guarantee that this turbulent behavior was the cultural legacy of compagnonnage. But in individual cases, Louisbourg's compagnons could cling to their status with pride and obstinacy, as we learn from the random documents that gave them voice.

The judicial archives for 1743 and 1744 record the trial of a stonecutter named Valérien Louis, accused of stealing building materials from royal construction sites and fencing them to a long list of local artisans. Louis was a native of Dijon, a city where compagnonnage was fully implanted by the late fifteenth century.[43] The son and godson of stonemasons, he bore the surnames Bourguignon and La Verdure. In 1742, aged twenty-five, he made a three-year commitment to Louisbourg's entrepreneur in return for a yearly salary of 300 livres, room, board, and return passage. He embarked for the city in La Rochelle, after a brief stay at an inn called *Les Trois Chandeliers* in the *rue du Marché*.

Louis, or Le Bourguignon, as he was called throughout his trial, was guilty but recalcitrant. In the end, his obstinate refusal to confess spared him the death penalty in favor of the galleys. Interestingly, he resisted attempts to treat him as an ordinary indentured servant at least as strongly as suggestions of his guilt. On at least five occasions, he informed the judge that he had come to Louisbourg as a "compagnon tailleur de pierre," and when the judge seemed unimpressed, he adamantly stated that "he was not indentured in the capacity of domestic but clearly in that of compagnon."[44]

That other compagnons may have felt the same way is suggested by their appearance in the court records, complete with unmistakable surnames and titles. In 1726, for example, Hierome Dupuy gave testimony in a theft case as Bayonnais l'Aimable, "compagnon serrurier" in the workshop of blacksmith Jacques Frican.[45] Since this twenty-four-year-old Gavot never appeared in Louisbourg's census records, he must have returned home after his expanded Tour de France.[46]

The court records also reveal that the daily life of journeymen in Louisbourg was organized in familiar ways. Master artisans, some of whom may have been former compagnons themselves, ran taverns and rooming houses for workers in their trades. Their wives acted as *mères*.[47] The wife of Bayonnais l'Aimable's master Jacques Frican presided over one such establishment, gaining notoriety in 1737 for serving a thief together with her regular clients Prêt à Boire, La Terreur, and Sans Souci.[48] Other masters whose wives ran taverns and inns included Pierre Lelarge, a carpenter from outside La Rochelle, Jean-Baptiste Laumosnier, a stonecutter from Paris, and Pierre Morin, also a stonecutter. Morin's inn housed not only workers from his atelier, but visiting artisans like Armand Clavier dit l'Angevin, a tailor who passed through Louisbourg in 1740 after a stint in Québec.[49]

There are no archival examples, comparable to that of Le Bourguignon, of a soldier-worker directly expressing pride in his status of compagnon. But there were few barriers between Louisbourg's military and civilian artisans. They drank together at the same workers' taverns, and sometimes they lodged there together also. Although Louisbourg provided barracks for its soldiers from an early date, there were never enough beds for the entire garrison. Some soldier-workers were forced to seek accomodation elsewhere. One soldier-worker from Laumosnier's atelier, Germain Le Parisien, also lived at his inn. He is known to us only by his surname, that of a Dévorant.[50]

An episode that occurred in Laumosnier's tavern in 1733 suggests that a common artisanal culture may have been shared by all of Louisbourg's tradesmen, whether they served in a civilian or military capacity. The incident, which is recorded in the judicial archives, took place late in the afternoon, on the last day of the Feast of Epiphany. A soldier named Nicolas Lebègue dit Brûlevillage, a butcher by trade, entered the home of Dame Berruchon with an accomplice. Although he did not steal anything particularly valuable, he did take a large quantity of multicolored ribbon. He proceeded imme-diately to Laumosnier's to find his friend Germain Le Parisien, and joined him for some eau de vie together with 12 or 15 other military companions.[51] According to Laumosnier, "while drinking together the said Brûlevillage took from his pocket some ribbon of different colors to make cockades which the said Brûlevillage gave to the said soldiers, and they asked the wife of the witness to make them the cockades, which she did." Further testimony and physical evidence revealed the ribbon to be red, white, blue, and yellow, the first four of the five colors of the compagnon.

Although this episode could be seen as an example of military particu-larism, since all of the participants were soldiers, it perhaps makes equal sense to view it in relation to compagnonnage. For while it was not customary for soldiers of the period to wear cockades, compagnons wore them as a matter of course.[51] Journeymen stonecutters, in specific, favored "flowery ribbons of various colors,"[52] just like those stolen from Dame Berruchon. Laumosnier, moreover, ran an atelier for stonecutters, and his wife dispensed hospitality to his workers. In making the cockades, la femme Laumosnier was behaving exactly like a good *mère des compagnons*.

In conclusion, the debate over social reproduction in the New World is enriched by enlarging our purview to include urban as well as rural institutions. In the case of the journeymen's compagnonnages, organizational strength did not travel well. On the other hand, established habits of journeyman mobility did contribute, if only temporarily, to the population of New France, while artisanal militancy and conviviality permeated and enlivened the culture of urban Louisbourg.

NOTES

1. Of the many works dealing with compagnonnage, see Pierre Barret and Noël Gurgand, *Ils voyageaient la France: vie et traditions des compagnons du Tour de France au XIXe siècle* (Paris: Hachette, 1980); Jean-Pierre Bayard, *Le Compagnonnage* (Paris: Payot, 1977); Luc Benoist, *Le Compagnonnage et les métiers* (Paris: PUF, 1966); Émile Coornaert, *Les Compagnonnages du Moyen Age à nos jours* (Paris: Éditions ouvrières, 1966); Raoul Dautry, *Compagnonnage par les compagnons du Tour de France* (Paris: Plon, 1951); E. Martin de Saint-Léon, *Le Compagnonnage: son histoire, ses coûtumes, ses règlements et ses rites* (1901; Paris: Librairie du Compagnonnage, 1977); Agricol Perdiguier, *Le Livre du compagnonage* [sic] (Paris, 1841); Daniel Roche, ed., *Journal de ma vie: Jacques-Louis Ménétra, compagnon vitrier au XVIIIe siècle* (Paris: Montalba, 1982).

2. It should be noted that compagnons were not alone in their adoption of surnames. According to André Corvisier, "The usage of surnames was frequent in the period. One could find them in every village, in every parish, in every collectivity . . ." However, the surnames of compagnons and soldiers were often distinct from ordinary sobriquets. The double nicknames of the Gavots and Dévorants were unique to compagnonnage. Author's translation of Corvisier, *L'Armée française de la fin du XVIIe siècle au ministère de Choiseul: le soldat*, 2 vols. (Paris: PUF, 1964), 2: 851; Martin Saint-Léon, *Le Compagnonnage . . .*, 112–14.

3. Martin Saint-Léon, *Le Compagnonnage* ... , 263; Perdiguier, *Le Livre du compagnonage*, 60–61.

4. Coornaert, *Les Compagnonnages* ... , 7. According to Luc Benoist, this domination increased to the point where "If, at the beginning of the eighteenth century, compagnonnage could count one affiliate for every three workers, at the end, it was in a position to forbid work to non-affiliates." Benoist, *Le Compagnonnage et les métiers*, 35. (Author's translations.)

5. Martin Saint-Léon, *Le Compagnonnage* ... , 87–91. The striking of a town was known as a damnation, or *mise en interdit*.

6. Coornaert, *Les Compagnonnages* ... , 49, 425–28.

7. Bayard, *Le Compagnonnage*, 177.

8. Agricol Perdiguier, *Mémoires d'un compagnon* (1854; Paris: Librairie du compagnonnage, 1964), 311.

9. On the organizations of compagnons overseas, see Bayard, *Le Compagnonnage*, 172, 181; Coornaert, *Les Compagnonnages* ... , 146.

10. Steven Kaplan and Cynthia Koepp, eds., *Work in France: Representations, Meaning, Organization, and Practice* (Ithaca: Cornell University Press, 1986), 85, 161.

11. Letters of the Minister to Hocquart, 22 April 1732, Archives nationales, Archives des Colonies (AC), B 57: 665; Minister to Hocquart, 6 May 1732, AC, B 57: 688 ; Hocquart to Ricouart, 17 October 1740, AC, C11A 73: 162; Prévost to the Minister, 28 October 1751, AC, C11B 30: 338; Minister to Lebrun, 20 January 1759, AC, B 110: 29; Minister to Mauclerc, 26 June 1759, AC, B 110: 432 [11]; Minister to Michel, 23 February 1759, AC, B 110: 442 [21]. Other journeymen carpenters were sent in 1749 and 1750. See Réal Brisson, *La Charpenterie navale à Québec sous le Régime français* (Québec: Institut québébois de recherche sur la culture, 1983), 114.

12. These contracts identified emigrants according to community of origin, age, and occupation. They stipulated a term of service (usually three years) in return for overseas passage, room and board, and some form of remuneration. Once the term expired, emigrants were free either to return to France, sometimes at the expense of the employer, or to prolong their stay in the colony.

13. Reproduced in Maria Mondoux, "Les Hommes de Montréal," *Revue de l'histoire de l'Amérique française* 2 (1948–49): 62–64. (Author's emphasis.)

14. They signed a five-year labor contract, but according to Marcel Trudel, four of them settled permanently in Canada. See Marcel Trudel, *Catalogue des immigrants, 1632–1662* (Montréal: Hurtubise HMH, 1983).

15. Témoignages de liberté au mariage, 1757–1820, *Archives du Séminaire de Québec* (ASQ), ms. 430. The documents from the years 1757–63 have been published in the *Rapport de l'archiviste de la province de Québec*, vols. 32–33 (1951–53): 5–159.

16. Author's translation of "Témoignages de liberté," *Rapport de l'archiviste de la province de Québec*, vols. 32–33 (1951–53): 48.

17. Jean-Claude Perrot, *Genèse d'une ville moderne: Caen au XVIIIᵉ siècle*, 2 vols. (Paris: Mouton, 1975), 1:171.

18. For example, Michael Sonenscher discovered that "A significant number of the 1,086 journeymen locksmiths who registered to find work in Rouen between 1782 and 1791 were soldiers." Michael Sonenscher, "Mythical Work: Workshop Production and the Compagnonnages of Eighteenth-Century France," in Patrick Joyce, ed., *The Historical Meanings of Work* (Cambridge: Cambridge University Press, 1987), 62. According to Agricol Perdiguier, the link between compagnonnage and military service persisted into the nineteenth century. See Perdiguier, *Mémoires*, 225.

19. "Témoignages de liberté," 47. Imprecision about an emigrant's real name sometimes gave way to ignorance, for example, when Jean Louis Maillet presented as witnesses "two men whose names he does not know and one of whom is, he says, from marseille, and the other from perigord with Whom he has lived for three [years]." Author's translation of "Témoignages de liberté," 86. The authorities responded to such situations by attempting to monitor, or even control, the use of surnames by these floating elements of the population. In Louisbourg, for example, judicial interrogations routinely began with a question about "name, surname, and origin."

20. Correspondence among compagnons was strictly forbidden by law, which probably explains the dearth of extant letters. According to Luc Benoist, "until the end of the 19th century, the archives of the cayennes [the gathering places of compagnons] were burned, except for the rolls, at the end of each year . . ." Benoist, *Le Compagnonnage et les métiers*, 9. See also Ulrich-Christian Pallach, "Fonctions de la mobilité artisanale et ouvrière: compagnons, ouvriers et manufacturiers en France et aux Allemagnes (XVIIᵉ–XIXᵉ siècles)," *Francia* 11 (1983): 398. On literacy rates in New France, see Marcel Trudel, *Histoire de la Nouvelle-France*, 3 vols. (Montréal: Fides, 1963-83), 3, pt. 2:49–52. The témoignages de liberté occasionally mention letters. For example, d'Arnonville's other witness spoke of "having seen Letters from his father written to him by

which it did not appear that he was married or engaged in any fashion whatsoever." "Témoignages de liberté," 47–48. (Author's translations.)

21. As André Corvisier has pointed out, military documents also tended to eschew corporate and caste distinctions in favor of a more functional definition of labor. Corvisier, *L'Armée française* . . . , 1: 459.

22. Barret and Gurgand, *Ils voyageaient la France* . . . , 343.

23. Benoist, *Le Compagnonnage et les métiers*, 32.

24. Germain Martin, *Les Associations ouvrières au XVIIIᵉ siècle (1700–1792)* (1900; Geneva: Slatkine-Megariotis Reprints, 1974), 47.

25. In 1756, for example, journeymen bakers were forbidden to move without a certificate from the master, delivered after 15 days notice, stating, "I certify that one _____ by name native of _____ new arrival may be received to work elsewhere." *Archives départementales* (AD), Charente-Maritime, B 6040. (Author's translation.)

26. Among them were Bishop Laval, Abbé Olier, and the baron de Renty. Olier, the founder of the Order of Saint-Sulpice, personally engineered both the condemnation of the compagnons by the Sorbonne and the organization of the Société Notre-Dame de Montréal; Renty was one of the society's associates. Under these circumstances, La Dauversière's recruitment of compagnons for Ville-Marie is perhaps best understood as a missionary effort. In any case, the secular missionary (and later saint) Marguerite Bourgeoys did succeed in converting them. "Shortly after their arrival in Québec," wrote the good sister, "these . . . men were changed like linen put to the wash." Cited in Ed. de Lorière, "Quelques notes sur les émigrants manceaux et principalement fléchois au Canada pendant le XVIIᵉ siècle," *Annales fléchoises* 9 (1908): 24. (Author's translation).

27. Letter of Saint-Ovide to the Minister, 24 November 1731, AC, C11B, 12: 26. (Author's translation.)

28. Brisson, *La Charpenterie navale* . . . , 79. Craft organization and ritual did exist in early Canada, but without exception it involved masters rather than compagnons. On artisan life in the St. Lawrence, see Marius Barbeau, "Confrérie des menuisiers de Madame Sainte Anne," *Archives de folklore* 1 (1946): 72–96; Marius Barbeau, "La Confrérie de Sainte-Anne," *Mémoires de la Société royale du Canada*, sect. 1, ser. 3, vol. 39 (1945): 1–18; Russel Bouchard, *Les Armuriers de la Nouvelle-France* (Québec: Ministère des Affaires Culturelles, 1978); Jean-Pierre Hardy and Thierry Ruddel, *Les Apprentis artisans à Québec, 1660–1815* (Montréal: Presses de l'Université du Québec, 1977); Renald Lessard, "De France à Nouvelle France:

la pratique médicale canadienne aux XVIIᵉ et XVIIIᵉ siècles, in *Les Dynamismes culturels en France et au Québec*, Colloque France-Québec, Rennes, 1988, *Annales de Bretagne et des pays de l'Ouest* 95 (1988); Édouard-Zotique Massicotte, "La Communauté des cordonniers à Montréal," *Bulletin des recherches historiques* 24 (1918): 126–27; Édouard-Zotique Massicotte, "La St-Éloi et la corporation des armuriers à Montréal, au XVIIᵉ siècle," *Bulletin des recherches historiques* 23 (1917): 343–46; Jacques Mathieu, *La Construction navale royale à Québec, 1739–1759, Cahiers d'histoire* 23 (Québec: Société historique de Québec, 1971); Peter Moogk, "Apprenticeship Indentures: A Key to Artisan Life in New France," *Canadian Historical Association/Société historique du Canada: Papers/Communications historiques* (1971): 65–83; Peter Moogk, *Building a House in New France: An Account of the Perplexities of Client and Craftsman in Early Canada* (Toronto: McClelland and Stewart, 1977); Peter Moogk, "Manual Education and Economic Life in New France," in James Leith, ed., *Facets of Education in the 18th Century*, vol. 67 of *Studies on Voltaire and the 18th Century* (1977): 125–68; Peter Moogk, "In the Darkness of a Basement: Craftsmen's Associations in Early French Canada," *Canadian Historical Review* 57 (1976): 399–439.

29. Benoist, *Le Compagnonnage et les métiers*, 38-39; Dautry, *Compagnonnage . . .* , 101–4.

30. Letter of L'Hermite to the Minister, 1 December 1714, AC C11B 1: 83. (Author's translation.)

31. Letter of Verville to the Conseil de la Marine, 19 June 1720, AC, C11B 5: 235. (Author's translation.)

32. Letter of Isabeau to the Minister, 30 November 1722, AC, C11B 6: 127. (Author's translation.)

33. Letter of Soubras to the Minister, 3 December 1714, AC, C11B 1: 94. (Author's translation.)

34. Letters of Lenormant to the Minister, 6 July 1736, AC, C11B 18: 85; Bigot the the Minister, 13 November 1744, AC C11B 27: 27; Prévost to the Minister, 13 July 1756, AC, C11B 36: 120.

35. Memorandum touching the revolt of the soldiers of Louisbourg on 27 December 1744, 1745, AC, C11B 27: 55.

36. Letters of Franquet to the Minister, 13 October 1750, AC, C11B 29: 314; Franquet to the Minister, 9 November 1754, AC, C11B 34: 226. (Author's translation.)

37. Letters of Franquet to the Minister, 13 October 1750, AC, C11B 29: 314; Franquet to the Minister, 9 November 1754, AC, C11B 34: 226.

38. Letter of Franquet to the Minister, 9 November 1754, AC, C11B 34: 228.
39. See Letter of Soubras to the Conseil de la Marine, 1717, AC, C11B 2: 258.
40. Letter of Soubras to the Conseil de la Marine, 13 April 1717, AC, C11B 2: 9. (Author's translation.) See also Letters of Verrier to the Minister, 1 November 1738, AC, C11B 20: 227; Duquesnel to the Minister, 2 June 1741, AC, C11B 23: 43.
41. Letter of La Forest to the Conseil de la Marine, 12 November 1717, AC, C11B 2: 274. (Author's translation.)
42. Complaints about taverns appeared in the administrative correspondence in 1714, 1715, 1717, 1718, 1720, 1721, 1722, 1738, 1739, 1741, 1742, 1749, 1753, and 1754. The list is not exhaustive.
43. See Paul Labal, "Notes sur les compagnons migrateurs et les sociétés de compagnonnage à Dijon à la fin du XVe siècle et au dèbut du XVIe siècle," *Annales de Bourgogne* (22) 1950: 187–92.
44. Trial of Valérien Louis dit Le Bourguignon for theft, 1743–44, *Conseil Supérieur de Louisbourg*, AC, G2 187: 128-334. (Author's translation.) As Steven Kaplan and Ulrich-Christian Pallach have shown, this issue had long been a prickly one for compagnons. Steven Kaplan, "Réflexions sur la police du monde du travail, 1700-1815," *Revue historique* 261 (1979): 23; Pallach, "Fonctions de la mobilité . . . ," 396, 404.
45. Trial of Jean-Baptiste Lahaye, François Dubois, Raymond Aulier dit Saint-Louis, and Charlotte Dumesnil for theft, Conseil Supérieur de Louisbourg, AC, G2 179: 129–428.
46. Census records of Ile Royale and Ile Saint-Jean, 1724-35, AC, G1 466.
47. On the importance of taverns and inns for French compagnons, see Daniel Roche, "Le Cabaret parisien et les manières de vivre du peuple," in Maurice Garden and Yves Lequin, eds., *Habiter la ville, XVe–XXe siècles* (Lyon: Presses universitaires de Lyon, 1984): 233–51; Jean Lecuir, "Associations ouvrières de l'époque moderne: clandestinité et culture populaire," in *Histoire et clandestinité du Moyen Age à la première guerre mondiale, Revue du Vivarais* (1979): 286–87; Martin, *Les Associations ouvrières . . .* , 78. The familiarity of masters with compagnonnage is discussed by Michael Sonenscher in *Work and Wages: Natural Law, Politics and the Eighteenth-Century French Trades* (Cambridge: Cambridge University Press, 1989), 308–9 and in "Mythical Work . . . " 42. The rituals of reception made clear that compagnonnage was a lifetime affiliation. See M. J. Pradelle, "Réception des compagnons menuisiers et serruriers du devoir de liberté sous l'Ancien Régime

à Toulouse," *Mémoires de l'Académie des sciences, inscriptions et belles-lettres de Toulouse*, 13th ser., 3 (1941): 136.

48. She testified that she served them "a quart of eau de vie, that after having drunk the said eau de vie they drank another two jugs or five bottles of wine." Author's translation of Trial of Mathurin Bunau for theft, 1737, Conseil Supérieur de Louisbourg, AC, G2 184: 454–517.

49. On the taverns of Laumosnier and Morin, see Trials of Nicolas Lebègue dit Brûlevillage and Thomas Béranger dit La Rozée for theft, 1733, Conseil supérieur de Louisbourg, AC, G2 182: 148–357; Louis Davory for theft, 1740, Conseil Supérieur de Louisbourg, AC, G2 186: 228–322. On Lelarge's tavern, see Christopher Moore, *Louisbourg Portraits* (Toronto: Macmillan, 1982), 152-53.

50. Trial of Nicolas Lebègue and Thomas Béranger, AC, G2 182: 148–357.

51. Trial of Nicolas Lebègue and Thomas Béranger, AC, G2 182: 148–357. The different witnesses could not agree on how many soldiers had been drinking at the inn. Brûlevillage said 12 to 15, Marche à Terre, another soldier, 15 to 20, and Laumosnier himself, eight to 10.

52. Accounts of the ceremonial life of Ancien Régime compagnons often mention large quantities of brightly colored ribbon. Sonenscher has called attention to the ribbons of the journeymen leather dressers of Troyes, and Germain Martin cited a comparable example from Orléans. See Sonenscher, "Mythical Work . . . ," 38–39, 265–66; Sonenscher, *Work and Wages . . .*, 306–7; Martin, *Les Associations ouvrières . . .*, 110.

53. Perdiguier, *Le Livre du compagnonage*, 37. (Author's translation.)

CHAPTER SEVEN

"Adieu pour cette année": Seasonality and Time in New France[1]

Jane E. Harrison

Au cours des XVIIᵉ et XVIIIᵉ siècles, les communications transatlantiques avec le Canada (en l'occurrence la colonie française le long du Saint-Laurent) étaient strictement saisonnières. Le présent document se place du point de vue des correspondants canadiens et montre que, s'ils trouvaient normal le rythme particulier des communications transatlantiques, leur acceptation dépassait de beaucoup la simple résignation devant une situation inévitable. Ce rythme était «normal» dans le sens le plus profond, c'est-à-dire que la grande partie de leur vie, et plus particulièrement les communications, était réglée par les saisons. L'aspect et la signification donnés aux saisons différaient d'un milieu à l'autre, puisque ces dernières étaient établies par des humains, en fonction d'influences complexes, où les conditions climatiques se mêlaient aux interventions et aux expériences humaines. En conclusion, le document explique la signification donnée au printemps, à l'été, à l'automne et à l'hiver, dans le contexte des communications transatlantiques.

On 27 July 1657, the Ursuline nun Marie de l'Incarnation wrote her son Claude a brief letter: the impending departure of the vessel which would carry it from Quebec to France left her little time. Thus she commented, "Ce mot est seulement pour vous témoigner la consolation que je reçois chaque année lorsque j'apprends de vos nouvelles." Her later letters, she promised, would respond to his.[2]

Though we know that Marie de l'Incarnation wrote a number of other letters to Claude in the summer and early fall of 1657 all but two have been lost which she wrote to him on 15 October.[3] In one of these she commented,

> Voici la derniere lettre que vous recevrez de moy cette année, parcequ'il ne nous reste ici qu'un vaisseau qui lève l'ancre pour partir. Celle-cy n'est qu'une réite-ration de celles que je vous ay déjà écrites en matière de mon affection pour vous, ne vous ayant rien mandé que pour l'amour que je porte à votre âme.[4]

The last vessel to sail from Quebec that year left the same day the letter was written.[5] Nine months later, on 11 July 1658, the first French vessel of the new shipping season arrived.[6] It was probably that vessel which brought Marie de l'Incarnation three letters from Claude: the first word from him in almost a year. She would respond on 24 August, expressing her hope: "J'espère vous écrire par tous les vaisseaux."[7]

Year after year, the pattern was the same.[8] In the spring and early summer of each year, Claude would write a series of letters to his mother which were dispatched on vessels sailing for Quebec. The letters arrived in the summer and early fall. Once the first vessels were in port, Marie de l'Incarnation began to write her letters. She would write as many as five or six times to Claude, dispatching the letters as the vessels, both merchantmen and the king's ships, set sail. By late October or November, as the weather grew colder and the danger of ice in the St. Lawrence River increased, the last vessels prepared to leave Quebec. It was time to say farewell. In the normal course of events it would be six months, and possibly longer, before she heard news of France again. "Voicy la dernière qui va partir," she wrote in 1671, "après quoy nous ne verrons plus que des glaces sur notre mer douce jusques au mois d'avril ou may."[9] The poignancy of the situation is reflected in the often repeated phrase with which she closes many of her letters: "Adieu pour cette année."[10]

The seasonal rhythm which characterized Marie de l'Incarnation's cor-respondence with Claude was typical of transatlantic communications to and from Quebec during the French regime. There were only occasional excep-tions: letters which travelled between France and Canada on the edges of the season or during the winter. Throughout the seventeenth and eighteenth centuries these exceptions were carried by mariners with connections in New England, Acadia, Placentia, and Louisbourg. Such alternative routes may have been useful for some writers,[11] but were never common. Most correspondents had to rely on a system of communications that was rigidly seasonal.

Correspondents accepted the seasonal rhythm of transatlantic communications as normal. Marie de l'Incarnation's phrase "Adieu pour cette anneé" neatly captures the sense of calm acceptance of the seasonal rhythm which imbues most extant letters from the French regime.[12] Canadians framed their correspondence firmly within those limits, reminding the recipients not to forget to write or it would be two years before they received news.[13] In place of the expectation that they would be able to send and receive transatlantic letters year round, correspondents developed a different set of expectations. Their ideal was to be able to receive and to send a series of letters each season by a number of vessels sailing at well spaced intervals during a shipping season which extended from early spring to late fall.[14]

At one level, this is neither surprising nor complicated. Correspondents had little choice: the freezing of the St. Lawrence was the overriding constraint. Historians have stressed this perspective, presenting the seasonal rhythm of correspondence as one of the immutable facets of life at Quebec: an inescapable by-product of the climate of this colony septentrional. The correspondent is by implication the victim of the weather.[15] The normalcy of the rhythm of communications, they might say, is rooted in its inevitability. Did the correspondents themselves understand their situation in such terms? The purpose of this paper is to explore the meaning of the seasonal rhythm of communications from the writers' perspective.[16]

Generally speaking, correspondents understood seasonal constraints as more than a simple accommodation to an unavoidable condition. For them, the seasonal rhythm of communications was "normal" in the more profound sense that they assumed and accepted that much of their lives would be seasonally structured. Time was understood at least in part as a seasonal phenomenon and in such a context the rhythm of communications possessed a deep resonance. That there would be a repeated rhythm to communications therefore made sense to them. The distinction, while fine, is important. It suggests that there existed more than a grudging acceptance of the inevitable; there was a fundamental ease with the seasonal rhythm of communications.[17]

Correspondents did not, however, embrace the silence of winter eagerly. Many worried about family, friends and associates in the period when they received no news.[18] Marie de l'Incarnation wrote in the fall of 1668 to Mère Marie de la Nativité, an Ursuline at Tours, commenting,

> Si nous vivons encore l'année prochaine vous me direz de vos nouvelles, et je vous dirai des miennes. . . . Cepandant je seray en peine de vous jusqu'à l'année prochaine, la grandeur de votre maladie m'en rendant l'issue douteuse et suspecte.[19]

What they brought to their circumstances was a particular mindset which allowed them to understand the rhythm of communications as far more reasonable than we could ever conceive it to be.

At the root of the way Canadian correspondents[20] saw the seasonality of correspondence as normal was their conception of time. In one respect correspondents had a clear, linear sense of calendar time; they dated their letters marking the passage of days and months.[21] There is, however, an important distinction between "le temps-mesure," the time of the clock, and "le temps vécu," lived time.[22] We can establish conventions to measure time but time itself possesses no intrinsic, constant meaning. Rather, our sense of time is formed from our experience. The way we pattern and comprehend time is something we create.[23]

As any community, the French colonists along the St. Lawrence River possessed distinctive notions of time, created by the complex interaction between environment, experience, action, and expectation. There was Church time, marked off by bells ringing the canonical hours of matins, prime, tierce, nones, vespers, and compline. On a larger scale, the Church calendar parcelled up the year into a series of Saints days, fasts, and celebrations.[24] Then there was market time, the time of the tides, and soldiers' time.[25] For many workers, the work day and work week possessed their own distinctive rhythms.[26] These and other activities and practices created distinct patterns and rhythms which helped shape the lives of people in the preindustrial era, and influenced how they understood time.

At Quebec, for instance, there was the seasonal rhythm of the world of the merchant. Dale Miquelon notes that "The Quebec merchants' busy season was framed by the arrival and departure of ships from France, Louisbourg, and the West Indies."[27] Vessels brought cargoes, invoices, and mail to Quebec. During the short period of the season of navigation, letters had to be read, goods sold, a return cargo secured, and the details of business discussed in a voluminous correspondence. The pace was frantic.[28] Comparatively, the winter and spring were a "slack season" for the Quebec merchant. The greater part of his business involved trade overseas and this was conducted during the season of navigation. At the same time, however, the merchant still had much to do. Local business correspondence was voluminous in winter and the merchant did much travelling.[29]

The affairs of merchants at Montreal also conformed to a seasonal pattern. Louise Dechêne comments: "The seasonal movement of incoming and outgoing stocks reflects the harmonious relationship between local commerce and the fur trade." Thus the substance and limits of the seasons for the Montreal merchant differed slightly from those of the merchant at Quebec. In the fall and again in the early spring, the merchant of Montreal took receipt of goods imported through Quebec. During the winter, taking advantage of relatively easy transportation, he stockpiled foodstuffs and other local goods. In the spring the merchant prepared to outfit the voyageurs who headed West in May. The summer was spent receiving furs. Then in September, the merchant set out for Quebec, to sell furs, settle accounts, and replenish stocks.[30]

There was a similarly pronounced seasonal rhythm to the agricultural calendar. In the spring, fields were ploughed, the kitchen garden tilled, and crops planted. During the summer, the rural family pursued a range of activities including fencing. Hay was cut in mid-summer. The other crops grew and ripened according to their own schedules with oats and corn ready last in late September or early October. The fields were then ploughed, animals slaughtered and other preparations made for winter. In the winter, grain was threshed and later transported, and firewood was cut.[31] Indeed, as Jacques Mathieu has commented "Ce temps de repos de la nature est un temps de préparation active des travaux à venir."[32]

In part as a result of the seasonal rhythm of agriculture, other facets of the lives of the population also possessed a distinctive seasonal rhythm. In the countryside at least, winter was a time of comparative leisure and, "accordingly, . . . a season of festivities."[33] Marriages and births also conformed to a seasonal pattern. Most Canadians married in the autumn and, less often, the winter. Most children were conceived between April and July.[34] Louise Dechêne feels that the link between the arrival of spring and conceptions was so direct that it was the fact that spring arrives three weeks earlier at Montreal than at Quebec which explained the peak of births at Montreal in May as opposed to June.[35]

The fur trade was characterized by a variety of different patterns but each possessed a clear and predictable seasonal rhythm. For example, Louise Dechêne notes that between 1708 and 1717, many traders and voyageurs left Montreal in the spring and returned in the late summer having spent four months going to Michilimackinac or Detroit and back. Others left in October or early November, spent the winter in the upper country and returned the following August or September. Either way, the canoes and their loads of furs arrived in the St.Lawrence in late summer and autumn.[36]

The seasonal rhythm of so many facets of their lives accustomed Canadians to think of time, at least in some instances, as measured not by the progression of days, weeks, and months, but by the movement of the seasons. This notion provided the context in which they readily accepted as normal the seasonal structuring of other activities. What made correspondents all the more willing to consider it reasonable that communications should be seasonally structured was the fact that communications between Europe and other communities on the western side of the Atlantic, which did not share the characteristic Canadian climate, also conformed to distinctive seasonal patterns.

Shipping to the French West Indies, for example, was highly seasonal. Most vessels arrived in the islands between November and June with the largest number clustered in the spring. This pattern was the product of a number of factors. Weather played a role: the vessels wanted to avoid the hurricanes of the late summer and autumn. Commercial considerations were also important. The first vessels to arrive in the fall could often secure high prices for their cargo of provisions. They would, however, have to wait to pick up a return cargo, for the sugar crop was not ready for export until January. Other vessels sailed later from France, as they waited to bring new wine from Bordeaux.[37]

In the Chesapeake, communications were dominated by the season of a single commodity, tobacco. Ian Steele distinguishes an early pattern which held from the 1630s to the 1690s. Vessels arrived before November to avoid the winter westerlies; merchants spent the winter assembling a cargo; and vessels left in the spring to avoid the perils of the summer season. Later, the pattern of shipping, and hence communications, changed. Autumn arrivals became less common. Instead, most vessels arrived in spring and left in late summer having spent far less time in the colony. The change was the result of a number of factors including the determination of those involved to decrease the length and expense of the layover. While the specific pattern of shipping had changed, however, it was still distinctly seasonal and short. Steele concludes that although the Chesapeake was accessible year round, "there was no provisions trade . . . luring English or colonial ships to venture in the off-season of the staple trade." Thus the season for trans-oceanic communications "coincided with the season for loading tobacco."[38]

To a lesser extent, shipping—hence communications—to the port of Boston also possessed a certain seasonal pattern. In this case, again according to Steele, shipping was not dominated by the seasons of any one commodity, but by the weather. The issue seems to have been more one of the perception of a necessary seasonal rhythm than the real need for it. Passages westward across the Atlantic were uncommon in the winter, but vessels sailed eastward from Boston in any month.[39]

The seasonal patterning of transatlantic communications to Canada was thus understood as "normal" in a double sense. First, correspondents were accustomed to thinking of time as intrinsically seasonal in many contexts. Second, they were accustomed to the idea of the seasonal structuring of communications and did not see the phenomenon as peculiarly Canadian. What they were not accustomed to was a single or uniform seasonal pattern. If time was understood as a progression of seasons, clearly in each context the particular limits of the seasons and the meaning attached to them differed. At the root of the seasons were variations in climate, yet their specific boundaries and meanings were defined in relation to the actions and experience of people. The seasons were socially defined—human seasons— created by the complex interaction between the environment and the people themselves. The world of communications allows us to see, in a specific context, how the seasons were created and how Canadians constructed the meaning of spring, summer, fall, and winter. In doing this, they added another layer to their understanding of time and made sense for themselves of the seasonality of communications.

Thus we see that spring was a season when the thoughts of Canadian correspondents turned to France. There, letters were being written for friends, relatives and associates living along the St. Lawrence. As Mme Bégon wrote at Montreal on 8 March 1749, "Voilà cher fils, tout ce que je sais et que j'éspère, si tu es en France, que tu vas te préparer à me donner de tes nouvelles."[40] It was a time of anticipation. Correspondents made careful note of the winds, waiting for a favourable one to carry the vessels and their cargo of letters up the river.[41]

The "season of letters" began when the first French vessels arrived in the St. Lawrence River.[42] This varied from year to year and was never predictable.[43] The season of correspondence at Quebec was as much a product of conditions, constraints, and concerns in France as it was the product of the climate in Canada. Merchants, for example, sent off their vessels when their cargo was ready; when the winds were favorable; and when other conditions dictated considerations. Correspondents themselves were aware of the extent to which vessels sailed in response to conditions in France rather than in Canada. Marie de l'Incarnation informed her correspondents that the first vessels sailed from Dieppe.[44] The financial commissary of war in New France, Doreil, reminded his correspondents in the mid-1750s that the first vessels always sailed from Bordeaux in early March with more leaving from there in April; as many or more vessels sailed from La Rochelle slightly later; while one or two left Bayonne, and at least one from Marseille, Nantes, and Le Havre at fairly predictable intervals.[45]

The arrival of the vessels possessed for many correspondents the qualities of an awakening, commented the *Relation* of 1633.

> Les lettres qu'on envoie en ces pais cy, sont comme des fruiets bien rares et
> bien nouueaux: on les reçoit auec contenement, on les regarde avuec plaisir:
> on les sauoure comme des fruiets du Paradis terrestre.[46]

Marie de l'Incarnation expressed the same sense of joy at a world being reconnected when she wrote to her brother in 1640: "C'est avec un extrême contentement que j'ay reçu votre lettre en ce bout du monde oú l'on est sauvage toute l'année, sinon lorsque les vaisseaux sont arrivez que nous reprenons notre lanque François."[47]

Once begun, the season of correspondence possessed a distinctive quality. It was a period of business, bustle, and preoccupation with transatlantic affairs. For Marie de l'Incarnation, the summer and fall months were exhausting. As Superior of the Ursulines she was required to maintain a vast official correspondence which could number more than two hundred letters each season.[48] She often complained that she was worn out by "la presse des lettres et des vaisseaux qui vont partir."[49] "Je suis," she commented in late October 1649,

> une pauvre créature chargée d'affaires tant pour la France que pour cette Maison. Trois mois durant ceux qui ont des expéditions à faire pour la France, n'ont point de repos, et comme je suis chargé de tout le temporel de cette famille, qu'il me faut faire venir de France toutes nos nécessitez, qu'il me faut faire payement par billets, n'ayant pas d'argent en ce païs, qu'il me faut traitter avec des Mattelots pour retirer nos denrées, et enfin qu'il me faut prendre mille soins et faire mille choses qu'il seroit inutile de vous dire, il ne se peut faire que tous les momens de mon temps ne soient remplis de quelque occupation . . .[50]

Her private letters to Claude and other family as well as to friends and associates were often written at night, in haste, and a few lines at a time.[51] On 4 October 1658 she wrote to Claude, "Je n'ay pas le temps de relire ma lettre, excusez mes fautes et l'empressement."[52] She rarely had the leisure time for writing that she wished she had, particularly to write to Claude.

Nearly a century later, the pattern was much the same. Mère de Sainte-Hélène commented in 1730: "l'automne en canada est une saison accablante, parce que toutes les affaires se font, on reçoit les lettres de france, on y répond très promptement on fait ses provisions, on payes ses dettes . . . ,"[53] "tout ce termine ici en un mois ou six semaines, c'est un Chaos ou on ne se connoit pas."[54] Another observer commented, "le temps des vaisseaux qui est une espèce de foire à Québec."[55] Correspondents continually complained that they were left with little time for anything but the pressing business of the season. Mme Aubert Beaucours commented in a letter to M. Lavaltrie, of Niagara on 18 October 1744, "M. de beaucours est bien mortifié Monsieur de ne pouvoir pas vous écrire par cette occasions estant très occupé les vessaux aitant-preste a partir il a tres peu de tant pour faire des lestre ille vous fait bien ces complim't."[56]

The winter, in contrast to the season of navigation, was a period of relative calm. "The ships weighed anchor from before Kebec the 7th of October of last year [1642]," noted the *Relation* of 1642–43. "Their departure produces a wonderful silence here and directs each man's attention to his own family, in deep tranquility."[57] The pace of life was more measured and many correspondents had greater leisure. It was during the winter, for example, that Marie de l'Incarnation took the time to write the letters which she had been unable to write the previous season, those which required a particularly thoughtful answer. Thus, when Claude asked her penetrating questions on spiritual matters, she often postponed a response until after communications closed. She would write him during the winter and send the letter the following summer. He then would not receive a response to a question posed in the spring of one year until the fall of the following year.[58]

Marie de l'Incarnation would also write letters before the correspondence season began in order to lessen the volume she would have to write once the vessels arrived. In 1671, she wrote to her son,

> Je vous écris ce peu de lignes avant que d'avoir reçeu de vos nouvelles, pour vous assurer de la sainte protection de Dieu sur vous, et sur moi en particulier qui suis en assez bonne santé pour mon âge, grâces à la divine Bonté. Et pour prévinir l'embarras de la décharge des vaisseaux.[59]

The winter was not, of course, a period of inactivity. Marie de l'Incarnation prepared dictionaries of native languages, managed the affairs of her community, and oversaw the teaching of aboriginal and French girls, among a broad range of activities. Mère de Saint-Hèlene was also busy during the winter. Each, however, defined the winter season in contrast to the season of navigation and correspondence: for them the calm and peace of winter was a relative measure, their activities different, not ended.

Time was thus marked not by the passage of days but according to the cycle of correspondence. The year itself was constructed according to their experience. For example, François Dollier de Casson divided his *Histoire de Montréal*, written in 1672 or 1673, into 32 chapters. Each chapter covered a year, but the year was defined as the time between the departure of vessels from Quebec one year and the next. Thus Chapter Two covers the period "Depuis le départ des vaisseaux du Canadas pour la France dans l'autonne de l'année 1641 jusques à leur départ du même lieu pour la France dans l'autonne 1642." This structure was chosen, according to the author, "parces que . . . tous les nouvelles de ce pays sont contenues chanque année en ce qui se fait ici depuis le départ des navires d'une année à l'autre et en ce qu'on reçoit de France par les vaisseaux qui en viennent." The structure, he commented, followed "l'ordre naturel."[60]

Correspondents generally followed the same structure, marking the passage of time from season to season and beginning the news they had to recount in their letters with what had happened since the last vessels sailed. Thus in a letter written in the spring of 1650, Marie de l'Incarnation told Claude "Je vous dirai donc, que depuis les lettres que je vous écrivis au mois d'Octobre dernier tout a été en paix en ce pais."[61] Indeed, when she promised to provide him as she so often did with "un petit récit de ce qui s'est passé cette année dans notre nouvelle France," she generally meant that she would tell him what had happened since the fall.[62]

To the modern observer, the seasonal rhythm of transatlantic communications to Quebec seems extraordinary. We cannot imagine a correspondence so narrowly constrained. Canadian correspondents during the French regime, however, considered their situation to be normal. That they did so was a product of the way in which they understood time in general and the rhythm of communications in particular. The seasonal patterning of their existence made sense to them because so many facets of their lives were similarly structured. They were accustomed to measuring and understanding time, at least in some contexts, as a progression of seasons. The seasonal rhythm of communications did not appear peculiarly Canadian because shipping and therefore the mails in other parts of the colonial Atlantic world were also rigidly seasonal.

It is clear that the seasonal rhythm of correspondence was not simply the product of the winter freeze. It was also determined by the complex interaction between environment and people. Vessels did not crowd the St. Lawrence River the first moment it was open any more than in the Chesapeake the seasonal rhythm of communications had been the "natural" product of the weather. The particular pattern of shipping was determined by a series of factors. The meaning of the seasons was similarly not "natural" but created from the particular circumstances in which correspondents found themselves. Thus for Canadian correspondents writing overseas, the spring was a period of anticipation, the summer was all bustle, the autumn brought closure, and the winter was a time of quiet and reflection.

NOTES

1. I would like to thank Paul Deslandes, Stephen Heathorn, Jeff McNairn, Charlie Trainor, Carolyn Podruchny, Allan Greer, Deborah Van Seters, Adam Crerar, members of the Early Canadian History Discussion Group, and members of the French Colonial Historical Society for their helpful comments on earlier versions of this paper.

2. Dom Guy Oury, ed., *Marie de l'Incarnation, Ursuline (1599-1672): Correspondance* (Solesmes: Abbaye Sainte-Pierre, 1971), [Hereafter Marie de l'Incarnation], 27 July 1657, 588–90.

3. See *Marie de l'Incarnation*, 15 October 1657, 594, 590 n.9.

4. Ibid.

5. *Journal des jésuites*, 220, cited in ibid., 594.

6. *Journal de jésuites*, 237, cited in ibid., 599.

7. *Marie de l'Incarnation*, 24 August 1658, 596–98.

8. Marie de l'Incarnation left France for Canada on 4 May 1639 when Claude was 20 years of age. He joined the Benedictines of Saint-Maur, becoming superior in 1652 and superior-general in 1668. He did not see his mother again for more than 30 years as she lived at Quebec, where she died on 30 April 1672. The only direct link between them was their letters. DCB, s.v., vol. 1, "Guyart, Marie;" see also Dom Guy Oury, "Introduction," *Marie de l'Incarnation*, ix-xxxviii.

9. *Marie de l'Incarnation*, 9 November 1671, 946; see also 15 October 1657, 594, and 590 n.9.

10. Ibid., 2 November 1660, 650.

11. While not commonplace, such references do exist in the literature. In early May 1726, for example, the chief military engineer, Chaussegros de Lery received a letter dated 6 November 1725 "par la voie de l'angleterre." *Inventaire des papiers de Lery*, vol. 1, 140–2. I have found no references to mails through Placentia in the winter.

12. There are occasional exceptions. Louis-Antoine de Bougainville railed against the distance that separated him from friends and family in France and found the silence of winter almost insupportable. Then again, he found little about his

situation which pleased him. See, in particular, 7 November 1756, 392 and 9
November 1757, 414, de Bougainville, *Ecrits sur le Canada: Mémoires-Journal-Lettres*, ed, Roland Lamontagne, (Quebec: Pélican, 1993).

13. The Hospitaller of l'Hotel Dieu of Quebec, Mère de Saint-Hélène, frequently
reminded Mme Hecquet, "Que quand vous manquez a me faire l'honneur de
mécrire une année, il faut que je jeaune deux ans du plaisir d'apprendre ce qui
vous regarde," "Lettres de Mère Marie-Andrée Duplessis de Hélène, Supérieur
des Hospitalières de l'Hôtel-Dieu de Quebec," *Nova Francia*, [hereafter cited as
"Mère de Sainte-Hélène"], vol. 3, 18 October 1733, 171–72. Marie de l'Incarnation
reprimanded Claude in September of 1640, "Je ne veux pas agir avec vous comme
vous faites avec moy. Hé quoy! avez-vous eu le courage de laisser partir la flotte
sans me donner un mot de consolation par une lettre de vostre part?" *Marie de
l'Incarnation*, September 1640, 115–16.

14. Each year Jean Dudouyt, procurator of the Séminaire de Quebec and its
representative in Paris, wrote Bishop Laval of Quebec a series of letters which he
dispatched by different vessels. The letters sent by Dudouyt through the early
1680s all show the same pattern. See, for example Archives du Séminaire de
Québec [hereafter ASQ], Carton N, no's 52, 53, 54, 57, 60, 62, 67, and 71. See
also Tremblay's correspondence with Canada, ASQ, Lettres N and O. This was
always Marie de l'Incarnation's ideal. In late September 1665, she told Claude,
"je me suis donné la consolation de vous écrire plusieurs Lettres" This was the
fourth of five letters she would send that year. *Marie de l'Incarnation*, September
1665, 754–6 and 29 October 1665, 758. See also, "Mère de Sainte-Hélène," vol. 5,
372–74; "Les lettres de Doreil," letters from the summer of 1755, *Rapport de
l'archiviste de la Province de Québec*, 1944–1945; and Archives of the University
of Montreal, Baby Collection, U12,258, 2 May 1747, Jean Veyssière to Pierre Guy.

15. The rigors of the Canadian climate are prominent in many studies of the colony.
Strangely, however, most studies completely ignore the existence of a seasonal
rhythm of communications. Those who mention the pattern present it as a simple
matter of correspondents responding to climate. Those who make the most
interesting observations concerning the seasonal rhythm of communications are
Dale Miquelon, *Dugard of Rouen: French Trade to Canada and the West Indies,
1729–1770* (Montreal: McGill-Queen's Press, 1978), 69–73; and W. J. Eccles,
Canada Under Louis XIV, 1663–1701 (Toronto: McClelland and Stewart, 1978),
28.

16. Who were these correspondents? Studies have shown that the literate population

of New France was small and largely urban. In the last decades of the seventeenth century, an estimated 49.9 percent of the population of the parishes of Montreal and Quebec could sign their name while 28.6 percent of the rural population could do so. R. Roy, Yves Landry, H. Charbonneau, "Quelques comportements des canadiens au XVIIe siècle d'après les registres paroissiaux," *Revue d'histoire de l'Amerique française* 31, no. 1 (1977): 66; Allan Greer, "The Pattern of Literacy in Quebec, 1745–1899," *Histoire Sociale/Social History* 11 (1978): in particular, 330–31 for Greer's summary of his conclusions.

    This discussion is largely based on private correspondence of which little has survived from the period of New France. The letters provide access to a tiny fraction of the relatively small group of letter writers spread out over almost one hundred years. The paper is thus meant to be suggestive rather than conclusive. What is striking, however, is the extent to which conditions remained broadly the same through the period under study.

17. My appreciation of this idea was first prompted by Ian Steele, *The English Atlantic, 1675–1740: An Exploration of Communication and Community* (New York: Oxford University Press, 1986), esp. p. 5.

18. See, for example, *Mére de Sainte-Hélène.*

19. *Marie de l'Incarnation,* 13 September 1668, 817.

20. In referring to the writers as Canadian correspondents, I do not mean to suggest that they would so have identified themselves. Many merchants, for example, would almost certainly not have thought of themselves as "Canadian." Yet they were resident in Canada and it is in this sense that I use the term.

21. That they did so is evidence of one facet of the way in which they understood time, according to G. J. Whitrow, *Time in History: Views of Time from Prehistory to the Present Day* (New York: Oxford University Press, 1989), 83–84. As late as the fifteenth century correspondents rarely dated their letters. If they did so, they dated them in relation to saint's days or the years of a monarch's reign. The way Canadian writers dated their letters suggests a greater interest in and appreciation for a linear marking of the passage of time.

22. Lucien Febvre, *Le problème de l'Incroyance en XVIe Siècle* (Paris: 1947), 431 cited in E. P. Thompson, "Time, Work-Discipline and Industrial Capitalism," in *Customs in Common* (London: Merlin Press, 1991), 358 n.1.

23. See, for example, Jacques Le Goff, "Au Moyen Age: Temps de l'Eglise et temps du Marchand," *Annales E.S.C.,* May–June 1960, 417–33; Martin Bruegel, "Time that can be Relied Upon: The Evolution of Time Consciousness in the Mid-Hudson

Valley, 1790–1860," *Journal of Social History* (American) (Spring 1995): 547–64; Andre Gingrich, "Time, Ritual and Social Experience," in *Social Experience and Anthropological Knowledge*, Kirsten Hastrup and Peter Hervik,eds., (London: Routledge, 1994), 166–79.

24. "Le calendrier religieux a rhythmé la vie de l'ensemble de la population." Jacques Mathieu, *La Nouvelle-France: les Français en Amérique du Nord, XVIe-XVIIIe siecle*, (Laval: Les presses de l'Université Laval, 1991), 172. Whitrow, *Time in History*, 108–10.

25. Mathieu, *La Nouvelle-France*, 177–78; Ken Donovan, Historian, Fortress Louisbourg suggested the importance of the patterns of the military day to structuring the affairs of soldiers and others in the community.

26. See, for example, Thompson, "Time, Work-Discipline and Industrial Capitalism."

27. Miquelon, *Dugard of Rouen*, 71.

28. See for example, Allana Reid, "General Trade Between Quebec and France During the French Regime," *CHR*, 1953 and also Kathryn A. Young, "Kin, Commerce, and Community: Merchants in the Port of Quebec from 1717 to 1745" (Ph.D. diss., University of Manitoba, 1991), 67–68.

29. Miquelon, *Dugard of Rouen*, 73.

30. Louise Dechêne, *Habitants and Merchants in Seventeenth Century Montreal*, trans. Liana Vardi (Montreal: McGill-Queen's, 1992), 104.

31. Ibid., 174–5; Allan Greer, *Peasant, Lord, and Merchant: Rural Society in Three Quebec Parishes, 1740–1840* (Toronto: University of Toronto Press, 1985), 28–33.

32. Mathieu, *La Nouvelle-France*, 179.

33. Greer, *Peasant, Lord, and Merchant*, 32–33.

34. Hubert Charbonneau, et al., *Naissance d'une population. Les Français établis au Canada au XVIIe siècle*. (Paris/Montréal: Institut national d'études démographiques/Presses de l'Université de Montréal, coll. "Travaux et documents," no. 118, 1987), 84.

35. Dechêne, *Habitants and Merchants . . .* , 56–7.

36. Ibid., 117–19.

37. Miquelon, *Dugard of Rouen*, 91 n. 4. Ian Steele, *The English Atlantic*, 25–40 argues in contrast that shipping to the English sugar islands was not seasonal. Rather, the sugar route functioned as a year-round highway between England and English North America, providing high-volume, year-round traffic. The difference in the pattern emphasizes the extent to which seasonal rhythms are far more than the mere product of environmental factors.

38. Steele, *The English Atlantic*, 41–51; 55.

39. Ibid., 60.

40. *Elisabeth Bégon*, 8 March 1749, 4.

41. Ibid., 28 April 1749, 119; 18 May 1749, 130; 20 May 1749, 131; 3 June 1749, 137–8. On 3 June 1749 she was finally able to write, "Voila un commencement de nouvelles" when a vessel arrived from the West Indies with news from France.

42. News of the arrival of the first vessels was often carried to Quebec from Tadoussac. Thwaites, *Jesuit Relations*, vol. 12, Le Jeune's Relation, 1637, 188; vol. 28, 1645–46, 231; 1646–7, vol. 30, 189. Sometimes letters were brought to Quebec before the vessel itself arrived in port. See, for example, NAC, Baby Collection, fol. 618, 11 June 1748 cited in Miquelon, *Dugard of Rouen*, 73 and also a comment by Gilles Proulx, *Between France and New France: Life Aboard the Tall Sailing Ships* (Toronto and Charlottetown: Dundurn Press in Cooperation with Parks Canada, 1984), 78. Such early delivery was not always possible, as is clear from two ordonnances governing the delivery of letters at Quebec. See NAC, M8145, "21 Juin 1727, Ordonnance au sujet des Lettres Missives addresser a la Colonie." and P. G. Roy, *Inventaire des ordonnances*, vol. 2, 20 July 1732, 126.

43. The earliest vessels arrived in May or June with most coming into the port in July or August. Occasionally a vessel arrived in September or even October. The specific dates on which vessels arrived can be traced in many primary sources. J.S. Pritchard, "Ships, Men, and Commerce: A Study of Maritime Activity in New France," (Ph.D. diss., University of Toronto, 1971), table 1: "Ship Traffic Between Quebec and France, 1645–1667," provides a quick summary over a period in which shipping varied considerably over time but the basic pattern of arrivals remained remarkably constant.

44. *Marie de l'Incarnation*, 4 September 1640, 104.

45. Doreil was responsible for the care and maintenance of the French regular troops in Canada, see *DCB*, vol. 3. On the matter of departures see his correspondence of 1755, "Les Lettres de Doreil," *Rapport de l'archiviste de la province de Québec, 1944–45*.

46. *Relations des Jésuites* (Coté, 1858), 1633, 1.

47. *Marie de l'Incarnation*, 4 September 1640, 102–3.

48. Ibid., 15 September 1644, 240. On 16 October 1666, she closed a letter to her son so that she could rest. The number of letters she had written had worn her out, she explained. She added, however, that she had no more than forty left, which she hoped to have ready to send by the last vessel.

49. Ibid., 30 September 1643, 199.

50. Ibid., 22 October 1649, 377–78.

51. Ibid., 30 September 1643, 202; Summer 1647, 320; 13 August 1650, 392–93.

52. Ibid., 4 October 1658, 606.

53. *Mère de Sainte-Hélène*, vol. 3, October 1730, 56.

54. Ibid., vol. 3, 28 September 1742, 289–90.

55. NAC, Col., C11A, vol. 49: 494, "Observations sur l'ordonnace de police de Dupuy sur les cagarets", 22 November 1726, cited in John Hare, Marc Lafrance, David-Thiery Ruddel, *Histoire de la Ville de Québec*, 23.

56. NAC, Baby Collection, 530, 18 October 1744, U6082. The letter writer signs "Ellony Celeron" and may be the cousin of her correspondent, M. Lavaltrie, who is identified as captain of the infantry commanding Niagara.

57. Thwaites, *Jesuit Relations*, 1642–43, vol. 23, 307.

58. See for example, ibid., 2 October 1655, 557–60.

59. Ibid., September–November 1671, 939. The disadvantage of writing so early was that there was nothing to respond to. Letters from France had yet to arrive at Québec.

60. François Dollier de Casson, *Histoire du Montréal*, Nouvelle édition critique par Marcel Trudel et Marie Baboyant, Cahiers de Québec, (Québec: Hurtubise, 1992), 46. The year, so defined, was of variable length. It was marked off not by some absolute standard but by the date on which the vessels left Quebec in the fall. The limits of the season therefore could change from year to year, depending on the pattern of shipping. The seasons of the colony were not the pure seasons of nature but human seasons.

61. *Marie de l'Incarnation*, 17 May 1650, 389. The letter went by way of the fisheries.

62. Ibid., 30 September 1643, 199.

CHAPTER EIGHT

Some Unresolved Issues: Lorette Hurons in the Colonial Context

Cornelius J. Jaenen

Cette communication se penche sur cinq questions importantes pour la Nation Huronne-Wendat: l'étendue du territoire des ancêtres et son statut vis-à-vis des autres nations amérindiennes; les effets de l'économie missionnaire sur son évolution; les origines de la réduction de Sillery; les droits et les privilèges découlant du Traité de Murray, 1760; le renouvellement du partage des territoires de chasse entre les Algonquins et les Hurons, le 26 octobre 1829. Ce que beaucoup d'autochtones réclament de nos jours, c'est un retour non à une vie traditionelle d'antan, mais un retour à la possession des territoires, de l'autonomie et du droit de disposer d'eux-mêmes. Nous croyons que ce survol peut nous offrir quelques indices de ce que sont les revendications et les réclamations de ce peuple huron d'aujourd'hui.

The Nation Huronne-Wendat occupied a special place in the colonial policies of both France and Britain. This most favored nation approach was evident in early eighteenth-century French dealings with the Huron Confederacy in the *pays d'en haut* and may have reflected the position it held in pre-contact times. Although the British, for obvious geo-political reasons, were more involved with the Iroquois League, especially the Mohawk component, they too had to take Huron interests into consideration in their evolving aboriginal policy after 1760. The special role of the Hurons must be seen in the context of general French policy with regard to aboriginal peoples in the Canadian sector of New France.

By the end of the French régime, it is clear that the aboriginal nations allied to the French interest enjoyed four fundamental liberties in their relations with the colonizing power: possession of their territories; freedom to circulate as they wished throughout the upper country, or *pays d'en haut,* beyond the riverine area of French colonization; the free exercise of their customs, including justice; and freedom of trade and exploitation of the resources of their territories. The French, as I have stated elsewhere, maintained their sovereignty over a vast expanse of the continent, to be sure, but through the recognition of the independence and self-determination of the aboriginal peoples in the region.[1]

The French colonial administration at Quebec (Montreal in the summer months) had accepted a number of conditions for the maintenance of such an *entente cordiale*: to defer any extensive settlement of the hinterland above Montreal; not to establish any forts, trading posts or mission stations in the upper country without the prior consent and co-operation of the aboriginal inhabitants concerned; never to impose military orders or discipline on bands of allied warriors; never to impose French laws and judicial procedures on aboriginal people without their consent, and to remove all cases proceeded with from the royal courts to the military tribunal presided by the Governor General; to distribute regularly the *présents du Roy* in recognition of the sharing of territories and resources with the Native nations; to consult at the highest military and diplomatic level, that of Governor General and commander-in-chief, with all and sundry native leaders and delegations at Montreal each year between June and September.[2]

The British conquerors of Canada were not able to disregard this relationship when they assumed control of the colony renamed Quebec. Prior to the conquest, in fact, several English observers of colonial affairs had commented favorably on the superiority of this French approach to native affairs in North America compared to the policies of the fifteen Anglo-American colonies.[3] Indeed, the creation of an Indian department, placing Indian affairs under imperial rather than colonial control in 1755, may indicate a move towards adoption of the French model. The British found it necessary to continue the main features of the previous French policy, especially when faced with such events as the Pontiac rising, the War of the American

Revolution and the outbreak of the French Revolution. One may wonder, considering this elaborate accomodation between European intruders and aboriginal inhabitants, what special recognition or most favored nation role the Hurons Confederacy, and later the Hurons of Lorette, their descendants, might enjoy.

The importance of the Hurons in relation to other aboriginal communities dates from pre-contact times. There is a tradition that the Hurons or Wendats possessed the entire region from Mackinac on the Great Lakes eastwards along the north shore of the St. Lawrence river to just below the site of the present city of Quebec. This was a hunting territory dotted with agricultural villages on its southern limits.[4] In 1773, a Huron chief told Daniel Claus, Sir William Johnson's deputy, that they "have been looked upon by all Indian Nations from Tadousack to Niagara as their Superiors and obeyed as such . . . being considered by all the Nations in the above Light & original Proprietors of this Country"[5] Nicolas Vincent, hunting north of the Huron reserve at Nouvelle Lorette, could tell a committee of the House of Assembly of Lower Canada in 1824 that he was hunting in his nation's ancient and traditional hunting grounds. He affirmed:

> La nation Huronne avoit autrefois . . . aucunes limites de chasse ni de pêche; ils étoient maîtres du pays à aller jusqu'au grands lacs; nos ancêtres ne permettoient à qui que ce soit de faire la chasse et la pêche sur leurs terres . . .[6]

The anthropologist, Bruce G. Trigger, concluded recently that in some sense the Hurons were indeed the direct descendants of the early Iroquoian peoples that inhabited this extensive northern region.[7]

Furthermore, the Laurentian Iroquoians that Cartier encountered at Stadacona and Hochelaga during his visits in 1535 and 1541 had disappeared by the time his nephews entered the St. Lawrence valley in 1580. There is archaeological evidence that many of them, especially women and probably children, were absorbed by the eastern tribe of the Hurons who occupied the Trent River drainage basin.[8] Although there is still debate about the disappearance of the Laurentian Iroquoians, a far more important issue confronts contemporary jurists. In the present context of land claims in south-eastern Ontario and southern Quebec, especially by various Algonkian groups and the Mohawks, the Huron claim has not yet been advanced. It is the first of several unresolved issues.

The second unresolved issue regards the nature and consequences of Jesuit missionary activity beginning in what has more recently been called Huronia, that is the region between Georgian Bay and Lake Simcoe where the Hurons' villages were located at the beginning of the seventeenth century. The Jesuits were long portrayed as altruistic bearers of civilization to presumably backward pagan tribes and for their great pains a number were rewarded with martyrdom. More recent scholarly investigation has been less laudatory. They were not poor, like the Récollets who preceded them, but enjoyed such privileges as free transport for themselves and their goods from France to their mission stations, royal subsidies, and revenues from their extensive properties. In Huronia itself, the Jesuits demanded pay for their services in valuable furs but paid for services rendered to them with trade goods which they imported free of freight and customs. Missionary involvement in a hidden trade has recently been called *l'économie missionnaire.*[9]

Evangelization resulted in growing dissension in the Huron Confederacy as about one third eventually adhered to the new religion while the majority faction maintained traditional beliefs and customs. The secular authorities in the colony supported missionary work by dealing with converted trading captains, hiring converts as guides and canoemen, and supplying firearms at first only to Catholics. Factionalism in the Huron community sapped the unity of the confederacy, brought social disorganization, and by 1647 resulted in threats of forcible expulsion of all the French from the upper country.[10] Georges Sioui, a Huron historian, has recently expanded on the hypothesis that serious depopulation resulted from epidemics introduced by traders, missionaries and trade goods. He has argued that this loss of population was a critical element in the eventual destruction of the Huron Confederacy in 1649–50.[11]

The Jesuits who perished in the final phase of the Iroquois-Huron war were not martyrs strictly speaking, because, as Father Charles Garnier wrote at the time, they were not killed "par un tyran qui persécute l'église." The Iroquois won the inter-tribal war through the successful application of some of the basic principles of warfare: preparatory intelligence, surprise, concentration of forces, and use of terror tactics to demoralize the enemy. Since the French did not come to the aid of their Huron allies in this war, some of the missionaries were sacrificed along with the Hurons.[12] The surviving missionaries put the torch to Sainte-Marie, their headquarters in the upper country, and became refugees like one remnant of Hurons who eventually tried to find asylum on the island of Orleans near the town of Quebec. It was long held that the Hurons had been the victims of Iroquois designs to extend their domination over all their neighbors, occupy their hunting territories and cut off French trade. More recently the Iroquois have been seen as wishing to extend the universal peace of Deganawidah to incorporate both the Hurons and the French, at least symbolically, in the Longhouse. That concept was, in a sense, the traditionalists' proactive response to Catholic evangelization.[13]

The third unresolved question, which arises out of missionary efforts to evangelize and gallicize the Hurons, concerns the seigniorial rights to Sillery, the first *réduction* in New France. This reserve (as it was later called) was modeled on the Paraguayan *reducciones* and was conceived as an institution to accelerate the assimilation of the aboriginal inhabitants in a socially controlled environment, or segregation.[14] Unlike the practice in Massachusetts, the institution in New France did not involve any surrender of Amerindian lands to make way for European settlement; the opposite movement took place as aboriginal peoples came voluntarily into the French seigniorial tract to take up lands in proximity of French farmers.

But Sillery differed from all the other *réductions* organized thereafter in the colony. When the Algonkian bands who first came to take up residence at Sillery left, the proprietary Company of New France granted it to new seigneurs in 1651—the aboriginal peoples consisting mostly of Huron refugees from the Huron-Iroquois war—with full seigniorial rights, except justice, and privileges such as the exclusive right to fish in the St. Lawrence bordering the reserve near Quebec. Five years later, Governor Jean de Lauzon issued an ordinance prohibiting all French colonists from purchasing reserve lands or from hunting and fishing there without the consent of their Jesuit guardians:

Ayant cy devant pour bonnes considérations estably les Reverends Pères de la compagnie de Jesus tuteurs et curateurs des sauvages de la nouvelle france n'ayant pas jugé les dits sauvages capables de regir ny gouverner le Bien *qui leur est donné*, il est faict inhibitions et defenses à qui que ce soit de traiter avec eux pour raison de *leurs possessions et choses qui en despendent* à peine de nullité des dites conventions.[15]

Although his decree reaffirmed the custodial rights of the missionaries it also repeated the possessory rights of the aboriginal incumbents to the seigneury of Sillery. After New France passed from company rule to royal government in 1663, the Compagnie des Indes Occidentales received the fur trade monopoly, and article 34 of the royal edict for its creation acknowledged the legal rights of converted Amerindians:

> les sauvages convertis à la foi catholique, apostolique et romaine sont censés et réputés regnicoles et naturels françois, et comme tels, capables de toutes successions, dons, legs et autres dispositions sans être obligés d'obtenir aucunes lettres de naturalité.[16]

In 1673, the Jesuits convinced the Hurons to move to better farm lands. Thus they moved to Ancienne Lorette and eventually to Nouvelle Lorette, their present location. These moves took them away from the rich soils along the St. Lawrence towards the sandy soils north-west of the French town. The rationalization was that they would be closer to their hunting grounds. Meanwhile, the Jesuits granted concessions at Sillery to French settlers, also holding the title to the new *réductions* to which the Hurons were relocated. Finally, in May 1680 the Sovereign Council at Quebec issued a decree recognizing Jesuit rights to Sillery which appear to have infringed on the original grant of the fief to the "Sauvages chrétiens." The colonial attorney-general, Ruette d'Auteuil, later protested this violation of the proprietary rights of the "Sauvages chrétiens."[17] The claim to the Sillery lands may yet come to the Supreme Court of Canada.

A fourth issue has been resurrected as a result of the Supreme Court ruling in the case *Sioui v. the Queen* [1990] which broadened the concept of what constitutes a valid and binding treaty. By the 1750s the French were allied with a majority of the aboriginal nations of northeastern North America through three major alliances: the Micmac-Abenaki alliance in the Atlantic region; the Seven Fires or Nations of Canada; the Three Fires Confederacy of the upper Great Lakes region. In the Seven Fires of Canada, or the seven villages of "domiciled natives" in the St. Lawrence valley between La Présentation [Oswegatchie/Ogdensburg] and Lorette [Québec], the Hurons of Lorette held the honored place of "uncles," the Nipissings at Lac des Deux-Montagnes [Kanesatake/Oka] as envoys to the Three Fires Confederacy and the Mohawks of Kanawake as envoys to the Six Nations Iroquois. The fires represented their mutual understanding and cooperation; the French were allies. So, protocol required that Montcalm and Bougainville in planning their strategy in the final conflict against Britain should consult the Hurons of Lorette, then proceed to Lac des Deux-Montagnes and Kanawake to consolidate the alliance. Bougainville left but a terse reference to these important visits:

> Mêmes propositions, mêmes réponses, même cérémonie [à Kanawake] qu'au lac des Deux-Montagnes et de plus celle de couvrir au nom du [Gouverneur] marquis de Vaudreuil la mort de deux chefs iroquois et celle de me présenter à la nation comme candidat à l'adoption.[18]

As it turned out, the visit to Kanawake was more important than the French officers imagined because, according to an established tradition, the Iroquois of Kanawake alone among the Seven Nations of Canada could prevail on the Six Nations to remain neutral in a war between Britain and France.

The role of France's Amerindian allies in the Seven Years' War has generally been overlooked. Nevertheless, before an outbreak of smallpox disrupted some of the war parties, at least 1800 warriors were active in the Laurentian valley between 1757 and 1759, 2100 in the Ohio valley and another five or six hundred in Acadia in support of the French armies.[19] After the fall of Louisbourg in 1758 and Quebec in 1759, the League of the Iroquois abandoned the policy of neutrality it had adopted at the signing of the Treaty of Montreal in 1701 and joined Anglo-Americans in the siege of Niagara. This move disturbed the allies of the French, including the Hurons of Lorette. In mid-February 1760 Iroquois delegates from La Présentation [Oswegatchie], Kanawake and Kanesatake "being deputed by 22 Nations in the French Interest" invited delegates from the Six Nations Iroquois to come to Kanawake so that they might ascertain their role in the international conflict.[20] The Amerindian allies of the French were coming to the conclusion that Britain would conquer New France, therefore they ought to seek some guarantees for their territorial rights, their hunting and fishing rights, and their customs and usages. General Amherst gave them the desired guarantees in a proclamation issued at Fort Oswego on 27 April 1760. It read:

I do assure all the Indian Nations that His Majesty has not sent me to deprive any of you of your Lands and Property; on the contrary, so long as you do adhere to his Interest and by your behaviour give proofs of the sincerity of your attachement to His Royal Person and cause, I will defend and maintain you in your just rights, and give you all the aid and assistance you may stand in need of to repress the dangers you may be liable to, from the Enemy [French] . . .[21]

The success of this declaration was manifested when the British forces reached the Sulpician *réduction* of La Présentation and nearby Fort Lévis on the upper St. Lawrence.

Delegates of the Seven Nations of Canada met with William Johnson at Oswegatchie and entered into a treaty whereby the British guaranteed, as the delegates later recalled, the "quiet and peacable possession of the Lands we lived upon, and let us enjoy the free Exercise of the religion we were instructed in; which Engagements we then firmly and mutually agreed upon."[22] On 8 September, Governor Vaudreuil, faced with what he called "la désertion totale des [miliciens] Canadiens et celle d'un grand nombre de soldats [de France]" and the fact that "les sauvages domiciliés avoient fait leur paix avec les Anglois," signed the capitulation of Montreal, marking the surrender of what remained of New France.[23] Vaudreuil remembered the "Indiens Alliés de sa Majesté tres Chrestienne" in Article 40 of the capitulation which stipulated they should be maintained in the lands they inhabited, but of course there were really no longer any such allies of the French!

The Hurons of Lorette were among those who had joined the British. On 5 September, three days before the capitulation of Montreal, the chief of the Huron warriors who were at Longueuil, on the south shore from Montreal, signed a treaty with General James Murray, British commander of the garrison of Quebec. It read as follows:

Par les présentes, nous certifions que le Chef de la tribu des Hurons, étant venu à moi pour se soumettre au nom de sa nation à la Couronne Britannique et faire la paix, est reçu sous ma protection lui et toute sa tribu; et dorénavant ils ne devront pas être molestés ni arrêtés par un officier ou des soldats anglais lors de leur retour à leur campement de Lorette; ils sont reçus aux mêmes conditions que les Canadiens, il leur sera permis d'exercer librement leur religion, leurs coutumes et la liberté de commerce avec les Anglais: nous recommandons aux officiers commandant les postes de les traiter gentiment.[24]

Some historians have claimed that this was only a *laissez-passer* but there exists no safe conduct which enumerates the broad range of guarantees contained in this remarkable document. The terms of the treaty, for that is what the agreement at Longueuil was, are quite significant.

First of all, the Hurons made peace with the British, by abandoning the French alliance and coming under British protection, without at the same time capitulating or surrendering any rights or privileges. They were now in a state of neutrality. Second, they were permitted to return peaceably to their "camp" at Lorette through a countryside now under military occupation by their former enemies. Third, they were to be received on the same conditions as the Canadian militia; i.e., they were not to be pursued for having taken up arms in spite of the fact they had fought side by side with the French at the battle of Ste-Foy earlier that year and were part of the French forces gathered for the defence of Montreal. Murray had issued a proclamation on 23 July threatening all who took up arms to resist the British invasion with "bloody vengeance . . . the ravaging of your lands, the burning of your houses, which will be the least of your miseries."[25] In addition to laying down their arms, the Canadian militiamen had to take an oath of neutrality, but there is no such requirement of the Hurons in the Murray Treaty. Fourth, and most important in establishing its treaty nature, they were accorded legal protection as well as military guarantees. They were granted the free exercise of their religion, the pursuit of their customs, and freedom of trade. On the basis of this solemn treaty the Hurons can claim the right to exercise both Catholic and traditional practices, to pursue without hindrance their ancestral customs and way of life. It is my contention that their customs can include matters established under the French régime such as exemption from taxation, control of their own judicial procedures, control of local affairs, education, healing arts, and hunting and fishing rights. Finally, the guarantee of "liberté de commerce" reiterated the freedom to trade without any obligation to observe the restrictions placed on colonists or to be subject to any levies, customs duties, etc. Under French rule, the authorities had never been able to prohibit aboriginal peoples from trading with the Anglo-Americans if they wished to do so. The Murray Treaty of 1760 enabled the Hurons of Lorette to make an advantageous transition from the French to the British regime. It also marks the beginning of a British policy of conciliation of "His Majesty's new subjects."

A fifth crisis erupted in the 1820s when the "domiciled" Algonkians and Abenakis of Lower Canada quarrelled over hunting territories which the Hurons of Lorette also claimed. The Hurons at Lorette never ceased to hunt and fish on lands distant from their village near Quebec. In 1815, the surveyor Joseph Bouchette, for example, found they were actively engaged in this traditional activity far to the north on both banks of the Jacques Cartier River.[26] In 1821 and 1824, before a committee of the House of Assembly, the Hurons reaffirmed that they continued to hunt seasonally over a vast expanse of territory.[27] In 1829 the Algonkians of Trois Rivières protested that the Abenakis, established in reserves on the south shore of the St. Lawrence since the French régime, were encroaching on their hunting grounds on the north shore. The Hurons intervened to announce that they had a long-standing agreement with the Algonkians to hunt eastwards from the St-Maurice River to the Saguenay and that the Algonkian hunting territory was the north shore of the St. Lawrence westwards from the St-Maurice. The Algonkians and Hurons then signed a solemn reaffirmation of their traditional division of territory which was officially recorded and approved by the Superintendant of Indian Affairs in the province, Juchereau Duchesnay, on 26 October 1829.[28] The Hurons had triumphed in yet another critical juncture in their colonial experience.

To employ the word "triumphed" would seem to suggest an issue resolved. Yet, this paper claims to deal with unresolved issues. The five crises arising in the colonial context that we have examined all have implications for the future history of the Lorette Hurons. The comprehensive land claims based on ancestral occupation by various northeastern groups are far from settled. The debate over the original occupancy of the Laurentian lowlands continues. So does the debate over the consequences, both short and long term, of missionary intrusion into the Huron community. Presently, there are some signs of a revival of traditional beliefs and practices in what was assumed to be a fervent Catholic community. The question of property rights to Sillery, for which there appears to be some evidence of Jesuit misappropriation of an initial seignorial grant to specific aboriginal peoples, may be resurrected. The rights that flow from a recently reaffirmed treaty—the Murray Treaty of

1760—have not all been established to date. Nor is the question of traditional hunting territories resolved as the Hurons take on the Quebec government in its attempts to restrict hunting, fishing and traditional religious rituals in what it has unilaterally declared to be a provincial park.

The entrenchment of aboriginal rights in the Canadian constitution is not an inconsiderable element in keeping these issues current. There are some indications that the Canadian federal government is being pressed into becoming the defender of Huron rights in the face of Quebec provincial intrusion into and violation of traditional rights and practices. New attitudes and concerns of the courts and legal profession indicate that the legacy of the French colonial régime has taken on new importance as the twentieth century draws to its close. Historians can only rejoice at this development.

NOTES

1. Cornelius Jaenen, "French Sovereignty and Native Nationhood during the French Régime," in J. R. Miller, ed., *Sweet Promises: A Reader in Indian-White Relations in Canada* (Toronto: University of Toronto Press, 1991), 19–42.
2. Cornelius Jaenen, "The Uniqueness of the French Relationship with Canada's Native Peoples, 1504–1763," in Aparnu Basu, ed., *Imperialism, Nationalism, and Regionalism in Canadian and Modern Indian History* (New Delhi: Manohar, 1989), 11–29.
3. An anonymous writer in *The Expediency of Securing our American Colonies* (Edinburgh: n.p., 1763) commented on French "superior dexterity in address and civility of usage." Thomas Mante, *The History of the Late War in North-America* (London: Strahan and Cadell, 1772) contrasted British racial prejudice, and ill-treatment of aboriginal peoples, with more tolerant and just French approaches.
4. James B. Finley, *Life among the Indians: or, Personal Reminiscences and Historical Incidents Illustrative of Indian Life and Character* (Freeport, N.Y.: Books for Libraries Press, 1971), 93–94. In 1857, Finley wrote: "So far as history and their traditions inform us, they were the original proprietors of all the country from Mackinaw, down the lakes to ⸮uebec, west to the Great Miami river, and north-west to Lake Michigan." On the basis of archaeological evidence James F.

Pendergast, "An In-Situ Hypothesis to Explain the Origin of the St. Lawrence Iroquoians," *Ontario Archaeology* 25 (1975): 47–55, has concluded that Iroquoian peoples did in fact occupy the entire region from below Quebec to the upper Great Lakes.

5. Milton W. Hamilton, ed., *The Papers of Sir William Johnson* (Albany: University of the State of New York, 1962), vol. 8, Journal of Daniel Claus, 26 July 1773.

6. *Appendices du XXXIIIe Volume des Journaux de la Chambre d'Assemblée de la Province du Bas-Canada, 1824* (Québec: Neilson & Cowan, 1824), Appendice R (A), 28 janvier 1824.

7. Bruce G. Trigger, *Les Indiens, la fourrure et les Blancs* (Montréal: Boreal, 1992), 202, 424. Jack Weatherford, *Native Roots. How the Indians Enriched America* (New York: Crown Publishers, 1991), 16, 24, 33, 167 contends that the Laurentian Iroquoians were Hurons. Father Vimont reported in 1642 that two Algonquian chiefs gave him a different version of Hurons claims to the St. Lawrence valley: "les Hurons, qui pour lors nous estoient ennemis, ont chassé nos ancêtres de cette contrée . . . et voilà comment cette Isle [Montréal] s'est rendue deserte." Barthélemy Vimont, *Relation de ce qui s'est passé en la Novvelle France en l'annee 1642* (Paris: Sebastien Cramoisy, 1643), 132–33.

8. "Huron sites contemporaneous with the disappearance of the St. Lawrence Iroquois contain a high percentage of the characteristic St. Lawrence Iroquoian pottery but little or no evidence of the equally distinctive pipes. This fact suggests that the influx of St. Lawrence Iroquoian peoples into the eastern Huron villages was not a voluntary move; otherwise, all items of their material culture, including the pipes, the characteristic bone arrowheads and other tools, would be present in the excavations. . . . It appears, then, that the agojuda, or 'evil men', that the Hochelagans told Jacques Cartier about referred to the Huron." J. V. Wright, *Quebec Prehistory* (New York: Van Nostrand Reinhold, 1979), 71–73. St. Lawrence Iroquoian pottery is totally absent from all Five Nations Iroquois archaeological sites. This absence would tend to undermine the Mohawk claim that the Laurentian Iroquoians were Mohawks.

9. Guy Laflèche, *Les Saints Martyrs Canadiens. Volume 3: Le Martyre de Jean de Brébeuf selon Paul Ragueneau* (Laval: Editions du Singulier, 1990), 126–30. We first drew attention to Jesuit interest in Canadian commerce in "The Catholic Clergy and the Fur Trade, 1585–1685," *Canadian Historical Association, Report 1970* (Ottawa: Canadian Historical Association, 1970), 60–80. Even Lucien Campeau, s.j., who has always vigorously denied that the Jesuits engaged in

commerce, had to admit to they handled large quantities of furs and trade goods in their missions: *Les Finances publiques de la Nouvelle-France sous les Cent-Associés, 1632–1665* (Montréal: Bellarmin, 1975), 78.

10. *Relation de ce qui s'est passé en la Nouvelle-France, én années 1647 & 1648* (Paris: Sebastien et Gabriel Cramoisy, 1649), 122–23. The problem of factionalism resulting from Jesuit intrusion into Iroquoian confederacies is also raised by Daniel K. Richter, "Iroquois Versus Iroquois: Jesuit Missions and Christianity in Village Politics, 1642–1686," *Ethnohistory* 32 (1985): 1–16.

11. There is a vast literature on epidemics in colonial times, but of special interest are K. H. Schlesier, "Epidemics and Indian Middlemen: Rethinking the Wars of the Iroquois, 1609–1653," *Ethnohistory* 23 (1976): 129–46; Dean R. Snow and Kim M. Lamphear, "European Contact and Indian depopulation in the Northeast. The Timing of the First Epidemics," *Ethnohistory* 35 (1988), 15–33. Georges E. Sioui, *For an Amerindian Autohistory: An Essay on the Foundations of a Social Ethic* (Montreal: McGill-Queen's University Press, 1992).

12. We have dealt with the question of supposed "martyrdom" in several publications, including "Amerindian Responses to French Missionary Intrusion, 1611–1760: A Categorization," in William Westfall, et al., eds., *Religion/Culture. Comparative Canadian Studies* (Ottawa: Association des Etudes canadiennes, 1985), 187.

13. The thesis of economic motivation for the war is found in George T. Hunt, *The Wars of the Iroquois: A Study in Intertribal Trade Relations* (Madison: University of Wisconsin Press, 1949). The most recent reinterpretation of Iroquois motivation is Matthew Dennis, *Cultivating a Landscape of Peace. Iroquois-European Encounters in Sevententh-Century America* (Ithaca: Cornell University Press, 1993).

14. The Spanish model was explained by Father Paul Le Jeune in *Relation de ce qui s'est passé en la Nouvelle France, en l'année 1637* (Rouen: Jean Le Boullenger, 1638), 300. Reductions were first organized in Brazil in 1549, but enjoyed greatest popularity in Paraguay after 1588.

15. Pierre-Georges Roy, éd., *Ordonnances, Commissions, etc. des Gouverneurs et Intendants de la Nouvelle-France, 1639–1706* (Beauceville: L'Eclaireur, 1924), vol. 1, Ordinance of M. de Lauzon, 12 May 1656, 12.

16. *Édits et ordonnances*, vol. 1, Edit de l'établissement de la Compagnie des Indes Occidentales, mai 1664, 46.

17. "Messrs. de Callières et de Champigny avaient accordés aux Jésuites plus qu'ils ne leur avaient demandé, mettant dans leur don en général, tous les droits

qu'avaient autrefois les Sauvages." *Rapport de l'Archiviste de la Province de Québec pour 1922–23* (Québec, 1923), Mémoire de Ruette d'Auteuil à Pontchartrain, 29 mars 1707, 30.

18. "Le Journal de M. de Bougainville," *Rapport de l'Archiviste de la Province de Québec pour 1923–1924* (Québec, 1924), 272.

19. The role of the Amerindian allies is examined in Gerald Thomas Dell, "French-Indian Alliances during the Final Phases of the Seven Years' War in North America," (Master's thesis, University of Guelph, 1978). Peter MacLeod has calculated their numbers and the effects of the smallpox epidemic on their participation: "Microbes and Muskets: Smallpox and the Participation of the Amerindian Allies of New France in the Seven Years' War," *Ethnohistory* 39, no. 1 (1992): 52–55.

20. James Sullivan, ed., *The Papers of Sir William Johnson* (Albany: University of the State of New York, 1921), vol. 3, Johnson to William Pitt, 24 October 1760, 188.

21. Randolph Boehm, ed., *Records of the British Colonial Office: The French and Indian War, 1756–1763* (Frederick, Md.: University Publications of America, n.d.), Proclamation of Jeffrey Amherst, 27 April 1760.

22. The only record of this Treaty of Oswegatchie, 25 August 1760, is found in Milton W. Hamilton, ed., *The Papers of Sir William Johnson* (Albany: University of the State of New York, 1962), vol. 7, 109–10. George F. G. Stanley wrote, without citing his evidence, in *New France: The Last Phase, 1744–1760* (Toronto: McClelland & Stewart, 1968), 258, that even before the capitulation of Montreal the Amerindian allies "had made peace with Amherst," and added, "To the Indian, his relationship with the Frenchman was that of ally—and an alliance was only as durable as French success in battle."

23. Abbé H.-R. Casgrain éd., *Journal des Campagnes du Chevalier de Lévis au Canada de 1756 à 1760* (Montréal: C. O. Beauchemin & Fils, 1889), 303–4.

24. The text is found in English in Arthur G. Doughty, ed., *An Historical Journal of the Campaigns in North-America, for the years 1757, 1758, 1759, and 1760 by Captain John Knox* (Freeport, N.Y.: Books for Libraries Press, 1970), 2:149. We have examined the copy held by François Vincent, direct descendant of Nicolas Vincent, who may have been the person who copied it from an original in the possession of Mme. Mahon, great-grand-daughter of General Murray, at Quebec on 28 January 1804. The official text established by the Supreme Court of Canada, Le Procueur-Général du Québec c. Régent Sioui, Conrad Sioui, Georges Sioui et

Hugues Sioui et le Procureur Général du Canada et la Fraternité des Indiens du Canada/l'Assemblée des Premières Nations, No. 20628, 24 mai 1990, 3.

25. Henri-Raymond Casgrain, éd., *Collection des manuscrits du maréchal de Lévis. Vol. IV: Lettres et pièces militaires, instructions, ordres, mémoires, plans de campagne et de défense 1756–1760* (Québec, 1891), Proclamation du 23 juillet 1760, 284.

26. Jospeh Bouchette, *The British Dominions in North America: or a Topographical and Statistical Description of the Provinces of Lower and Upper Canada* (London: Longman, Rees, Orme, Brown, Green & Longman, 1832), 1:402. "A partir des hauteurs de chaque côté de la rivière [Jacques Cartier] s'étendent de vastes forêts à travers lesquelles il y a différents sentiers tracés par les Indiens, et surtout ceux du village de Lorette qui considèrent les terres à une distance immense vers le nord comme consacré à leurs chasses."

27. *Appendices des XXIXᵉ et XXXᵉ Volumes des Journaux de la Chambre d'Assemblée du Bas-Canada, 1820–21* (Québec: Neilson & Cowan, 1821), Appendice U, No.1, 12 février 1821; *Appendices du XXXIIIᵉ Volume des Journaux de la Chambre d'Assemblée du Bas-Canada, 1824* (Québec: Neilson & Cowan, 1824), Appendice R(A), 28 janvier 1824, 29 janvier 1824.

28. National Archives of Canada, ser. C, vol. 268, Procès-verbal du 26 octobre 1829, 724–39. There is also a certified copy of the agreement, signed by Duchesnay, in the Archives de la Nation Huronne-Wendat, Wendake.

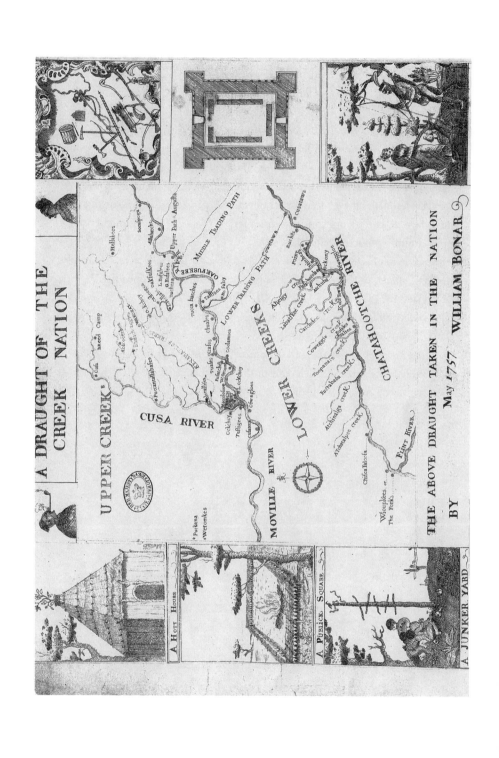

A DRAUGHT OF THE CREEK NATION

UPPER CREEKs

CUSA RIVER

MOVILLE RIVER

MIDDLE TRADING PATH

OAKFUSKEE RIVER

Upper Path to Augusta

LOWER TRADING PATH

LOWER CREEKS

CHATAHOOTCHE RIVER

FLINT RIVER

THE ABOVE DRAUGHT TAKEN IN THE NATION
May 1757 WILLIAM BONAR
BY

A HOTT HOUSE

A PUBLICK SQUARE

A JUNKER YARD

A Cartographic Adventure: William Bonar in the Creek Nation during the Seven Years' War

Laquita Thomson

Dans les guerres secrètes d'intrigue, un simple objet peut suffire à donner des indices aux protagonistes des camps en présence. Le «dessin de la nation Creek», de William Bonar et datant de la guerre de Sept Ans, est justement l'un de ces objets. Il s'agit d'une carte exceptionnelle, illustrée de scènes de la vie des Creek, et qui montre le fort Toulouse, situé en Louisiane, et ses alentours. Outre les différentes structures du village, les armes utilisées et les autochtones, on peut voir l'important fort sur le plan stratégique dans l'une des scènes représentées sur la carte. Le présent document porte plus particulièrement sur les circonstances et les événements liés à l'établissement de cette carte; il raconte notamment le travail effectué par Bonar pour le compte d'une délégation anglaise envoyée en reconnaissance au fort Toulouse, sa capture par les soldats du capitaine Montaut de Montberaut et leurs alliés indiens, son évasion et son retour à Charleston avec la carte. Cet incident montre que, en matière de commerce, de diplomatie, d'espionnage et de subterfuges divers, les rapports entre les Indiens et les Européens étaient comparables à petite échelle à ce qu'ils étaient dans la guerre menée à plus grande échelle dans le Nord.

Exploding cannons, sabre-wielding soldiers, and battlefield bluster did not characterize the Seven Years' War in Louisiana's southern backcountry. Instead, it was more a clandestine war of intrigue and diplomatic foibles, though there was always a potential for a European and Indian blood bath. The following story from 1756–57 relates a seven-month mission of spying and counterspying, all pursued in the hope of extending imperial influence in trade and diplomacy. At the center of the story is a rare artifact: a decorated map drawn during 1757 by one of the British players in this drama, William Bonar.[1]

The tale and the artifact are testaments to colonial intrigue, as well as to ethnographic explorations in the society of mid-eighteenth century Indians. The setting is the country around Louisiana's Fort Toulouse, in what is now Alabama. The main players are the French at Fort Toulouse, the various Indian tribes and their headmen who lived near the fort, and British agents Daniel Pepper and William Bonar.

Charleston officials immediately appreciated the importance of Bonar's map, which is decorated with vignettes of Indian life. It was valued not so much for its artistry but for its military usefulness, in that it offered a plan of the strategically important French post known as Fort Toulouse.[2] At the time, few maps existed of the area. The most detailed ones were made by the French and showed the area as belonging to Louisiana.[3] With the war heating up, an overall view with the relative positions of the Creek Indian villages was important for strategists back in Charleston and in London. While traders had known the location of important Indian villages for half a century, William Henry Lyttelton, the new royal governor of South Carolina, had no such intimate knowledge of Indians and their country. It really did not matter that the map was badly distorted; what mattered was that it depicted the center of the territory—complete with major waterways, trading paths, villages, and fort—which Charleston and Savannah hoped to wrest from New Orleans and Mobile.

The map was drawn by William Bonar, a young Scotsman. It is a 22-inch by 18-inch ink drawing on paper, signed and dated May 1757, most likely indicating the date of its completion. The map was unusual for its time in that its maker drew it on the spot. The most famous mapmakers of the period did not venture into the field, but depended on a compilation of extant maps and reports from the field for their information.[4] Errors were passed from one map to the next many times over. Bonar might have had access to crude traders' or Indian agents' maps, but he likely did not have any published ones to copy. He obviously wanted to get all the villages on his draft and still make it as large and readable as possible; hence the distortion. The most obvious problem is with the rivers. The Coosa and Tallapoosa are fairly accurate;

however, he drew the Chattahoochee flowing east and west instead of north and south. The pivot of the map is the French fort, Toulouse. He also indicated the three major Indian trading paths.

If Bonar's cartographic skills were primitive, his artistic ability was refined. It was not unusual to see a map with an intricately drawn compass rose or the legend contained in a cartouche surrounded by flora and fauna native to the place of the map. Bonar's map, however, is almost incidental to his elaborate vignettes which are at times historical and decorative, and at other times current and instructive. Bonar obviously wanted to show that he could draw, and that he could be useful to his king and governor in their fight against the French.

Bonar's entry into the Indian nations was courtesy of Captain Daniel Pepper, a forest diplomat and Indian agent appointed by South Carolina for a special mission. It was common practice for the governors of the southern colonies to send hardy and knowledgeable backwoodsmen as envoys to the Indians. From 1735 until 1745, Pepper had been the officer in charge at Fort Moore, a defensive stockade on the South Carolina side of the Savannah River on the trade path from the Indian nations to Charleston.[5] Pepper was also likely involved in the Indian trade.[6] But as the French and Indian War escalated, and rumors of impending strikes came to South Carolina and Georgia, he was appointed by South Carolina's Governor Lyttelton to go to the Creek nation to deliver some friendly "talks" on behalf of the governor; to ascertain whether Britain's Indian alliances were holding; and to gather whatever French intelligence he could.[7]

Pepper probably made the acquaintance of William Bonar for the first time in Augusta during September or early October, 1756, though he may have known him in Charleston a few years earlier. Bonar was at loose ends at the time, possibly running from debt. Nonetheless, Pepper recognized in Bonar qualities he could use to get his own job done, and hired him in Augusta as a secretary to do his personal business. Whether Pepper paid Bonar personally, or whether he placed him on the South Carolina expense account for this mission is not totally clear. Most likely he paid him personally since he had hired several others in connection with his expedition to the interior—an interpreter and several packhorsemen—and later discharged them. From a letter of 7 May 1757, we know that Pepper had Bonar doing more important and specialized tasks than mere packhorseman or runner of messages.[8]

It is probable that Pepper did not undertake this mission to the Indians solely for political reasons. He had been in the Creek Nation before, and among the 31 packhorses starting out from Augusta, he acknowledged that three carried provisions and ". . . Luggage belonging to the people [those in the horse train]."[9] He does not say exactly how many carried presents for the Indians. Some could have carried personal goods for trade, the proceeds from which he would pay Bonar. Perhaps Bonar himself carried some goods for trading. This arrangement is not unlikely as Pepper was not paid in advance, and in fact, was still waiting to be paid for his mission two years later when the colony owed him 2197 Pounds ". . . for Services in the Indian Nations."[10]

Pepper gave a diary-like account of his trip to Governor Lyttelton in a series of letters from which Bonar's activities can also be tracked. They left Augusta on 13 October 1756 with the 31 packhorses, their own mounts, as well as extra mounts. There must have been no fewer than 40 horses and four or five men in addition to Pepper and Bonar. After an uneventful journey they arrived on 5 November at the main town, Ockchoys, just across the Coosa River from Fort Toulouse. The Ockchoy town was headed by an Indian identified as Gun Merchant; the head warrior was known as Mortar. For most of the seven months Pepper and Bonar spent in the Nation, Mortar was away visiting with the Cherokees. Mortar was openly pro-French and Gun Merchant was a master at playing the British and French against one another to his own advantage. Pepper did not trust Gun Merchant, so he spent most of the time in his village trying to divine what plots and machinations the French and their allies were hatching. Gun Merchant was always friendly to Pepper's face, yet invariably vague when questioned and secretive about his actions.[11]

When the British convoy came into the Ockchoys on 5 November, Gun Merchant, who had been apprised of their coming, flew flags, fired guns, and beat drums. Pepper asked him to send word to the headmen of the other villages, as well as to their British traders, that he would be delivering a talk from the governor. November 12 was agreed on as the day for delivering the talk. When the day arrived, Pepper first read his commission from the governor, as it was common practice for Indians and Englishmen to establish their authority before any formal conversations took place. Along with Pepper and Bonar, there were two interpreters, six traders and about 38 Indians from 14 tribes present.[12] After the reading of the governor's talk, there was some discussion, and then the presents were distributed. Pepper's assessment was that everyone went home satisfied.[13]

Pepper had accomplished one of his main objectives, delivering the governor's talk. Thus he was free to spend the next few months seeking intelligence on the French and repairing damage caused by covert French actions. A primary concern was secret meetings held at Fort Toulouse with various tribes, mainly Cherokees and Choctaws. Both the French and the British had Indian spies in every tribe, and while several served as double agents, both countries had some very loyal allies who would always provide information for them. For example, Mortar was definitely in the French interest, while Wolf of Muccoloussus was a fierce partisan for British interests. For a while, Louis Lantagnac, a disaffected Frenchman turned British trader, then French returnee, was successful in his subterfuges with both sides.[14] By the time of Pepper's arrival in the Nation, however, the British no longer trusted Lantagnac. Pepper wrote: ". . . Mr. Lantanniact makes a Practice of Riding about the Nation carrying what Reports he can to the Fort, and indeed I find the French have free Egress and Regress among them so that [he] seem[s] to act in a double capacity to hold us by one Hand and the French by the other."[15]

Pepper monitored all the comings and goings on the river near the fort. As the fort was supplied from Mobile via water, Pepper realized that their supply situation was somewhat precarious. British goods, by way of comparison, had to come overland from Augusta, yet the British organization and structure was much better. Moreover, the native peoples tended to prefer the British trade goods to those of the French. The Creeks had suffered a famine the year before, so the British had extra bargaining power in 1756-57, which they used to drive harder bargains than the French. In addition, as the French constantly pointed out to the Indians, the British demanded land. Both sides would pay for scalps of their enemies, and rum was used by unscrupulous traders on both sides, though there were laws in South Carolina and Georgia against it. Pepper personally saw it as a dangerous practice. If the appeal of the French was that they were more interested in diplomatic ties than in land, their trading system was both less efficient and less reliable than the English one. Indians usually had to go to the French fort or to Mobile to do their trade, whereas all the larger villages had a resident English, or more often, Scots trader who likely had an Indian wife and children, and who had a warehouse to carry on the trade.[16]

For the first several months of his stay, Pepper was constantly stymied in his efforts to find out what was going on at the French fort. "I have made all the Enquiry possible as to the Strength and present Situation of the Alabama Fort, and by Reason of their Apprehensions of Danger by my coming up [to the Nation] find it difficult to come at an exact Account."[17] Again on 7 April 1757 he wrote from the Muccolassees, where he had gone to confer with their head warrior, Wolf: "I have not been able to learn any Thing the French are carrying on here though I have Spies in every Corner, but shall continue to observe their Motions and keep your Excellency advised accordingly."[18] The situation had become more acute by 25 April when Pepper was back at the Ockchoys. He had been apprised of a meeting in New Orleans with the French governor, Kerlerec, and the Cherokees and Shawnees, and felt that something big was afoot and that his hosts were involved: "I use my utmost Endeavors to watch their [French] Motions and the more so as I am afraid there is some underhand Dealings carried on between the Gun Merchant, the Mortar, and the French Fort, unknown to any other of the Head Men in the Nation. I am partly confirmed in this from private Messages from the Gun to the Fort (which I come to the Knowledge of for all his Cunning) and some alteration in his Talk which of late seem to tend that Way."[19]

Pepper, a military man for many years, was not one to sit by to see how things turned out. He had been hinting at and openly suggesting various military actions to the governor for some months. For example, in a 21 December 1756 letter, he wrote in relation to the pro-French Shawnee Indians: "Querie: In case I could in Conjunction with the Traders prevail upon this Nation [the Creeks] to [invite]them to a Ballplay and Knock them in the Head, would your Excellency approve of it, and would it not be laudable to counterplot them in their Machinations and to follow the Law of Nature in self Preservation?"[20]

By early May, however, Pepper had come upon another plan made possible by the war. As early as December 1756 he had this intelligence: "Some Indians who were lately at the Alabama Fort tell us when they were there the [French] Officer was swearing against the English in a great Rage and upon their enquiring the Reason from the Linguester he told them that the English had taken their large House Canoe with Money to pay the Soldiers by which he meant the Pay Ship."[21] That New Orleans, Mobile, and by extension, Fort Toulouse were suffering extremely from British naval activity can be seen from

Kerlerec's letters to the Minister of Marine in Paris. Kerlerec wrote in January 1757, "I find myself more and more in the most critical position. We have no more merchandise for the trade with the Indians or for their presents. The nation of the Choctaws is openly grumbling. The Alabamas who serve as a barrier between the British and us, and all the other different nations of this continent are not contented either. I am appeasing them as much as I can by fine words . . . but they must have something real if we wish to make them dissatisfied with the English. . . ."[22] And on 13 March 1757, "All the King's warehouses are empty. This is the time to deliver the presents to the Choctaws, Alabamas, and other nations, as they all loudly announce."[23]

These ciphered pleas were subject to falling into British hands and some did so. Pepper exults: "Your Favor of 29th March gives me a good Deal of Satisfaction, thereby receiving the agreeable Information of the Success of the Jamaica Sloop taking and bringing in a French Prize, bound from New Orleans to La Rochelle, whereby Your Excellency has been acquainted of the Transactions . . . mentioned in the Pacquet to the Minister of the Marine from the Governor of Louisiana."[24]

The desperate situation of the French fort made it a prime target for Pepper's intrigue. The British traders had ample goods in their various warehouses practically within sight of the fort, while the French had little left to give their Indian allies, whose fidelity was directly tied to the presents they received. Perhaps Pepper could have waited out the French, but such was not his style. He had a method to appraise the fort and he used it. He wrote: "I privately sent him [William Bonar] in Disguise as a Packhorseman to take a View of the Alabama Fort which he effected and assures me it is a place of no Strength and might at any time be surprized by a very small Body of Men."[25] There is no documentation from the French indicating that they recognized Bonar. They may have known that he was in Pepper's employ and was not a legitimate packhorseman. If that was the case, however, their desperate straits must have affected their judgement, because they let him walk in the fort and out again.

Whatever confusion the French were experiencing at the time, and whatever glee Pepper and Bonar gained from the reconnaissance mission were dispelled a few days later. From a reference to a lost letter of 20 May, we may assume that the French claimed that Bonar had defected and walked back into their fort on his own. In a surviving letter of 25 May, Pepper said, "As to

Mr. Bonar, I am well convinced the French way laid him and carried him to the Fort in the Night, notwithstanding they procured a Creek Indian in their Interest to say he met him and that he went of his own Accord, that they, the French, wanted him to return which he refused, therefore he was immediately sent down to Moville."[26]

If the French did not know Bonar at the time of his disguised entry to deliver goods, which probably would have taken no more than an hour, no doubt their Indian allies soon enough gave them a full story as to his identity. Since Bonar lived at the Ockchoys too, Gun Merchant would have known that he did Pepper's business including making a map of the surrounding area. The French, however, could not walk into Ockchoys and take Bonar, and Gun Merchant, who was pretending allegiance to the British, could not overtly deliver him to the French, so they had to wait for a chance to capture him. They got it when Bonar went to Lachlan McGillivray's to wait for some things he had sent for from Mr. Spencer's.[27] Perhaps these were trade goods for his own profitable use, or perhaps it was paper on which to draw a map of the adjacent Lower Creek country. At any rate, Pepper, in an attempt to convince Lyttelton that Bonar was kidnapped by the French, wrote: "Bonar did not carry the least Thing with him except what he had on his Back which were his very worst cloaths he had, and he rode his worst Horse, leaving his favorite one in the Yard at the Ockchoys."[29] Pepper also stated that at McGillivray's place Bonar had asked a young Indian who was going back to the Ockchoys to wait for him, but he refused. The Indian likely knew what was about to happen.

This was a crisis and Pepper knew it. Whether Bonar was kidnapped or had defected, Pepper wanted him back. "I applyed to the Gun Merchant to demand him, but he told me that the Path was open to French and English, and he could not do any Thing in it."[30] This fickle friend of the British had shown his true colors, so Pepper then applied to Wolf who effected the rescue. On 27 May, Pepper wrote a quick note to Lyttelton, "I have now the very agreeable News to tell you that Mr. Bonner [sic] is retaken from the French, who were guarding him down to Moville. The Wolf at my Request sent a Party of Indians who came up with him within a Day's Journey of the said Place, and brought him back though he is not with me yet."[31]

Mortar finally arrived back from the Cherokees on 28 May 1757. Knowing his importance in the nation, Pepper had been waiting for him. In the tactical game of one-upmanship, Mortar kept Pepper waiting for another three days. On 31 May, Mortar finally said he was ready to hear the governor's talk (which Pepper had delivered the previous autumn to the other headmen). Mortar had two Cherokees with him and argued every point of the talk, and, as Pepper reported to Lyttelton, "he . . . behaved with the most intolerable Impudence and Presumption and by his whole Behaviour confirms me in the Suspicion I entertained of his being greatly in the French Interest. . . ."[32] Pepper obviously was eager to leave the nation. He had accomplished all that he could, and Mortar's presence made his situation more dangerous. When he arrived back in South Carolina in late June, Bonar and Bonar's map called the "Draught of the Creek Nation" most likely accompanied him. Governor Lyttelton reported to the Board of Trade on 3 November 1757:

> Mr. Pepper our agent is returned having procured me many useful Informations and I hope much Improved our affairs in that country. [D]uring the time he was there he employed a spy to reconnoitre Alabama Fort: This man was taken and carried to the Fort from whence a party was employed to conduct him to Mobille but Mr. Pepper found means to send a number of the Indians after him who rescued him and brought him back safe. [H]e has given me a plan of the Fort as accurate as he could do from memory by which it appears to be a place of very little strength. . . .[33]

The draft Bonar brought back to Charleston from the Indian country was classical in design, meaning that he tried to make it symmetrical. Bonar's map, if halved, mirrors itself in its structural elements. Each of the six vignettes is exactly proportional to the central section, and every one is close to a golden mean rectangle.[34] The central section itself becomes a perfect square when the title and signature sections are deleted from the top and bottom. The small decorative vignettes on right and left of the title section are each small squares.

The order in which Bonar drew his vignettes is unknown. However, since the purpose of the map was to identify Creek villages, the logical next step after the map would have been to draw the three left-hand vignettes giving visual form to the most important public aspects of a typical Creek village: the ceremonial center containing the town house or hot house, a square ground or summer council space, and chunkey yard.[35] Though there are some problems with giving Bonar's three left-hand drawings these public designations, he was certainly not unaware of them and may have meant to depict them.

The vignettes on the right side of Bonar's map may also be instructive, but they are more decorative and contain some historical references. For example, the upper-right vignette has a border of serpentine shell- and paisley-like forms surrounding a field of weapons of war. By 1757 most Indians were using muskets, at least, for hunting and war. Rifles were even beginning to replace muskets by this time. Nonetheless, Bonar places the emphasis on the historical weapons of the Indians. A bow, arrows with quiver, tomahawk, hatchet, and spear fill most of the panel. In the lower section are a gun and sword. While all of these older weapons were still available as implements of war, Bonar was perhaps taking a nostalgic or romantic view of the frequency of their use at this point in time. In the stylized forest of the lower right panel Bonar has pictured a woman and a hunter/warrior. Though the warrior carries the obsolete bow and arrows, he also carries a gun and the woman is wrapped in a duffle and has French or English ribbons in her hair. Bonar flanked his title with the profiles of a pipe-smoking man and a heavy-featured woman, certainly not idealized.

The center right vignette, the plan of the fort, gave the map its power when it was first created, and has continued to the present time to attract attention. The fact that this panel is so out of character with the rest of the drawing is one reason, but another is that the plan of the fort has come to be the theoretical basis for the creation of the map. Fort Toulouse, the farthermost French outpost in the Indian country, and sitting on territory also claimed by the English, was the nexus for all backcountry intrigue, and had been so since it was built in 1717. Bonar's having been inside it made him a hero, and he awarded himself a trophy by including it on his draft. The simplicity of this elevation could not have been of great strategic use, though it does place the barracks and other interior structures. It is like an enlarged detail of the pivot-point of his map, and would have been a perfect reminder to Governor Lyttelton that Bonar's services could prove valuable, especially in light of the fact that he would have given a verbal account at the time he presented his draft to the governor.

Bonar's map reached London two years after its creation. Bonar himself was given a militia command at Fort Johnson in Charleston by 1759. Nothing else of his life is known except that he died on 7 July 1767. It is unknown whether he ever made another drawing. His testament is his existing "Draught of the Creek Nation," carefully preserved for over two and one quarter centuries. The map is a monument to his youthful courage and observation.It is an important artifact from the Southeastern theatre of the Seven Years' War and is a memorial to the social and cultural legacy of the colonial Southeast.

NOTES

1. This map, "A Draught of the Creek Nation" is in the British Public Record Office, CO700/Carolina 21. It has been reproduced in various publications, most recently as endpapers and details in Kathryn E. Holland Braund, *Deerskins and Duffles: The Creek Indian Trade with Anglo-America, 1685–1815* (Lincoln: University of Nebraska Press, 1993). My main sources for the story are British since the French did not elaborate on the artifact nor the incident and men involved in the artifact's creation, as these details would likely have been an embarrassment to them.

2. Fort Toulouse was known by various names. The French called it Toulouse or "aux Alibamons." The Creek Indians knew it as Franca Choka Chula or the old French trading house. The British called it the French Fort or the Alabama Fort. It was located near the confluence of the Coosa and Tallapoosa rivers about 250 miles from Mobile by water. It was in the midst of the Upper Creek Nation, the Alabamas being the tribe in the immediate vicinity of the fort. At the time of Bonar's visit, the French commander at the post was Captain Montaut de Montberaut. See Daniel H. Thomas, *Fort Toulouse: The French Outpost at the Alabamas on the Coosa* (Tuscaloosa: University of Alabama Press, 1989), 42-61. See also Milo B. Howard, Jr. and Robert R. Rea, eds., *The Mémoire Justificatif of the Chevalier Montault de Monberaut*, (Tuscaloosa: University of Alabama Press, 1965).

3. The best description of mapmaking in the South for this period is William P. Cumming, *The Southeast in Early Maps* (Chapel Hill: University of North Carolina Press, 1962), 38–51. Noted mapmakers included the Frenchman Guillaume Delisle and the Englishman John Mitchell.

4. John Mitchell's 1755 "A Map of the British and French Dominions in North America" relied heavily on Barnwell's map of the southeastern region. William

P. Cumming, "Mapping of the Southeast: The First Two Centuries," *The South-eastern Geographer* 4 (1966): 18 n.20.

5. Larry E. Ivers, *Colonial Forts of South Carolina 1670–1775* (Columbia: University of South Carolina Press, 1970), 28–30.

6. Most garrison commanders operated general stores in their forts. Ibid., 34. Within the context of this story Pepper sent packhorses with goods into Fort Toulouse, the stronghold of his enemy. Patricia Galloway suggests that this was common practice in this area and that ". . . Pepper probably made a handsome profit on it that he didn't report to Charles Towne." Letter to the author, 31 January 1992.

7. Pepper to Lyttelton, 18 November 1756, in William L. McDowell, Jr. ed., *Documents Relating to Indian Affairs, 1745–1765,* [Hereafter: *Indian Affairs Documents*] (Columbia: University of South Carolina Press, 1970), 252-57.

8. Pepper to Lyttelton, 7 May 1757, *Indian Affairs Documents,* 373

9. Pepper to Lyttelton, 30 November 1756, *Indian Affairs Documents,* 295.

10. Lyttelton to Board of Trade, 14 April 1759, Noel Sainsbury, comp., *Records in the British Public Records Office Relating to South Carolina, 1711–1782,* South Carolina Department of Archives and History, Columbia, Microfilm Roll #9, 183. (Hereafter: *BPRO Documents*). This "2197 Pounds" was South Carolina current money, not British pounds sterling.

11. *Indian Affairs Documents,* 364, 367.

12. Ibid., 257.

13. Ibid., 254.

14. Lantagnac's activities are covered in several sources including: Robert S. Cotterill, *The Southern Indians* (Norman: University of Oklahoma Press, 1954), 30; Thomas, *Fort Toulouse,* 31. For French/Indian alliances during this time see Michael Foret, "On the Marchlands of Empire: Trade Diplomacy and War on the Southeastern Frontier, 1733–1763" (Ph.D. diss., College of William and Mary, 1990), 209–33

15. Pepper to Lyttelton, 18 November 1756, *Indian Affairs Documents,* 255.

16. For the Creek Trade, see Braund, *Deerskins and Duffles.* For an overall description of commerce in this area see Daniel H. Usner, Jr. *Indians, Settlers and Slaves in a Frontier Exchange Economy* (Chapel Hill: University of North Carolina Press, 1992). Older useful works dealing with trade are Verner W. Crane, *The Southern Frontier 1670–1732,* (Durham: Duke University Press, 1928) and Nancy M. Miller Surrey, *The Commerce of Louisiana during the French Regime, 1699–1763* (New York: Columbia University Press, 1916). An advantage of the French trade centers

was that they provided gun maintenance, a service which was usually unavailable through the British traders. Pepper realized the appeal of this service and requested Lyttelton to add it. *Indian Affairs Documents*, 299.

17. Pepper to Lyttelton, 21 December 1756, *Indian Affairs Documents*, 299.

18. Pepper to Lyttelton, 7 April 1757, *Indian Affairs Documents*, 365.

19. Pepper to Lyttelton, 25 April 1757, *Indian Affairs Documents*, 367. Louis Billouart de Kerlerec was the French governor of Louisiana from 1753 to 1762.

20. Pepper to Lyttelton, 21 December 1756, *Indian Affairs Documents*, 298. Patricia Galloway, an Indian specialist, in a letter to the author, 31 January 1992, scoffs at the possibility of success in such a scheme. She says that the British were only tolerated in the region because of their trade goods and that the Indians would not have permitted any scheme which would have created an imbalance in their dealings with either the French or the British.

21. Ibid., 299

22. Kerlerec to DeMachault d'Arnouville, 28 January 1757, Dunbar Rowland, A.G. Sanders and Patricia Galloway, eds., *Mississippi Provincial Archives 1749–1763, French Dominion* (Baton Rouge: Louisiana State University Press, 1984), 5:180.

23. Kerlerec to DeMachault d'Arnouville, 13 March 1757, *Mississippi Provincial Archives*, 5: 182.

24. Pepper to Lyttelton, 7 May 1757, *Indian Affairs Documents*, 369–70.

25. Ibid., 373.

26. Pepper to Lyttelton, 25 May 1757, *Indian Affairs Documents*, 378.

27. Lachlan McGillivray was a Scots trader who had a trading post and plantation within a few miles of Fort Toulouse. He was married to Sehoy Marchand, a Creek princess, and was the father of Alexander McGillivray. He acted as a forest diplomat on many occasions for the British. He also owned property and trading interests in Augusta. Mr. Spencer was probably John Spencer, another English trader based in nearby village. See Edward S. Cashin, *Lachland McGillivray, Indian Trader: The Shaping of the Southern Colonial Frontier* (Athens: University of Georgia Press, 1992).

28. Pepper indicated that "when [Bonar] has finished" his draft of the Upper Creek Nation he will do "a like Draught of the Lower Towns . . ." Pepper to Lyttelton, 7 May 1757, *Indian Affairs Documents*, 373.

29. Pepper to Lyttelton, 25 May 1757, *Indian Affairs Documents*, 378.

30. Ibid.

31. Pepper to Lyttelton, 27 May 1757, *Indian Affairs Documents*, 380.

32. Pepper to Lyttelton, 28 June 1757, *Indian Affairs Documents*, 388.

33. Lyttelton to Board of Trade, 3 November 1757, *BPRO Documents*, Microfilm Roll #9, 315.

34. Worked out in the first century B.C. and used in design ever since then, a golden mean rectangle is one considered "ideal." In it the longer side is equal in length to the diagonal of a square whose side is equal to the shorter side of the rectangle. Bonar's schooling would most likely have included drafting or mechanical drawing in which he would have learned about his. Perhaps he had no measuring instrument with him in the Nation and eyeballed what appeared to be golden mean rectangles on his "Draught."

35. Charles Hudson, *The Southeastern Indians* (Knoxville: University of Tennessee Press, 1976), 218.

CHAPTER TEN

Établir ses enfants au XVIIe siècle: Élénore de Grandmaison (1619–1692) et sa descendance[1]

Claire Gourdeau

In New France, under the French regime, the principal objective of the couples who had come to the new country with the intention of settling there permanently was to establish a descent. The Custom of Paris governing inheritance procedures according to the quality of the property, whether noble or common, allows certain interpretations to be made with respect to the complexity and particularities of each family situation upon the death of one of the parents.

The purpose of this article is to examine the personal undertakings of Éléonore de Grandmaison, which, together with family strategies, allowed her to establish each of her nine children from two different marriages. It also seeks to underscore the compelling example of a woman, who in spite of the limited room to manoeuvre afforded by marriage in the seventeenth century, was quite familiar with the law and its subtleties as well as the limits governing its application.

Les discours institutionnels et les pratiques familiales montrent que l'établissement de la descendance constitue l'un des objectifs principaux de la formation des couples aux XVIIe et XVIIIe siècles. Dans l'ensemble, les règles qui régissent la Coutume de Paris se révèlent explicites à ce sujet. En effet, les parents, selon l'esprit de cette loi, ne sont que les gardiens du patrimoine qu'ils transmettront à leurs enfants afin que ceux-ci assurent la continuité de la lignée et contribuent de leur mieux à l'augmentation de ce patrimoine qu'ils lègueront à leurs descendants.

Le consensus est cependant loin d'être fait sur les diverses modalités de transmission. Il semble qu'il y ait autant de variantes dans les modèles que de contextes familiaux différents, résultant d'une complexité de comportements due aux aléas politiques, économiques ou démographiques. La plupart des ouvrages sur la question traitent des successions foncières et articulent les modèles de transmission autour des axes du partage égalitaire ou inégalitaire, de l'établissement ou du non-établissement d'un, de plusieurs ou de tous les enfants, du rôle des parents, de celui du réseau d'alliances, des solidarités.[2]

Le cas d'Éléonore de Grandmaison et de sa descendance couvre toute la seconde moitié du XVIIᵉ siècle, allant même jusqu'au début du XVIIIᵉ siècle. Le contexte est celui des débuts de la colonie et du régime seigneurial en Nouvelle-France et réfère aux deux premières générations de cette famille. Comportant des situations complexes, ce cas offre l'avantage de mettre en relation un éventail de gestes susceptibles d'éclairer la stratégie d'ensemble préconisée par Éléonore de Grandmaison dans l'établissement de ses enfants.

Il a fallu dépouiller bon nombre d'actes notariés pour tirer au clair la succession d'Éléonore de Grandmaison. Une première série, ses contrats de mariage et ceux de ses enfants, fournit une foule d'informations sur la reproduction sociale d'un groupe spécifique, celui des gens de la petite noblesse et de la bourgeoisie au XVIIᵉ siècle. En effet, la plupart des familles connues à Québec, soit pour leurs activités prestigieuses au sein de l'élite dirigeante, ou comme associées à la classe marchande-bourgeoise montante de la colonie, sont reliées de près ou de loin à Éléonore de Grandmaison et font partie de son réseau d'alliances. L'identité de ses conjoints successifs, de ses enfants et la liste, souvent longue, des témoins qui assistent à la signature de leurs contrats de mariage, révèlent un tissu social serré, où pouvoir et prestige s'entremêlent aux alliances parentales. Ces documents témoignent également des biens fonciers et financiers apportés par chacune des parties, et, le cas échéant, des mesures adoptées par les parents pour établir leurs enfants.

Une seconde série de documents éclaire la question de l'acquisition et de la transmission des biens. Elle consiste en différents actes notariés tels les concessions, traités, accords, échanges, ventes, donations, testaments et inventaires après décès, qui, en plus de souligner des moments importants dans l'établissement des enfants, rendent compte des événements qui ont influencé les stratégies successorales des parents. Ces actes sont d'autant plus révélateurs qu'ils stipulent les clauses, les raisons et les conditions rattachées à chacune des transactions.

Pour étayer notre démonstration, nous établirons d'abord sommairement la structure démographique de la famille, étape essentielle pour comprendre le processus d'établissement de la descendance, et énumérerons succintement les différents éléments constituant le patrimoine foncier de cette famille. Après avoir apporté quelques précisions sur le droit coutumier, nous observerons les moments et les modes de transmission des biens fonciers d'Éléonore de Grandmaison.

STRUCTURE DÉMOGRAPHIQUE DE LA FAMILLE

Éléonore de Grandmaison, née vers 1619 est originaire du Nivernais. Les registres du navire qui l'amène en Nouvelle-France, avec la flotte de juin 1641, mentionnent qu'elle est de condition noble, âgée de 22 ans, déjà veuve d'un premier mari, et remariée à François de Chavigny de Berchereau, de souche noble, originaire de la Champagne.[3] De l'union d'Éléonore de Grandmaison et de François de Chavigny, six enfants naîtront, cinq filles et un garçon; ils composent le premier lit. Quelques mois après le décès de Chavigny, survenu en 1651, Éléonore de Grandmaison convole en troisième noces avec Jacques Gourdeau de Beaulieu.[4] Ils auront quatre enfants, trois fils et une fille, qui forment le deuxième lit. (Voir tableaux 1 et 2).

TABLEAU 1
Conjoints de Éléonore de Grandmaison.

DATE DU MARIAGE	NOM DU CONJOINT	LIEU DU MARIAGE
Vers 1635	Antoine Doudier de Beauregard	France
Vers 1640	François de Cavigny de Berchereau	France
1652	Jacques Gourdeau de Beaulieu	Ile d'Orléans, Québec
1663	Jacques Cailhaut de la Tesserie	Québec

TABLEAU 2
Enfants issus des unions d'Éléonore de Grandmaison.
Mariage avec François de Chavigny, sieur de Berchereau (vers 1640 en France)

PRÉNOM	DATE DE NAISSANCE	DATE(S) MARIAGE	AGE(S) AU MARIAGE
Marie-Madeleine	1641	1662	21 ans
Marguerite	1643	1656 et 1671	13 ans et 28 ans
Geneviève	1645	1660 et 1680	15 ans et 35 ans
Charlotte	1647	1668 et 1709	21 ans et 62 ans
Élisabeth	1648	1667	19 ans
François	1650	1675 et 1699	25 ans et 49 ans

Mariage avec Jacques Gourdeau de Beaulieu, 13 août 1652, Ile d'Orléans

PRÉNOM	DATE DE NAISSANCE	DATE(S) MARIAGE	AGE(S) AU MARIAGE
Antoine	1655	1685	30 ans
Jeanne-Renée	1658	1686	28 ans
Jacques	1660	1691	31 ans
Pierre	1662–1670	—	—

Le quatrième et dernier époux d'Éléonore de Grandmaison, Jacques Cailhaut de la Tesserie, arrive en Nouvelle-France avec la flotte de 1661. Il accompagne le gouverneur Davaugour, dont il est le lieutenant. Son contrat de mariage le décrit comme «fils aîné et principal héritier de deffunct Samuel de Cailhaut, escuyer, sieur de la Grosardière».[5] Décédé à l'âge de 44 ans, il ne laissera pas de descendance, mais il apportera sa contribution à l'établissement des enfants d'Éléonore.

CONSTITUTION DU PATRIMOINE FONCIER

Pour résumer les avoirs fonciers d'Éléonore, mentionnons que la plupart de ceux-ci lui proviennent de François de Chavigny, père des six enfants du premier lit. Ils consistent en deux emplacements à Québec et à Sillery, et en la seigneurie de Chavigny à Deschambeault, d'une lieue de largeur sur trois de profondeur. A ces trois lots, concédés par la Compagnie des Cent-Associés avant le départ de Chavigny pour la Nouvelle-France, s'ajoutera, en 1649, l'arrière-fief Beaulieu à l'Ile d'Orléans, mesurant 40 arpents de front sur toute la largeur de la pointe ouest de l'ile.[6]

Quant au troisième époux d'Éléonore, Jacques Gourdeau de Beaulieu, il se fait concéder en 1662, un emplacement de maison à la basse ville de Québec, rue St-Pierre.

Enfin, Éléonore de Grandmaison hérite, au décès de son quatrième époux, Jacques Cailhaut de la Tesserie, d'un arrière-fief de 15 arpents de front appelé La Grosardière situé à l'Ile d'Orléans.[7]

DROIT COUTUMIER ET PARTAGE

Une première observation se dégage à l'étude des actes notariés passés par Éléonore de Grandmaison, sur plus de 50 ans: nous sommes devant une femme qui reconnaît l'importance du document écrit et conservé dans un greffe, à une époque où les ententes verbales et les papiers rédigés sous seing privé sont légion. Au cours de sa vie, le notaire se présentera chez elle entre 75 et 100 fois. De ce chiffre, une trentaine d'actes sont directement liés à la transmission de ses biens. Afin d'aborder les manières et les moments privilégiés par Éléonore pour transmettre son patrimoine, il apparaît utile d'apporter quelques éclaircissements sur certains aspects de ses contrats de mariage. Précisons que celle-ci, en choisissant de se remarier à chaque occasion que lui offre le destin, se montre soucieuse de préserver les droits de ses enfants des deux lits.

Au décès de chacun de ses époux, Éléonore de Grandmaison peut, si elle le désire, continuer la communauté de biens entre elle et ses enfants ou y mettre fin. Dans les deux cas, elle devra en faire dresser «bon et loyal inventaire» devant notaire. Mais, qu'elle poursuive ou qu'elle mette fin à la communauté, la moitié des biens lui reviendra, tandis que l'autre moitié sera divisée entre ses enfants. Ces parts seront administrées par Éléonore elle-même, assistée d'un tuteur «subrogé»[8] jusqu'à la majorité des enfants. Pour que prenne fin cette communauté cependant, il faut que l'inventaire soit déclaré «clos» devant notaire. Advenant un bilan négatif de l'inventaire de la communauté, les parties peuvent y renoncer.

Éléonore de Grandmaison, au décès de François de Chavigny, choisit de laisser «ouverte», autrement dit de continuer la communauté de biens entre elle et ses six enfants mineurs. A son remariage avec Jacques Gourdeau de

Beaulieu, elle forme une seconde communauté de biens qui se superpose à la première, ce qui ne lèse en rien les enfants du premier lit, comme le stipule la Coutume de Paris:

> Les acquêts de la première communauté sont le propre héritage des enfants, qui doivent retourner à leurs héritiers du côté et ligne, lesquels par conséquent ne doivent point être mis en une nouvelle communauté; autrement ce seroit donner occasion à l'aliénation d'iceux; ce qui est défendu par nos coutumes.[9]

Le même processus vaut pour les quatre enfants du deuxième lit, les Gourdeau de Beaulieu, lorsque, au décès de leur père, Éléonore décide de se remarier encore une fois. L'inventaire des biens de la communauté se montre déficitaire cette fois, ce qui prive les enfants de leur part d'héritage paternel. Nous verrons plus loin quelles actions seront entreprises par Éléonore pour remédier à cette lacune.

La dernière union entre Éléonore de Grandmaison et Jacques de Cailhaut de la Tesserie est effectuée en séparation de biens, chose qui paraît assez rare pour l'époque. Éléonore, alors âgée de 44 ans, ne prévoit sans doute plus avoir d'enfants. Ce choix s'avérera avantageux autant pour Éléonore que pour ses enfants des deux lits. D'une part, Jacques Cailhaut de la Tesserie, arrivé seul dans la colonie et donc sans héritier potentiel, décide de participer financièrement à l'établissement de ses beaux-enfants en y consacrant son argent personnel. D'autre part, en décédant sans postérité, ses avoirs reviennent à son épouse et contribuent, par le fait même, à augmenter la part d'héritage maternel des enfants.

LES MODES ET LES MOMENTS DE TRANSMISSION

Le destin a donné longue vie à Éléonore de Grandmaison, ce qui lui a permis d'échelonner l'établissement de ses enfants sur une période étendue et de compléter le cycle familial. En établissant des relations entre les différents actes retracés, nous sommes à même de fournir une analyse partielle de sa stratégie successorale.

C'est au moment du mariage des enfants du premier lit que se traduisent l'impact et l'importance des alliances matrimoniales de leur mère Éléonore de Grandmaison sur leur propre établissement. A la signature du contrat de mariage de sa fille Geneviève de Chavigny, (tableau 3) Éléonore et son époux d'alors, Jacques Gourdeau de Beaulieu versent conjointement une dot de mille livres, «le tout payable en meubles et bestiaux ou autres effets du pays, en une fois payée», incluant «une place et maison située au lieu et proche la fontaine Champlain».[10] De même, Élisabeth et Charlotte de Chavigny recevront chacune, lorsqu'elles prendront mari, une somme de 1000 livres provenant de leur beau-père Jacques Cailhaut de la Tesserie.[11]

TABLEAU 3

Unions des enfants d'Éléonore de Grandmaison.
(a) Les Chavigny

PRÉNOM	NOM DU CONJOINT DATE MARIAGE	REMARQUES
Marie-Madeleine	Jean LeMoyne, 1662	Sans contrat, registre de la paroisse. Concession à l'époux de la seigneurie de Ste-Marie au Cap-de-la-Madeleine en 1672; augmentée des ilets de Sorel en 1711. Achat d'un arrière-fief dans Boucherville en 1702. Le couple a 10 enfants.
Marguerite	1. Thomas Douaire de Bondy, 1656	1. Noble, écuyer, gentilhomme ordinaire de la chambre du roi. La mairée est âgée de 13 ans. Le couple aura 6 enfants.
	2. Jacques-Alexis Fleury Deschambault, 1671	2. Noble, juge civil et criminel, procureur du roi et lieutenant général à Montréal. La couple a 7 enfants.
Geneviève	1. Charles Amiot, 1660	1. Marchand à Québec. Elle est âgée de 15 ans. 3 enfants.
	2. Jean-Baptiste Couillard de L'Espinay, 1680	2. Anobili, capitaine des gardes de la Ferme, procureur du roi à la prévôté, lieutenant général de l'Amirauté de Québec. Sans postérité.
Élisabeth	Étienne Landron, 1667	Pâtissier et cuisinier, bourgeois, échevin en 1682. 16 enfants.
Charlotte	1. René Breton, 1668	1. Marchand-bourgeois. Le couple a un seul enfant.

François	2. Jean Girou, 1709	2. Elle est âgée de 62 ans.
	1. Antoinette de	Il a un enfant naturel avec une autre
	Poussans de L'Hôpital,	femme en 1674.
	1675	1. Elle accouche 5 mois plus tard d'une
	2. Geneviève Guyon-	fille dont Frontenac est le parrain.
	Després, 1699	2. Elle lui donne 10 enfants. Il fonde
		cette nouvelle famille à près de 50 ans.

(b) Les Gourdeau de Beaulieu

PRÉNOM	NOM DU CONJOINT DATE MARIAGE	REMARQUES
Antoine	François Zachée, 1685	Militaire, puis commerçant (fourrure). Il épouse une veuve avec 2 enfants. Sans postérité.
Jeanne-Renée	Charles Macard, 1686	Marchand-bourgeois, membre du Conseil Supérieur de la N.F. Procureur général au Conseil Souverain (6 enfants tous décédés en bas âge).
Jacques	Marie Bissot, 1692	Marchand-bourgeois, seigneur de Beaulieu (I.O.). Il épouse une veuve avec 3 enfants. Le couple en aura 6 autres.

Pour établir sa fille Marguerite, Éléonore de Grandmaison choisit d'autres moments que le mariage. Neuf ans après sa première union avec Thomas Douaire de Bondy, Marguerite reçoit de sa mère une terre de quatre arpents située sur l'arrière-fief de Beaulieu à Ile d'Orléans. Cette terre est concédée au couple «en plein fief», c'est-à-dire sans aucune charge ni redevance.[12]

En 1672, Éléonore, profitant du remaniement seigneurial initié par Jean Talon, double la superficie de sa seigneurie de Chavigny près de Trois-Rivières, en y ajoutant le fief de La Chevrotière. Marguerite et son second époux, Jacques-Alexis Fleury Deschambault[13] échangent, en 1683, leur terre de l'Ile d'Orléans contre l'entière seigneurie de Chavigny qui prendra le nom de Deschambault.[14]

La stratégie mise en oeuvre par Éléonore apparaît clairement ici. Au fil des événements vécus par ses enfants et tout en tenant compte de leurs goûts personnels, il semble évident, par le biais de ces différentes transactions, qu'elle s'affaire à installer les Chavigny sur la seigneurie de Deschambault et de réserver ses arrière-fiefs de l'Ile d'Orléans aux Gourdeau de Beaulieu.

LA PART DU FILS

François de Chavigny est le sixième enfant du premier lit mais le seul garçon. Il jouit donc, malgré son rang de naissance du droit d'aînesse. Tout comme sa soeur Marguerite, sa mère l'établit d'abord, à l'âge de 18 ans, sur «une habitation sise en l'Isle d'Orléans, seigneurie de Beaulieu, contenant quatre arpents de terre de front du côté du nord, traversant ladite Ile d'Orléans en profondeur avec droits de chasse et de pêche, sur laquelle il y a sept arpents en labour et le surplus complanté de hauts bois . . . ».[15] Peu avant son premier mariage, François de Chavigny échange cet héritage contre le fief La Chevrotière.[16]

Pourquoi Marguerite et François de Chavigny choisissent-ils de délaisser les belles et bonnes terres de l'Ile d'Orléans, situées près de Québec, et dont l'exploitation est assez avancée? L'hypothèse la plus plausible réside dans la qualité des titres qui y sont rattachés et non dans la qualité des sols. De souche noble, les Chavigny préfèrent sans doute être seigneurs de fiefs, même s'ils sont peu exploités, et pour lesquels ils rendront foi et hommage directement au roi, via son représentant dans la colonie. Les terres de l'Ile d'Orléans, quant à elles, ne sont que des arrière-fiefs et obligent leurs tenanciers à porter foi et hommage au seigneur principal. Mentionnons que les questions de prestige sont très importantes à l'époque.

La stratégie d'établissement des enfants du deuxième lit diffère grandement des Chavigny car les Gourdeau de Beaulieu n'ont rien reçu au décès de leur père, celui-ci n'ayant laissé que des dettes et aucun bien noble. En compensation de cette lacune, leur mère a dû consentir de nombreux efforts pour établir ses trois enfants survivants, Antoine, Jeanne-Renée et Jacques.

A son mariage avec une veuve en 1685, le fils aîné du deuxième lit, Antoine Gourdeau de Beaulieu, apporte donc ses propres deniers, qui consistent en «la somme de seize cents livres, qu'il a déclaré provenir des profits faits dans son voyage tant au nord qu'à l'Acadie et de la part qu'il a eue de son camp de traite aux Outaouais».[17] Pour sa part, Éléonore lui réserve, par droit d'aînesse, l'arrière-fief de Beaulieu, situé à l'Ile d'Orléans, en plus d'accorder à la future épouse une part d'enfant.[18]

Antoine ne se montre guère intéressé par l'activité terrienne. Marchand prospère à Québec, il cumule également des charges militaires et civiles.[19] A cet égard, il ne se démarque pas de ses contemporains. Un traité passé entre Éléonore et son fils Antoine en 1690[20] révèle que celui-ci renonce à son droit d'aînesse et à son titre de seigneur, en échange de compensations monétaires qui lui seront versées par ses cohéritiers, c'est-à-dire sa soeur Jeanne-Renée et son frère Jacques. C'est à ce dernier qu'échoient les deux arrière-fiefs de l'Ile d'Orléans, Beaulieu et La Grosardière.

Bien qu'il soit impossible d'évaluer exactement le montant que chacun des trois enfants a reçu, il est néanmoins permis de croire qu'Éléonore a tenu compte des goûts personnels de ses enfants du second lit. Jeanne-Renée, qui épouse un riche marchand, reçoit la maison de la basse-ville, rue Saint-Pierre, tandis que Jacques hérite des arrière-fiefs de Beaulieu et de la Grosardière à l'Ile d'Orléans. En compensation de cette donation, Jeanne-Renée devra verser 600 livres à Antoine, tandis que Jacques, pour sa part, paiera 2000 livres à son frère aîné.

Afin de conserver son patrimoine, Éléonore de Grandmaison avait fait reconstruire le manoir seigneurial de Beaulieu, rasé par le feu à deux reprises, en 1652 et en 1663. Quant à sa maison de la basse-ville, seul bien laissé par Gourdeau de Beaulieu, sa valeur ne couvrait pas le montant des dettes laissées à son décès. De plus, elle avait été également incendiée en 1682. En la faisant rebâtir à ses frais,[21] Éléonore éponge les dettes de la succession et fait donation de ladite maison à sa fille Jeanne-Renée pour son mariage. Le droit coutumier régissant les donations stipule qu'avant de donner quoi que ce soit à l'un de ses enfants, Éléonore doit faire la preuve, devant notaire, que le bien lui appartient en propre et que la donation ne lèse aucun des cohéritiers. Le contrat de mariage de Jeanne-Renée, dans lequel est détaillée la donation, explique donc que sa mère, face à une communauté de biens déficitaire à la mort de Jacques Gourdeau de Beaulieu, avait quand même accepté d'en payer les dettes. Éléonore pouvait donc disposer de la maison à son gré.[22]

A cette donation sont assorties d'autres conditions. D'une part, Éléonore stipule que cette maison demeurera dans les propres de sa fille ou, autrement dit, qu'elle n'entrera pas dans la communauté de biens. D'autre part, en acceptant cette donation, Jeanne-Renée s'engage à renoncer à toute autre part d'héritage à venir. Son contrat de mariage précise qu'elle ne pourra «prétendre d'entrer en aucun partage avec ses frères» pour les arrière-fiefs de l'Ile d'Orléans.

Antoine et Jacques sont absents au mariage de leur soeur Jeanne-Renée. A leur retour, ils se présentent donc devant le notaire pour apposer leur signature à un codicille du contrat de mariage de Jeanne où ils acceptent l'entente, et précisant qu'ils ne devront prétendre à aucun moment retirer des rentes ou des sommes pouvant provenir de cette propriété.

A son décès, en 1692, Éléonore de Grandmaison, qui vit chez sa fille Jeanne, ne possède pratiquement plus rien. Les articles énumérés dans son inventaire de biens après décès sont de peu de valeur et consistent en quelques hardes et objets usés. Ils reviendront à Jeanne-Renée, tel que prévu dans son contrat de mariage et ce, «pour les bons et agréables services qu'elle luy a toujours rendus».[23]

CONCLUSION: UNE TRANSMISSION PROGRESSIVE ET SANS EXCLUS

Quelques constats se dégagent à l'étude de la transmission des biens d'Éléonore de Grandmaison. Parmi eux, la connaissance du droit matrimonial est déterminante. Ayant survécu à ses quatre époux, c'est à elle qu'incombent la gestion et la répartition de la part des héritiers. En choisissant de continuer ou de renoncer à la communauté de biens entre elle et ses enfants, Éléonore protège les avoirs des Chavigny et travaille à la reconstitution de ceux des Gourdeau. Le mode de transmission observé ici révèle non seulement sa volonté de favoriser l'établissement de chacun de ses enfants mais démontre également les résultats positifs de gestes posés consciemment et graduellement.

Éléonore s'adapte aux circonstances et au cycle de vie familiale de ses enfants. La transmission s'effectue progressivement et principalement au moment de leur mariage, ce qui ne l'empêche pas de reconsidérer les choix de chacun en procédant à des échanges ou à des consultations au moment du partage. En effet, ses contributions, sans être strictement égalitaires, sont comparables et adaptés aux besoins et aux goûts des uns et des autres. Généreux et prudent, l'apport au mariage des enfants d'Éléonore suscite, de la part des nouvelles familles alliées, des engagements sociaux et financiers avantageux.

Par le traité de 1690, dressé un an avant sa mort, Éléonore de Grandmaison complète l'établissement des enfants du second lit, mettant ainsi fin à sa vie active. A cette date, toutes ses affaires sont, pour ainsi dire, liquidées. Le fruit du travail de toute une vie, résultant de ses initiatives personnelles ajoutées aux stratégies familiales, est ainsi réparti équitablement entre ses enfants.

NOTES

1. Cette communication reprend les résultats d'une recherche plus exhaustive portant le même titre et parue dans l'ouvrage collectif *Espaces-temps familiaux au Canada aux XVIIe et XVIIIe siècles*, sous la direction de Jacques Mathieu, Alain Laberge et Louis Michel, Université Laval, CIEQ (Centre Interuniversitaire d'Études Québécoises), collection «Cheminements», 1995, 45–68.
2. A ce sujet, les actes du colloque de Veyrier-du-Lac tenu en 1991 sur la reproduction familiale en milieu rural France-Québec, XVIIIe–XXe siècles et regroupés dans le collectif *Transmettre, Hériter, Succéder* (Lyon: Presses Universitaires de Lyon, 1992), nous offrent de nombreux exemples. En particulier, pour la région de Québec sous le Régime français, les articles de Geneviève Postolec, 43–53; de Jacques Mathieu, Alain Laberge, Lina Gouger et Geneviève Postolec, 121–33; et enfin, de Louis Lavallée, 213–30.
3. Marcel Trudel, *Catalogue des immigrants 1632–1662* (Montréal: Hurtubise HMH, 1983), 102.
4. Archives nationales du Québec [ANQ], extrait des registres de baptêmes, mariages et sépultures de la paroisse Notre-Dame de Québec pour les années 1621–1679, 117, acte de mariage; ANQ, greffe du notaire Rolland Godet, contrat de mariage daté du 30 juillet 1652.
5. ANQ, greffe du notaire Guillaume Audouart, 10 octobre 1663.
6. Pierre-Georges Roy, dans *La famille de Chavigny de la Chevrotière* (Lévis: L'Action sociale Limitée, 1916), 9 et ss., décrit les différents lots accordés à François de Chavigny de Berchereau avant son départ pour la Nouvelle-France.
7. A l'origine, Tesserie possédait cet arrière-fief en co-propriété avec Louis Péronne de Mazé. Lorsque ce dernier rentra en France en 1665, il céda sa moitié à Tesserie. ANQ, greffe du notaire Pierre Duquet, 14 mai 1665; ANQ, greffe du notaire Gilles

Rageot, Acte de foi et hommage de Jacques de Cailhaut, sieur de la Tesserie à Mgr de Laval pour son fief de la Grosardière, 26 mars 1668.

8. Personne désignée en dehors de la famille pour représenter les intérêts des héritiers et pour surveiller la gestion du tuteur, dans le cas présent, de la tutrice. A la mort de ses époux, Éléonore de Grandmaison devient, en effet, la tutrice de ses enfants. La Coutume, soucieuse de préserver leurs droits lui adjuge un second: «Par plusieurs Loix, la mère qui n'a point demandé dans l'an au Magistrat un tuteur à ses enfants, est privée de leur succession.» Claude de Ferrière, *Corps et Compilation de tous les commentateurs anciens et modernes sur la Coutume de Paris* (Paris: Nicolas Gosselin, 1714), vol. 2, «Tuteurs», art. 11, 1019.

9. ANQ, Claude de Ferrière, *Commentaire sur la Coutume de la prévôté et vicomté de Paris* (Paris: Les Libraires Associés, 1788), vol. 2, 104, article «Communauté de biens».

10. ANQ, greffe du notaire Guillaume Audouart, Contrat de mariage de Geneviève de Chavigny et Charles Amiot, 12 avril 1660.

11. ANQ, greffe du notaire Gilles Rageot, Contrat de mariage de Élisabeth de Chavigny et Étienne Landron, 2 octobre 1667; greffe du notaire Pierre Duquet, Contrat de mariage de Charlotte de Chavigny et René Breton, 3 novembre 1668. Dans son cas, le contrat stipule: «mille livres tournois, argent de France».

12. ANQ, greffe du notaire Pierre Duquet, Concession de Éléonore de Grandmaison à Thomas Douaire de bondy, 1er juin 1665.

13. ANQ, greffe du notaire Romain Becquet, Contrat de mariage de Marguerite de Chavigny, veuve de Thomas Douaire de Bondy avec Jacques-Alexis Fleury Deschambault, 18 novembre 1671.

14. ANQ, greffe du notaire François Genaple, Échange entre Éléonore de Grandmaison, Jacques-Alexis Fleury Deschambault et Marguerite de Chavigny, 25 octobre 1683.

15. C'est la description qu'en dresse le notaire dans l'acte d'échange de 1674. ANQ, greffe du notaire Romain Becquet, Échange entre Éléonore de Grandmaison, veuve Tesserie et François de Chavigny la Chevrotière, 7 avril 1674.

16. Ibid.

17. ANQ, greffe du notaire François Genaple, Contrat de mariage de Antoine Gourdeau de Beaulieu et Françoise Zachée, veuve Claude de Saintes, 30 novembre 1685.

18. Ibid. «Et à l'égard de ladite future épouse, pour l'amour et l'affection qu'elle porte aux futurs époux, elle [Éléonore] l'admet à partager dans ses biens propres et

d'acquêts qu'elle peut avoir, pour pareille part et portion qu'un de ses enfants pourra amender venant à sa succession après son décès, suivant la Coutume de Paris».

19. Lieutenant de la Compagnie colonelle du Régiment de Québec dans l'armée de La Barre en 1684; contrôleur à la réception des castors du bureau de la Ferme à Québec. René Jetté, *Dictionnaire généalogique des familles du Québec des origines à 1720* (Montréal: Presse de l'Université de Montréal, 1983), 521.

20. ANQ, greffe du notaire Gilles Rageot, Traité entre Éléonore de Grandmaison veuve Tesserie et Antoine Gourdeau de Beaulieu, 11 septembre 1690.

21. ANQ, greffe du notaire Gilles Rageot, Marché de maison entre Éléonore de Grandmaison et René Allary, 19 novembre 1682.

22. ANQ, greffe du notaire François Genaple, Contrat de mariage de Charles Macard et de Jeanne-Renée Gourdeau de Beaulieu, 7 décembre 1686: «[. . .] laquelle maison ladite Dame de Grandmaison de la Tesserie a fait rebâtir après l'incendie de cette dite basse-ville arrivé en décembre 1682, en la place d'icelle qui y avait été bâtie pendant la communauté qui était entre elle et le défunt sieur de Beaulieu, sur ledit emplacement, à laquelle communauté ayant renoncée, après l'inventaire des biens d'icelle, elle avait néanmoins acquitté les dettes passées de la succession dudit défunt. Et, puisque [. . .] ladite succession lui est débitrice de plus grande somme que ne peut valoir ledit terrain sur lequel est édifiée la dite maison et qu'ainsi elle lui appartient avec ledit terrain sans que ses deux fils puissent prétendre aucune part».

23. ANQ, greffe du notaire Gilles Rageot, Testament d'Éléonore de Grandmaison, en dernières noces veuve de Jacques Cailhaut de la Tesserie, 19 novembre 1691.

PLAISANCE - INVENTAIRE - NOM: - DATE:

Alimentation conservation	ameublement	civilisation	domestique	luxe	maritime	vêtements
assiette-étain	armoire	balance-cuivre	blanchet	cave-vin	amarre	bas
assiette-faillance	banc	chocolatière-cuivre	étoffe	chambres (3-5)	aviron-chaloupe	bonnet-enfant
baril	chandelle		gargousse-poudre	cheminée-double	barriques-sel	camisole-toile
barrique	chandelier-léton	livre			bottes	camsecon-toile
biscuits	chandelier-cuivre	pinte	gillets-bassin	galon-argent	cable-chaloupe	capot
boeuf		poid-plomb	guenilles	jardin	chaffaud	change
bouteille-terre	chandelier-fer-blanc	porte-feuille	peigne-corne	tasse-argent	chaloupe	chapeau
bouteille-ver		quart	raquettes		compas-hyvoire	chemises
caisse	coffre	rasoir	savon		croos	chemises-femmes
cannette faillance	coffre-armoire	romaine-anglaise	serviettes		demi-chaloupe	coiffes-taffetas
chaudière-bière	coffre-plume	tabac	toile		fil-voile-ret	coiffes-toile
chaudière-cuivre	couverture-laine		vergettes		grapins	cravatte
chopine	drape-lit				grave	cravatte-mousseline
couteaux-table	étoiles-oreiller				magasin-cabanne	culotte-de-peau
couve-plat	fauteuil				mats-chaloupe	culotte-enfants
cuillère-étain	lit				mats-misène	culotte-soie
cuillères-fer-blanc	matelat				misène	dentelle
eau-de-vie	miroir				morue-verte	gants
écuelle-étain	nappe				peau-loup-marin	gillet-femme
farine	paillasse				quart-goudron	habits-enfants
fourchette-acier	penture				quintaux-morue	habits-pelletrie
fourchette-bois	pot-chambre				ret-anglais	hardes
fourchette-fer	table-bois				scène-treille	jupe
gobelet	table-tôle				voiles-chaloupe	jupon
gri-fer	tapisserie					juste-a-corps
huilière-étain	traversin					manteau
jarre-d'huile	vesselier					mouchoir-couleur
lard						mouchoir-blanc
mélasse						perruque
pain						poignets-femme
passoire-cuivre						robe-chambre-femme
poêle						souliers
pois						tablier
poivre						veste
plats-étain						
plats-fer-blanc						
plats-terre						
pot-confiture						
pot-fer						
pots-terre						
quart						
salière						
verre						
vin de al						
vin-terrier						

Transmission du patrimoine dans une colonie de pêche: analyse préliminaire des inventaires après-décès à Plaisance au XVIIIe siècle

Nicolas Landry

The relative scarcity of Acadian colonial documents has resulted in a new generation of Acadian historians turning to micro-history. This research is of that nature because it deals with a type of document that is very rare in the Acadian archival corpus, the after-death inventory. Inspired by the work of other historians, we decided to do a preliminary analysis of seven after-death inventories found in notarized documents from Plaisance (now Placentia). This study involved creating a sample of the degree of wealth in the main social classes of the colony; that is, the merchants, the habitant-fishermen, the civil administrators and the fishermen, with a view to adjusting our data collection and analysis methods before looking into all of the available documentation. Our work is related to the development of two parallel projects: the social history of French sedentary fishery in America and a social and economic monograph of Plaisance.

La relative rareté des documents coloniaux acadiens, a favorisé l'éclosion de la micro-histoire chez une nouvelle génération d'historiens et d'historiennes en Acadie. Après les grandes synthèses événementielles de la première moitié du XXe siècle,[1] l'ouvrage de Andrew Hill Clark ouvrait de nouveaux horizons de recherche sur l'époque coloniale acadienne.[2] Publiée durant les années 1960, cette recherche en géographie historique présentait une interprétation renouvelée ayant recours à une approche plus thématique, surtout par le biais des recensements.

C'est dans ce sillon que des auteurs comme Naomi Griffiths et Jean Daigle adopteront des sujets tels l'évolution sociale des Acadiens, ou encore leur implication dans le commerce avec l'extérieur.[3] A compter de la fin des années 1960, le grand projet de recherche guidant la reconstruction de la forteresse de Louisbourg allait mettre au jour des types de documents jusque-là peu utilisés dans l'historiographie acadienne, entre autres les inventaires après-décès. Il en découla subséquemment quelques ouvrages soulignant la grande richesse de ces documents, d'ailleurs exploités depuis les années 1950 en France et ensuite au Québec.[4] Comme le soulignait récemment Louis Lavallée, l'histoire sociale, depuis une trentaine d'années, s'est surtout développée par le biais des études basées sur les minutes notariales. Plusieurs historiens les utilisèrent dans l'espoir de reconstituer le tissu social d'Ancien Régime. Bref, cette documentation se prêtait bien à l'histoire sérielle chère à Pierre Chaunu. La communication présentée par Ernest Labrousse à Rome en 1955, représente un peu l'acte fondateur des multiples recherches qui allaient subséquemment utiliser les minutes notariales, jusque-là négligées par les historiens. Depuis ce temps, de nombreux textes méthodologiques proposent des façons d'aborder l'utilisation de l'inventaire après-décès par exemple.[5]

Cependant, comme le souligne Dominique Bouchard, l'exploitation des inventaires après-décès soulève d'épineux problèmes méthodologiques. Bouchard reconnaît qu'il existe un grand nombre de tentatives intéressantes, mais difficiles à intégrer. Incidemment, l'auteur nous prévient que l'exploitation de cette source exige un fastidieux travail de «repérage, de dépouillement et d'analyse qu'un chercheur isolé ne pourra jamais en saisir plus qu'une infime partie».[6] Pourtant, considérant la composition des inventaires, on serait porté à croire qu'ils permettraient d'évaluer aisément la fortune. Rappelons-le, l'inventaire n'est ni plus ni moins qu'un recensement en principe exhaustif des éléments composant le patrimoine mobilier et immobilier d'un ménage. C'est dans l'espoir de pallier aux lacunes des inventaires que Bouchard adopte la méthode de Micheline Baulant, permettant de «synthétiser... un inventaire à partir de la présence ou de l'absence d'un certain nombre de caractéristiques».[7]

Baulant a recours à un indice du niveau de vie, qui est une liste d'éléments choisis en fonction de leur fréquence d'apparition dans les inventaires. Il s'agit ensuite de déterminer la présence ou l'absence de chacun d'eux dans les actes étudiés. Christian Dessureault et John Dickinson ont adapté l'indice de Baulant au contexte canadien. C'est cette version que Bouchard applique à son échantillon en utilisant une liste des éléments de l'indice du niveau de vie divisée en cinq grandes catégories que sont les objets de première nécessité, de la vie domestique, du confort, de civilisation et de luxe.

Une deuxième option méthodologique provient d'une recherche menée par Jean-Pierre Hardy, destinée à comparer le niveau de richesse et quelques aspects de la vie matérielle des artisans de Québec et de Montréal à l'aide principalement des inventaires après-décès.[8] Il effectue une compilation des objets relatifs au système de chauffage, la batterie de cuisine, la vaisselle, le mobilier et les objets de décor. Son échantillon se compose de 39 inventaires entre 1740 et 1755. Il présente ses résultats par l'entremise de six tableaux cumulatifs. Comme exemples, citons les comparaisons des valeurs et des quantités moyennes par famille pour l'équipement domestique, la comparaison entre les deux villes et entre les fortunés et les moins fortunés en ce qui a trait à la vaisselle et le mobilier.

Plus récemment, on assiste à un certain renouvellement d'intérêt dans l'utilisation des documents coloniaux, entre autres, les inventaires après-décès. Ceci, relativement à une importante tentative de réinterprétation de l'histoire coloniale acadienne. Il s'agit d'une approche qu'on pourrait qualifier de micro-historique puisqu'elle s'attarde à l'étude de groupes sociaux, de familles ou d'individus. Je me permets de signaler les travaux de thèses de Maurice Basque portant sur la famille Robichaud et ceux de Josette Brun et de Nicole Boucher qui touchent le rôle des femmes d'affaires et des marchands à Louisbourg.[9] Ces chercheurs ont eu l'occasion de constater la richesse des informations contenues dans les inventaires. Les historiens et historiennes de Parcs Canada à Halifax et à Louisbourg, ont également produit quelques travaux faisant usage des inventaires. Bien qu'ils ne soient pas tous publiés, le chercheur aurait intérêt à les consulter dans leur totalité.[10]

Bien que plus familier avec l'historiographie des pêches du XIXe siècle, je tente néanmoins d'élargir mon champ d'étude en abordant l'étude de Plaisance, importante colonie de pêche française jusqu'en 1713. La perte de cette colonie de pêche lors des négociations du Traité d'Utrecht forcera la France à se rabattre sur l'Ile Royale.[11]

En appendice d'une récente thèse de maîtrise, Roland Plaze aborde l'hypothèse d'une étude socio-économique de Plaisance.[12] Elle s'appuie essentiellement sur les archives notariales de Plaisance conservées dans la série G3, du fonds des colonies. A la différence de l'Acadie péninsulaire,[13] il existe heureusement des archives notariales plus riches pour Plaisance et Louisbourg, permettant peut-être de démontrer que leur population était organisée comme une véritable société et non pas seulement comme un poste de pêche ou militaire. Peut-on ainsi espérer mettre en relief la très grande richesse de telles sources, ainsi que les énormes possibilités d'études qu'elles ouvrent pour une connaissance plus raffinée de Plaisance et de Louisbourg sous le Régime français?[14]

Entre autres avenues de recherche, Plaze mentionne l'analyse des répertoires notariés pour établir des rapports entre l'activité notariale et l'activité économique afin de cerner les structures sociales de la colonie.[15] Suite à l'analyse du répertoire notariés de Plaisance, Plaze identifie 860 actes pour la période 1696-1713. La moyenne s'établit à 160 par an de 1709 à 1711. A noter qu'il ne s'y trouve que vingt inventaires après-décès. Il a également subdivisé ce total en 21 types d'actes représentant 92,30% de l'ensemble de l'activité notariale de la période étudiée. On retrouve ainsi les quatre grandes catégories que sont les opérations de crédit, l'activité économique, le droit de la famille et l'activité maritime, se composant elles-mêmes de plusieurs sous-catégories qui serviront de point de départ pour notre recherche préliminaire.

TABLEAU 1

Répartition des catégories d'actes notariés de Plaisance 1696–1713

OPÉRATIONS DE CRÉDIT	ACTIVITÉS ÉCONOMIQUES
quittances	ventes
oblications	marchés
saisies	associations
comptes	engagements
cautionnement	sociétés
protêts	estimations
requêtes	affrètements
sommations	
sentences	
arrêts	

DROITS DE LA FAMILLE	ACTIVITÉS MARITIMES
mariages	enquêtes
inventaires	interrogatoires
requêtes	rôles d'équipages
donations	requêtes
testaments	protêts
mise sous scellés	déclatations (pièces)
renonciations de succession	procurations

Une lecture encore plus serrée des inventaires d'actes devrait cependant nous aider à mieux cerner les grands axes de recherche pouvant échafauder une démarche d'histoire sociale et économique de Plaisance. De fait, la petitesse du corpus documentaire comparativement à d'autres régions françaises d'alors et la courte histoire de Plaisance, permettront une approche davantage microscopique. Les raisons d'être de cet établissement sont bien connues mais l'on en sait beaucoup moins sur ses habitants et sur les rapports qu'ils entretenaient entre eux. Les conclusions préliminaires de cette recherche pourraient laisser supposer un portrait sensiblement similaire aux résultats de travaux antérieurs pour d'autres régions. Cependant, le caractère maritime de Plaisance laisse présager de nouvelles avenues de recherche rattachées aux exigences de la vie maritime du XVIIIe siècle. Théoriquement, certains aspects de notre recherche seraient transférables à une démarche plus globale incluant l'Ile Royale.

La conclusion sommaire de Plaze est que le notariat de Plaisance n'est pas confiné dans le droit familial et qu'il traduit une forte activité économique. Il existe bel et bien une société dynamique à Plaisance s'apparentant davantage à une colonie qu'à une simple garnison militaire.[16] Cette conclusion débouche sur une hypothèse de recherche voulant que l'on puisse en connaître davantage sur les structures sociales de Plaisance à partir des contrats de mariage (âge des époux, lieux d'origine, revenus, profession, dot). On en apprendrait ainsi sur la qualité des époux et de leurs parents pour possiblement arriver à dresser un classement socio-professionel provisoire.

Bien que la série G3 offre un éventail assez intéressant de projets en micro-histoire, nous nous limitons ici à une analyse préliminaire de sept inventaires après-décès également utilisés par l'historienne Brenda Dunn de Parcs Canada.[17] Ceci dans le cadre d'un projet d'interprétation de Castle Hill, situé sur l'ancien emplacement de Plaisance. Le projet visait à répertorier les types d'objets composant le mobilier et les ustensiles d'une maison d'habitant-pêcheur à Plaisance au XVIIIe siècle. Bien que notre objectif demeure une étude complète des contrats de mariage, testaments et inventaires de Plaisance, nous estimons que cette analyse préliminaire offre une indication utile, permettant de roder nos méthodes de cueillette et d'analyse. Dans sa recherche, Dunn offre deux catégories sociales reposant sur l'identification d'une occupation. Cependant, la prudence exige que l'on signale la possibilité, pour ces individus, d'exercer plus d'une occupation. Nous nous en tenons cependant aux occupations identifiées par Dunn. Toutefois, nous entretenons un doute sur le statut de Gabriel Barnetche. En effet, le contexte documentaire nous porte à croire qu'il était habitant-pêcheur et non pas compagnon-pêcheur. Il affiche d'ailleurs les meilleures rendements chez les individus de la catégorie B.

TABLEAU 2

Catégories socio-économiques attribuées par Dunn

Catégorie A: Marchands/entrepreneurs de pêche/fonctionnaires

NOMS	COMMENTAIRES
Sébastien Soudeval	Commandant de l'Ile Saint-Pierre, habitant à Petit Plaisance
Gaspard Zemard	habitant-pêcheur, tué lors d'une prise dune frégate anglaise
Marguerite Aubert	Habitant-pécheur, veuve de Abraham Pichart, entrepreneur de pêche

Catégorie B: Pêcheurs et Autres

NOMS	COMMENTAIRES
Louis Josselin dit Lachapelle	Compagnon-pêcheur, habitant à Pointe-Verte (noyé)
Robert Tebaux	Compagnon-pêcheur
Christophe Moisant	Compagnon-pêcheur
Gabriel Barnetche	Habitant-pêcheur ou compagnon-pêcheur (?) déserteur aux Anglais

Nous nous sommes donc inspiré des approches méthodologiques de Dominique Bouchard et de Jean-Pierre Hardy pour établir notre propre grille de cueillette de données, en fonction des réalités socio-économiques de Plaisance. C'est ainsi que nous sommes arrivés à sept catégories que sont: alimentation et conservation, ameublement, civilisation, domestique, luxe, maritime et vêtements. On peut donc dire qu'à l'exception des objets reliés aux activités de pêche, les autres catégories de notre grille se rapprochent de celles utilisées pour l'étude des inventaires du Canada. L'annexe 1 donne un exemple de la grille de cueillette. Bien qu'elle doive être adaptée au fur et à mesure du le dépouillement des autres inventaires nous estimons avoir développé un concept de cueillette assez fiable. A l'heure actuelle, les sous-catégories de l'annexe 1 se répartissent comme suit.

TABLEAU 3

Répartition quantitative des sous-catégories d'entrées

CATÉGORIES	SOUS-CATÉGORIES
Alimentation-conservation	45
Ameublement	25
Civilisation	11
Domestique	11
Luxe	6
Maritime	24
Vêtement	34
TOTAL	156

A la suite du dépouillement des sept inventaires, nous obtenons un premier tableau compilatif du nombre d'objets classifiés dans chaque catégorie pour chaque personne. Nous avons dressé la liste selon les catégories sociales A (marchands-entrepreneurs de pêche et fonctionnaires) et B (pêcheurs-autres) adoptées par Dunn.

Le tableau 4 doit nécessairement se lire à la fois à l'horizontale et à la verticale. C'est ainsi que l'on dénombre un total de 659 entrées d'objets, d'articles ou de denrées, pour une moyenne de 94,1 par personne. C'est dans le domaine de l'alimentation-conservation que l'on en retrouve le plus grand nombre soit 193, pour une moyenne de 48,5, suivi du domestique avec 21,4 et

du maritime avec 21,6. La catégorie vêtements se chiffre à 19,6 et l'ameublement à 11,1. Pour ce qui est de la valeur en argent attribuée à chaque inventaire,
le total se chiffre à 1 181 livres pour une moyenne de 236, 2 livres.

Nos résultats appellent toutefois à la prudence. Par exemple, prenons le
nombre de vêtements chez Bernatche et Zemard. Dans le cas du premier, c'est
probablement tout ce qu'il avait au moment de sa mort. Mais pour Zémard,
il faut comprendre que les possessions inventoriées sont celles toujours en
place, un an après sa mort et, qui plus est, après le remariage de sa veuve. Il y
a fort à parier qu'une bonne partie des vêtements ayant survécus à Zémard
soient dispersés.

Si l'on reprend le même raisonnement en examinant les statuts de chacune
des sept personnes impliquées, on peut théoriquement remettre en question
la classification avancée par Dunn. En fait, outre Magdeleine Aubert qui
totalise 308 entrées, les deux autres personnes de la catégorie A ne se détachent
certes pas des quatre individus de la catégorie B. On pense, entre autres, à
Louis Josselin dit Lachapelle chez qui on dénombre 145 entrées et une valeur
de 533 livres!

Il nous faut cependant reconnaître les limites de notre échantillon en
constatant que seuls les inventaires de Magdeleine Aubert et Gabriel
Barnetche déclarent des entrées dans les sept catégories. Le choix de
l'inventaire de Lachapelle s'avère cependant très approprié pour le projet de
Dunn, puisqu'on y dénombre 109 entrées reliées à la catégorie maritime. Pour
sa part, l'inventaire de Aubert est certes le plus pertinent pour avoir une
fenêtre sur les objets familiers de nos ancêtres puisqu'on y repère 110 entrées
dans la catégorie alimentation-conservation, 69 dans le domestique et 79 dans
le vêtement.

Il n'est pas sans intérêt de se pencher plus attentivement sur la situation
de quatre des personnes touchées par les sept inventaires. Dans le cas de Louis
Josselin dit LaChapelle, un premier inventaire[18] nous apprend qu'il habitait
chez la veuve Mechin, à la Pointe Verte. Il se serait noyé en compagnie de
Matturin Galtine et Augustin Morua. Ces trois pêcheurs revenaient en
chaloupe de l'Ile de Colinet où ils étaient allés avec cinq autres équipages,
pour y hiverner et s'y préparer à y faire la pêche de la morue. Dans un
deuxième document,[19] on constate que l'année suivante, la valeur des effets
de LaChapelle se chiffrent à 553 livres, dont une partie sera remise au Sieur
Bellefeuille et une autre au Sieur Bertero.

TABLEAU 4

Compilation des catégories d'entrées (objets ou autres) dans sept inventaires après-décès de Plaisance

Noms	catégorie	rédaction	alimentation\ conservation	ameublement	civilisation	domestique	luxe	maritime	vêtement	total	valeur (livres)
Zemar	A	1711	—	7	—	—	3	8	3	21	—
Aubert	A	1713	110	29	6	69	7	8	79	308	—
Sourdeval	A	1710	11	17	5	14	—	—	—	47	332
Barnetche	B	1713	56	17	4	19	5	3	11	115	173.80
Moisant	B	1711	—	3	—	2	—	1	10	16	91
Tebaux	B	1711	—	1	—	—	—	1	5	7	52
Lachapelle	B	1710	16	4	1	3	2	109	10	145	533
Total	7		193	78	16	107	17	130	118	659	1181.10
Moyenne			48.5	11.1	4	21.4	4.2	21.6	19.6	94.1	236.2

Notre deuxième cas est celui de Magdeleine Aubert, veuve de Abraham Pichaut. Le 2 décembre 1713, on apposait les scellés dans la maison de la défunte Aubert. En plus de posséder une propriété très bien garnie pour les standards sociaux de Plaisance, on constate aussi un billet de louage du magasin et d'une chambre aux Sieurs Sapie et Lagardère à 150 livres par an, en date du 6 août 1711. On retrouve également le brevet de l'habitation, grave et terrain, qui lui furent accordés par le roi sur la concession faite par DeBrouillan, gouverneur de Plaisance, en 1695 et 1696. Pouvant aussi nous renseigner sur les relations entre marchands et engagés à l'époque, se retrouvent un engagement et un billet du Sieur Lartigue à Jean Peris Pichaut, datés respectivement de 1709 et 1711, pour les salaires.[20]

Quant à Bernardine Paquiau, veuve du défunt Sieur Leroy, son cas illustre la complexité de certaines situations se retrouvant dans les inventaires. Du 28 octobre au 30 décembre 1709, cinq documents distincts retracent les étapes administratives suivant le décès de Paquiau, incluant l'inventaire, la vente des effets, meubles et papiers, la mise des scellés et la protection de la maison. Tout ceci sous la bienveillance des administrateurs Durand La Garenne et Costebelle.[21] Les choses se compliquent cependant l'année suivante suite à une requête du Sieur Charles Lucas, écuyer et Seigneur de Leszeaux. Il réclame les biens et effets de la défunte Leroy se trouvant chez des particuliers et dont il a besoin pour établir les enfants de la défunte, qui sont à sa charge. Il estime cette somme à 996 livres.[22]

Notre dernier cas touche un militaire, soit Sébastien de Sourdeval, commandant aux Iles Saint-Pierre. Du 7 au 9 mai 1710 se déroulaient les démarches de Catherine Labaudy, sa veuve, comme quoi elle renonçait à la succession de son mari et demandait que l'on fasse l'inventaire des biens du défunt.[23] Quelques mois plus tard se tenait la vente judiciaire, par le notaire Basset, des objets et effets ayant appartenus au défunt.[24]

Les résultats de notre étude préliminaire gagnent en intérêt si on les associent à ceux de Hardy. En effet, nous avons dressé un tableau comparatif partiel de quinze sous-catégories en termes du nombre moyen par foyer. Nonobstant la petitesse de notre échantillon, nous constatons tout de même certains rapprochements entre quelques sous-catégories telles les fourchettes, les serviettes, les tables, coffres, nappes, lits et couvertures.

TABLEAU 5

Eléments de comparaison dans quinze sous-catégories d'entrées
(nombre moyen par foyer)

SOUS-CATÉGORIES D'ENTRÉES	QUÉBEC	MONTRÉAL	PLAISANCE
Plats	5	—	8,6
Assietts	18,7	—	19
Couteaux	1,2	0,1	17,5
Fourchettes	6,1	6,3	5,5
Cuillères	6,3	—	1,2
Pots	2,1	1,4	5,3
Serviettes	34,8	17,7	29
Tables	1,9	2	1
Coffres	1,1	0,5	2,1
Nappes	13,5	11,4	7,5
Couchettes	1,6	1,2	1,2
Couvertures	3,1	2,6	2,3
Draps	7,7	7,7	1
Traversins	1,4	0,7	1
Oreillers	1,7	1,4	4

Comme Hardy, nous nous sommes aussi penchés sur la valeur des habitations. C'est ainsi que Hardy arrive à établir qu'à Montréal et ce, jusque vers 1725, une maisonne de bois vaut entre 1 500 et 2 000 livres.[25] Cette maison contient le plus souvent qu'une seule pièce. Les quelques informations disponibles pour Plaisance permettent d'inventorier neuf ventes de maisons pour une valeur totale de 12 363 livres, soit une moyenne de 1 373 livres par vente. Par exemple, le 6 juillet 1696, Vital Paris vendait une maison et une grave, située au goulet de Plaisance, à Jean de Jaldaye pour un total de 2 400 livres.[26] Par contre, en 1703, Sébastien de Sourdeval s'entendait avec Marie Milon, pour une transaction incluant maison, grave, jardin, four et chaffaux pour seulement 650 livres, le tout situé à Petit Plaisance.[27] La maison la plus chère se détaille à 4 000 livres et est située sur la pointe de la Grande Grave. En 1706, le bourgeois et marchand Jean de Jalday la vendait à Jean Chevalier, maître armurier au Fort Louis.[28] Dans trois des sept inventaires, on dénote deux maisons comptant jusqu'à quatre ou cinq pièces. En effet, la maison de

Marie Sceau compte cinq chambres, une cheminée double, un jardin, avec trois magasins ou cabanes,[29] tandis que celle de la veuve Abraham Pichaut compte deux chambres à coucher avec en plus une «Cabanne des gens» comprenant aussi deux chambres.[30] Quant à Gabriel Barneche, sa demeure comprend trois pièces dont la cuisine, une chambre à coucher et une autre pièce faisant usage de salle a dîner.[31]

Bien que se limitant à un échantillon plutôt modeste, cette brève étude devrait nous permettre de solidifier nos repères méthodologiques. C'est ainsi que nous tenterons d'intégrer la balance des données des autres inventaires de Plaisance, pour compléter cette tranche de notre projet sur cette colonie de pêche. Notre portrait socio-démographique des habitants de la colonie sera encore davantage éclairé, lorsque s'ajouteront les informations tirées des testaments et des contrats de mariage.

Cependant, il est indéniable qu'il n'est pas suffisant de simplement classifier les objets d'inventaires; il faut aussi questionner l'ensemble de la documentation. Les liquidations, les comptes et les dettes actives et passives, autant de pistes qui devront être exploitées dans le cadre d'un projet d'histoire socio-économique de la colonie.

NOTES

1. Nous ne donnons ici que quelques exemples. Emile Lauvrière, *La Tragédie d'un peuple: histoire du peuple acadien de ses origines à nos jours* (Paris: Brossard, 1922). John Bartlet Brebner, *New England's Outpost: Acadia Before the Conquest of Canada* (New York: Columbia University Press, 1927). Robert Rumilly, *Histoire des Acadiens* (Montréal: Fides, 1955). De date plus récente, Michel Roy, *L'Acadie des origines à nos jours: essai de synthèse historique* (Montréal, Québec\Amérique, 1981).

2. Andrew Hill Clark, *Acadia: The Geography of Early Nova Scotia to 1760* (Madison, The University of Wisconsin Press, 1968).

3. Jean Daigle, «Nos amis les ennemis: relations commerciales de l'Acadie avec le Massachusetts, 1670–1711», thèse de Ph.D., University of Maine (Orono), 1975. Naomi E.S. Griffiths, «The Golden Age: Acadian Life, 1713-1748», *Histoire sociale/ Social History* 17, no 33 (1984): 21–34. Du même auteur, *The Context of Acadian History, 1686–1784* (Montreal, McGill-Queen's University Press, 1992).

4. Nous nous limitons à trois exemples récents. Jean-Pierre Hardy, «Quelques aspects du niveau de richesse et de la vie matérielle des artisans de Québec et de Montréal, 1740–1755», *Revue d'histoire d'Amérique française* [*RHAF*] 40, no 3 (1987): 339–72. Louis Lavallée, «La vie et la pratique d'un notaire rural sous le régime français: le cas de Guillaume Barette, Notaire à la Prairie entre 1709–1744», *RHAF* 47, no 4 (printemps 1994): 499–520. Dominique Bouchard, «La culture matérielle des Canadiens au XVIIIᵉ siècle: Analyse du niveau de vie des artisans du fer», *RHAF* 47, no 4 (printemps 1994): 479–98.

5. Louis Lavallée, «La vie et la pratique d'un notaire rural sous le régime français: le cas de Guillaume Barette, notaire à La Prairie entre 1709–1744», *RHAF* 47, no 4 (printemps 1994): 499–500.

6. Dominique Bouchard, «La culture matérielle des Canadiens au XVIIIᵉ siècle: Analyse du niveau de vie des artisans du fer», *RHAF* 47, no 4 (printemps 1994): 479–80.

7. Micheline Baulant, «Niveaux de vie et reproduction sociale. Les paysans de la région de Meaux (1751–1790)», dans Gérard Bouchard et Joseph Goy, ed., *Famille, économie et société rurale en contexte d'urbanisation (XVIIᵉ–XXᵉ siècle)* (Montréal, Centre universitaire SOREP, 1990), cité par Bouchard, "La culture matérielle . . . ," 480.

8. Jean-Pierre Hardy, «Quelques aspects du niveau de richesse et de la vie matérielle des artisans de Québec et de Montréal, 1740–1755», *RHAF* 40, no 3 (1987): 339.

9. Maurice Basque, «Les stratégies de la reproduction sociale de deux familles de notables acadiens de 1640 à 1867: le cas des d'Entremont et des Robichaud», Thèse de doctorat, Université Laval (en cours). Josette Brun, «Des femmes d'affaires à Louisbourg, 1713–1745», thèse de maîtrise, Université de Moncton (1994). Nicole Boucher, «Les rapports patron-clients dans les promotions militaires à Louisbourg, 1713–1745», thèse de maîtrise, Université de Moncton (en cours).

10. Par exemples, Linda Hood, «La chirurgie et les chirurgiens de l'Ile Royale», *Histoire et Archéologie*, no 6, Parcs Canada (1979): 238–389 et G. Proulx, «Aubergistes et cabaretiers de Louisbourg, 1713–1758», Parcs Canada, travail inédit no 136, 1972.

11. Corinne Laplante, «Le Traité d'Utrecht et l'Acadie; une étude sur la correspondance secrète et officielle qui a entouré la signature du traité d'Utrecht», thèse de M. A. Université de Moncton, 1972.

12. Roland Plaze, «La colonie Royale de Plaisance 1689–1713: impact du statut de colonie royale sur les structures administratives», thèse de M. A., Université de Moncton, 1991.

13. A ce sujet voir Jacques Vanderlinden, «A la rencontre de l'histoire du droit en Acadie avant le dérangement: premières impressions d'un nouveau venu», *Revue de l'Université de Moncton* 28, no 1 (1995): 47–80.

14. Plaze, "La colonie Royale . . . ," 205.

15. Ibid, 207.

16. Ibid, 213–14.

17. Brenda Dunn, «A First Look at Notarial Records for Terre-Neuve», Parks Canada, Atlantic Regional Office (ARO 0135 (b0-ref.) December 1985. Je voudrais remercier Eloi DeGrâce pour m'avoir signalé ce document.

18. France, Archive Nationales, G3, 8\176, Pièce 145, 5 décembre 1710.

19. G3, 8\176, Pièce 1, 8 janvier–9 août 1711.

20. G3, 8\176, Pièces 119, 2 décembre 1713 et Pièce 120, 12-13 décembre 1713.

21. G3, 7\175, Pièces 267; 28 octobre, 288; 11 décembre, 289; 12 décembre, 290; 13 décembre et 294; 30 décembre 1709.

22. G3, 8\176, Pièces 16; 20 octobre, 125; 31 octobre 1710.

23. G3, 8\176, Pièces 12-13–14, 7–9 mai 1710.

24. G3, 8\176, Pièce 143, 2 décembre 1710.

25. Jean-Pierre Hardy,"Quelques aspects du niveau de richesse . . . ," 348.

26. G3, 7\175, Pièce 1, 6 juillet 1696.

27. G3, 7\175, Pièce 10, 12 avril 1703.

28. G3, 7\175, Pièce 87, 4 novembre 1706.

29. G3, 8\176, Pièce 148, 3 novembre 1711.

30. G3, vol. 2055, Pièce 145, 2 décembre 1713.

31. G3, vol. 2055, Pièce 78, 22 septembre 1713.

CHAPTER TWELVE

La succession de Louis Bélanger, seigneur de Bonsecours (1724–1741)

Tommy Guénard

The study, which deals with New France in the early eighteenth century, seeks to identify the processes involved in settling the estate of seigneur Louis Bélanger, with particular emphasis on demographic "events." In fact, the transmission practices are influenced by many demographic factors, including the age of the parents upon death, the number of children, the age difference between them, their marital status and the proportion of boys and girls. Family data played an important role in the "fate" of the estate. In this case study of a Canadian seignorial family, we will try to identify the different strategies open to the parents in passing on property to their heirs. We will see that a quick death and early widowhood have consequences for land division and for individuals that are many and that they are expressed in a multitude of notarized documents.

La transmission du patrimoine a des effets tangibles dans la construction du paysage rural en Nouvelle-France au XVIIIᵉ siècle. Elle a façonné à sa manière le panorama des seigneuries de la vallée laurentienne. Les pratiques des transmissions successorales sont cependant influencées par de nombreux facteurs, tels l'âge des parents au décès, le nombre d'enfants, l'écart d'âge entre eux, leur statut matrimonial ou la proportion de garçons et de filles.[1] Ainsi, les données démographiques jouent un rôle important dans la transmission du patrimoine foncier. Plus précisément, nous avons voulu savoir comment s'opère une succession seigneuriale et de quelle façon les événements ou accidents démographiques influencent la répartition du patrimoine ainsi que le contrôle seigneurial.[2]

Au départ de notre étude se trouve un événement démographique normal, le décès en 1724, à l'âge de 69 ans, de Louis Bélanger, seigneur de Bonsecours. La question de la succession paraît si simple et si réglée qu'elle n'entraîne même pas d'acte de partage entre la veuve et les enfants. Pourtant, c'est un document de 1741, dix-sept années plus tard qui expliquera le partage de la seigneurie. Entre temps, un accident démographique, le décès hâtif de l'héritier présumé, en 1727, bouleversera la logique et les stratégies familiales de la transmission. Cet exemple fait ainsi ressortir les circonstances qui pouvaient affecter la transmission, les choix qui s'offraient aux familles, les décisions prises, ainsi que la nécessaire et constante reconstruction des cohérences familiales face au patrimoine foncier.

L'insertion d'un tel événement dans une logique d'ensemble oblige, à la manière de la microhistoire, à relever toute la documentation disponible et à reconstituer les rapports entre les gestes familiaux.[3] Une fois établi le contexte légal qui préside à la transmission des biens,[4] il faut procéder à une reconstitution de la démographie et de l'histoire de la famille, en s'appuyant, en particulier, sur les dictionnaires généalogiques et les contrats de mariage.[5] A leur tour, les propriétés foncières font l'objet d'un relevé exhaustif que les actes de donations, de ventes et d'échanges permettent d'établir de façon assez satisfaisante. Car il faut également compter avec les silences de la documentation. Et Louis Bélanger n'a pas été très disert, comme le montre sa déclaration de foi et hommage en 1723: « . . . propriétaire de son chef . . . , et pour le tout, ayant acquis, par accommodement et eschange verbal, les parts et portions de . . . ».[6]

La connaissance étendue des dossiers familiaux livre toutefois suffisamment de renseignements précis pour tenter, malgré certaines incertitudes, de cerner les rapports d'une famille à son patrimoine foncier et de dégager la nature et la cohérence des choix effectués.[7]

La Coutume de Paris précise clairement la répartition d'un patrimoine foncier entre la veuve et les enfants. La veuve en reçoit la moitié mais sa part est tenue en usufruit et passe aux enfants à sa mort. A la différence de la succession roturière, la succession seigneuriale divise la part des enfants de la manière suivante: le fils aîné hérite de la moitié du reste de la seigneurie et l'autre moitié est répartie également entre les autres enfants [tableau 1]. La

Coutume attribue aussi au fils aîné la possession du manoir seigneurial avec la cour attenante à ce dernier. Les droits seigneuriaux sont soumis au même mode de partage.[8]

TABLEAU 1

Partage entre veuve et héritiers d'une succession seigneuriale selon la coutume de Paris

Veuve	Fils aîné	Enfant	Enfant	Enfant

LA SUCCESSION DE LOUIS BÉLANGER

A sa mort, le 1er octobre 1724, Louis Bélanger laissait un beau patrimoine à ses héritiers. Il avait cependant dû faire beaucoup d'efforts pour éviter de laisser leur transmettre une seigneurie fragmentée entre lui et ses cohéritiers.

La seigneurie de Bonsecours avait été concédée en 1677 à François Bélanger, père de Louis. À la mort de François, vers 1691, elle fut partagée entre ses trois garçons (Charles, Jacques et Louis) et ses cinq filles. Charles, le fils aîné qui était entré en possession de la moitié de la seigneurie, décéda un an plus tard. Le fils aîné de Charles, François, hérita alors de la moitié des biens de son père tandis que ses frères et soeurs se partagèrent la seconde moitié. En 1699, Jacques, fils de François et frère de Charles, décédait à son tour. Louis devenait ainsi le seul survivant masculin de la famille dans sa génération.[9] En 1723, après un long processus de rachat, d'échanges et de transactions de toutes sortes, effectuées la plupart du temps verbalement, Louis parvenait à rentrer en possession du fief de Bonsecours et en devenait le seigneur primitif.

Outre une seigneurie remembrée, Louis Bélanger laissait en héritage un patrimoine foncier relativement considérable à ses enfants, soit une terre domaniale de sept arpents de front sur deux lieues de profondeur et deux terres en roture: la première de 10 arpents de front sur deux lieues de profondeur et la seconde, de six arpents de front sur 42 arpents de profondeur [tableau 2]. De son mariage avec Marguerite Lefrançois étaient nés 13 enfants, dont sept étaient déjà décédés lors de la succession en 1724;[10] il en restait donc six, soit deux garçons et quatre filles : François, le fils aîné, Pierre, Élizabeth, Marie-Madeleine, Françoise et Marie-Marthe [tableau 3].

TABLEAU 2

Bonesecours 1723: Patrimoine foncier de la famille Louis Bélanger

fleuve Saint-Laurent

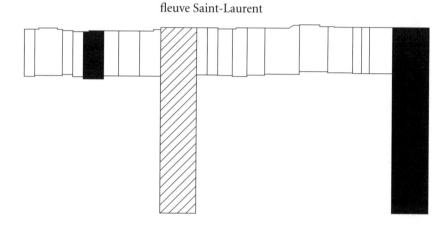

■ Terres faisant partie du patrimoine foncier de Louis Bélanger

▨ Domaine

Échelle: front 1 cm pour 8,2 arpents
         profondeur 1 cm pour 27,45 arpents
Source: Aveux et dénombrements du Régime français

TABLEAU 3

*Schéma généalogique de la famille Bélanger**

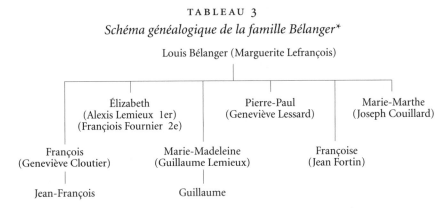

Louis Bélanger (Marguerite Lefrançois)

Élizabeth (Alexis Lemieux 1er) (Françiois Fournier 2e)	Pierre-Paul (Geneviève Lessard)	Marie-Marthe (Joseph Couillard)

François (Geneviève Cloutier)	Marie-Madeleine (Guillaume Lemieux)	Françoise (Jean Fortin)
Jean-François	Guillaume	

*Ce schéma ne retient que les principaux enfants ayant particpé à la succession de Louis Bélanger.

La forme que prend une succession est d'abord influencée par de nombreux éléments, dont les facteurs démographiques et plus particulièrement l'âge au décès des parents. En effet, cette dernière donnée agit un peu comme une loterie en introduisant une large part d'incertitude sur la durée des mariages et en créant de fortes différences entre les ménages. Tantôt elle précipite la transmission des biens d'une génération à l'autre. tantôt elle la retarde.[11]

La durée de l'union joue un rôle appréciable sur le mode de transmission pratiqué. À cet effet, Sylvie Dépatie constate que «les partages interviennent plus fréquemment dans le cas d'unions prématurément brisées et, à mesure que le mariage se prolonge, les parents ont de plus en plus tendance à avoir recours à la donation».[12] Dans le cas étudié, les observations de S. Dépatie semblent se confirmer. Louis Bélanger décède le 1er octobre 1724, à l'âge de 69 ans, et tout laisse supposer qu'il y a eu donation au fils aîné, François. La documentation fait toutefois défaut ici, puisqu'aucun acte de donation n'a été retrouvé concernant la succession de Louis Bélanger, mais l'analyse des dossiers familiaux et des différents actes notariés autorise cette conclusion.

L'âge de la veuve et des enfants au décès de Louis Bélanger sont des éléments essentiels pour saisir la forme que prend la succession. Lorsque son mari décède, Marguerite Lefrançois est âgée de 59 ans. L'âge de la veuve est déterminant car elle aurait pu se remarier, la succession risquant d'impliquer alors deux familles. Dans le cas des Bélanger, Marguerite est trop âgée pour avoir d'autres enfants et, de toute façon, ne se remarie pas.

En ce qui a trait aux enfants, leur âge au décès du père est assez élevé.[13] La succession étant survenue tardivement, le cycle familial arrivait à sa fin, c'est-à-dire que chacun était prêt à s'établir ou l'avait déjà fait. D'ailleurs, lors du décès de Louis Bélanger, le 1er octobre 1724, seuls Pierre et Marie-Marthe n'étaient pas mariés.

En effet, François qui avait épousé Geneviève Cloutier en 1711, habitait et exploitait le Domaine de Bonsecours,[14] Élizabeth s'était mariée en 1710 avec Alexis Lemieux et habitait à la Rivière-du-Sud. Marie-Madeleine et Françoise profitèrent d'un mariage double en 1723 pour s'unir respectivement à Guillaume Lemieux et à Jean Fortin. La première alla s'établir à Berthier et la seconde à l'Islet-Saint-Jean.

Le processus d'établissement des enfants était donc pratiquement terminé. La mort du père semble d'ailleurs avoir eu pour effet d'en accélérer le parachèvement: Pierre se marie en 1724 et Marie-Marthe en 1725. La conclusion d'alliances matrimoniales était devenue pressante. De fait, si l'on considère le rapprochement dans le temps des quatre derniers mariages, on peut avancer l'hypothèse que certaines alliances ont été conçues pour dégrever le patrimoine familial. En effet, l'union double de Françoise et de Madeleine en 1723 et celles de Pierre et de Marie-Marthe en 1724 et 1725 s'insèrent dans une période où la succession paternelle était au centre des préoccupations, comme si le désir d'en conserver l'intégrité n'avait pas été étranger à la conclusion de ces alliances.

Le mariage de Pierre, le second fils, semble avoir été un élément-clé dans la stratégie de la transmission du patrimoine de Louis Bélanger. Sa position est délicate car son avenir n'a pas été planifié en fonction de l'exploitation et de la gestion du patrimoine familial. Comme tous les enfants puînés, son avenir demeure hasardeux et incertain, car ils doivent se construire une nouvelle existence en dehors de l'espace familial.

Dans le cas de la famille Bélanger cependant, les enfants ont profité d'alliances capables de leur assurer un avenir sécuritaire. Pierre, qui se marie un mois seulement après la mort de son père,[15] bénéficie d'une alliance très avantageuse avec la famille Lessard en s'unissant à Geneviève le 11 novembre 1724. Cette famille, que nous pouvons qualifier de «seigneuriale», offre en effet une belle alternative à Pierre Bélanger qui n'a aucun avenir sur la terre familiale, réservée à son frère aîné François.

Le choix de cette alliance n'est probablement pas étranger au statut de la famille Lessard ainsi qu'à l'apport foncier fourni par l'épouse au moment du mariage.[16] Ce choix a sans doute également été influencé par les liens qui existaient entre les deux familles.[17] De plus, le père de Geneviève, Pierre Lessard, était un homme bien pourvu qui possédait le fief Lessard, situé juste derrière la seigneurie de Bonsecours. Malgré le faible développement de cette seigneurie, le fait demeure que Pierre Lessard était propriétaire d'un fief et que sa position dans la société différait de celle du simple habitant.[18] Pierre Bélanger entrait donc dans une famille faisant partie de l'élite rurale, ce qui était prometteur pour son avenir. Nonobstant les avantages évidents procurés à Pierre Bélanger par son mariage, il faut se demander si, malgré tout, cette alliance matrimoniale ne s'est pas réalisée à la suite d'une «exclusion» plus ou moins pressentie par celui-ci. La position de Pierre, dans la succession de son père, ne correspondait pas à ses intérêts. En ce sens, son mariage avec Geneviève Lessard s'est avéré la meilleure solution.

Suite au mariage de Pierre, il ne restait plus que Marie-Marthe à la charge de la veuve Lefrançois-Bélanger. Un an plus tard, soit le 18 novembre 1725, une alliance était conclue avec la prestigieuse famille des Couillard. Marie-Marthe Bélanger épousait Joseph, seigneur en partie de l'Islet Saint-Jean et fils de Louis Couillard, l'époux de sa défunte soeur Marguerite.

Tout indique que le décès de Louis, étant survenu tardivement, la succession avait été prévue en faveur de François qui, vraisemblablement s'occupait déjà du patrimoine familial avant la mort de son père.[19] Son décès, le 1er octobre 1724, semble avoir provoqué la conclusion d'alliances matrimoniales visant, dans un premier temps, à alléger le fardeau du fils aîné et, dans un deuxième temps, à assurer un meilleur avenir aux enfants qui n'étaient pas encore mariés. On remarque donc une certaine inégalité entre les héritiers. En effet, bien qu'ils aient tous été pourvus de la même somme au moment du mariage, soit 100 écus en avancement d'hoirie, la gestion du patrimoine familial semblait destinée à un seul héritier.

UNE DETTE D'HONNEUR

D'ailleurs, la succession avait été tellement bien organisée par Louis Bélanger, que suite à son décès, un document notarié intitulé «Acte de partage», vient confirmer sa volonté concernant l'implication d'un étranger dans la succession. Dans ce document daté du 12 novembre 1724, il est précisé que:

vue les bons et loyaux services que Louis Langelier a rendu depuis plusieurs années en la maison dudit sieur Louis Bélanger [...] le deffunt sieur Bélanger a voulu faire donation part et entière et irrévocable au dit Langelier de un arpent de terre de front sur la proffondeur qui est d'une demie lieu de terre à prendre et détaché d'une concession qui lui appartenait. . . . Comme le dit sieur Bélanger est décédé sans avoir pu accomplire et effectué la sus dite donation, les sus dits Reconnaissants [les héritiers de Louis Bélanger] sus nommés ont déclaré et déclare par les présentes vouloir accomplir et effectué la sus dite donation suivant et conformément à la dite intention du deffunt sieur Bélanger.[20]

Louis Langelier est alors âgé de 27 ans. Il est le troisième fils de Charles et Françoise Destroismaisons qui habitaient la seigneurie de Bonsecours jusqu'à leur décès survenu en 1717 pour le premier et en 1715 pour la seconde. La famille de ces derniers se compose en 1724 de quatre garçons et de six filles [tableau 4].[21] Concernant François, il se marie en 1721 à Saint-François Ile d'Orléans, où il demeure.

TABLEAU 4

Age des enfants de Charles Langelier au décès de Louis Bélanger

	ENFANTS	ÂGE EN 1724		ENFANTS	ÂGE EN 1724
1.	François	30	6.	Geneviève	17
2.	Louis	27	7.	Madeleine	17
3.	Elisabeth	25	8.	Marthe	16
4.	Louise	23	9.	Pierre	14
5.	Joseph	21	10.	Angélique	12

L'attribution de cette terre survient durant une période d'activité notariale intense pour Louis Langelier. Outre le partage des Bélanger le 12 novembre, il avait conclu, deux jours auparavant, un échange avec sa soeur Élizabeth.[22] Cet acte lui permettait de concentrer ses biens fonciers, consistant en une part de la terre familiale, héritée de son père ajoutée à la parcelle voisine que les héritiers Bélanger lui allouaient. Le 13 novembre 1724, il passe encore chez le notaire pour épouser Geneviève Fortin.[23]

Il est important de souligner la signification d'un tel partage avec un étranger dont le statut social semble très humble. Quelle est la valeur morale de cette action? Rien n'obligeait les héritiers de Louis Bélanger à respecter cette donation. Pourtant, ils n'hésitent pas à honorer la volonté de leur père. Il est difficile de saisir la signification réelle de cette donation car les sources manquent. Cependant, l'hypothèse selon laquelle ce cas représenterait une redevance morale ou un concept élargi de la famille demeure vraisemblable. Le sens moral aurait primé sur la Coutume.

L'INFLUENCE DES ÉVÉNEMENTS DÉMOGRAPHIQUES DANS LES SUCCESSIONS

La succession de Louis Bélanger ne révèle rien d'exceptionnel. Le décès survenu à un âge assez avancé, la majorité des descendants est déjà installée et les deux enfants restants quitteront, à leur tour, sans délai, peut-être même un peu précipitamment, pour le second fils, alors âgé de 24 ans seulement. Dans cette succession, chacun a eu droit à sa part. L'aîné, déjà responsable en grande partie du domaine, prend naturellement le relais de son père. Les règles successorales le favorisent et il gère les trois quarts du patrimoine foncier familial original.

Un accident démographique, son décès prématuré à l'âge de 40 ans, brise ce bel ordre et ramène inopinément dans le décor ce second fils, Pierre, qui semblait avoir fait son deuil du patrimoine familial.

LE DÉCÈS DU FILS AÎNÉ

Le fait que François Bélanger, fils aîné de Louis et de Marguerite Lefrançois, soit l'héritier principal entre dans l'ordre des choses, conformément aux dispositions de la Coutume de Paris. Du reste, au cours des dernières années, il avait participé, avec son père, à l'exploitation et à la gestion du patrimoine foncier familial. A son tour, il était amené à assumer la responsabilité de ses avoirs fonciers, à les préserver et, si possible, à regrouper les parcelles léguées aux autres enfants. Sa mort, survenue trois ans après celle de son père Louis, laissait dans le deuil son épouse Geneviève Cloutier, âgée de 38 ans et ses neuf enfants, cinq garçons et quatre filles, dont l'âge variait de huit mois à 15 ans [tableau 5].

TABLEAU 5

Age de la femme et des enfants de François Bélanger
lors de son décès le 12 novembre 1727

NOM	ÂGE EN 1727	NOM	ÂGE EN 1727
Geneviève Cloutier	38 ans	Marie-Françoise	9 ans
Jean-François	15 ans	Pierre-Paul	8 ans
Jean-Baptiste	13 ans	Marguerite-Ursule	5 ans
Geneviève	12 ans	Joseph	2 ans
Marie	11 ans	Pierre	8 mois

Du coup, le nombre d'ayants droit au patrimoine seigneurial se multiplie par deux. Marguerite Lefrançois, femme de Louis Bélanger, conserve la jouissance en usufruit de la moitié de la seigneurie. Geneviève Cloutier, la veuve de François, dispose, elle, des revenus sur la moitié des biens du décédé, soit sur le huitième de la seigneurie. Le reste est divisé en une infinité de parcelles entre les autres héritiers. Un acte de partage, daté du 18 avril 1730, confirme la part de chacun.[24]

Jean-François, fils aîné et principal héritier, le prochain seigneur de Bonsecours, n'a que 15 ans au décès de son père. Il est trop jeune pour assurer la responsabilité de gestion de la seigneurie. Il faut donc trouver un palliatif à l'absence d'homme mûr et responsable pour présider aux destinées de la famille et préserver son patrimoine. C'est la figure de Pierre, deuxième fils de Louis Bélanger qui émerge alors.

TABLEAU 6

Part revenant aux ayants droit suite au décès de François Bélanger,
le 12 novembre 1727

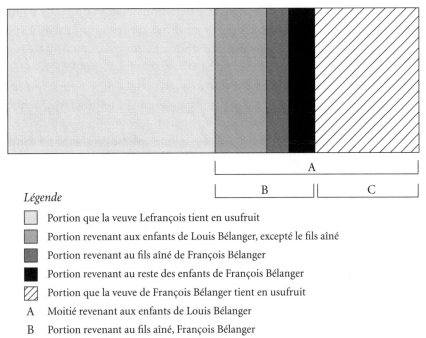

Légende

☐ Portion que la veuve Lefrançois tient en usufruit

▨ Portion revenant aux enfants de Louis Bélanger, excepté le fils aîné

▨ Portion revenant au fils aîné de François Bélanger

■ Portion revenant au reste des enfants de François Bélanger

▨ Portion que la veuve de François Bélanger tient en usufruit

A Moitié revenant aux enfants de Louis Bélanger

B Portion revenant au fils aîné, François Bélanger

C Portion se divisant entre Pierre, Élizabeth, Françoise, Madeleine et Marthe Bélanger

PIERRE BÉLANGER, GESTIONNAIRE DU PATRIMOINE FAMILIAL

En 1724, la succession avait été organisée en fonction du fils aîné, François. Pour cette raison, Pierre se voyait, en quelque sorte, exclu de la jouissance du bien familial. Son avenir se serait probablement déroulé dans la seigneurie voisine, à l'Islet Saint-Jean, si son frère n'avait été emporté si tôt. La mort de François et les stratégies de sa mère, Marguerite Lefrançois, veuve de Louis Bélanger, le ramènent dans la seigneurie de Bonsecours.

Pierre Bélanger réapparaît à un moment assez significatif. En effet, trois jours avant la réunion de tous les héritiers pour l'acte de partage, soit le 15 avril 1730, sa mère lui concède une terre en «bois debout» de 4 arpents de front sur 40 de profondeur, par billet fait sous seing privé.[25] Ce geste de Marguerite Lefrançois, qui survient quelques jours seulement avant le partage, n'est sûrement pas l'effet du hasard. Suite au décès de François en 1727, il devenait capital pour la veuve de Louis Bélanger, maintenant âgée de 65 ans, de ramener à Bonsecours son fils Pierre afin de lui confier, outre les destinées de la famille Bélanger, l'exploitation de la terre principale,[26] en attendant que Jean-François soit en mesure d'exercer ses droits d'héritier principal. Cette concession de Marguerite constituerait donc une sorte de compensation à son fils Pierre pour la fonction de gestionnaire qu'elle lui demande de remplir. Craint-elle le remariage de Geneviève, encore assez jeune pour avoir un deuxième lit d'enfant? Désire-t-elle éviter un éventuel imbroglio? Quant à Pierre, sa situation à l'Islet Saint-Jean lui déplaît-elle? Pourquoi choisit-il de revenir à Bonsecours? S'agit-il pour lui d'une promotion sociale? Voilà plusieurs questions qui surgissent et qui mériteraient une analyse plus approfondie.

Quoi qu'il en soit, à partir du moment de cette concession du 15 avril 1730, Pierre se fait de plus en plus présent à Bonsecours. De plus, tout indique que Marguerite Lefrançois ait fait une donation à son fils Pierre, entre l'acte de partage du 18 avril 1730 et la date de son propre décès survenu le 31 août 1735, à l'âge de 70 ans.[27]

Nous pouvons remarquer, en examinant l'aveu et dénombrement de 1739 [tableau 7], qu'une partie de terre est détachée de la concession de 10 arpents de front que possédait Louis Bélanger au nord est de la seigneurie. Cette parcelle de 2,9 arpents de front, appartient à Pierre par concentration de sa part d'héritage avec celle que sa mère lui cède par donation. Cette parcelle est celle qui a le plus de valeur sur la terre. Elle regroupe, en plus d'une maison de pierre, une grange, une étable, une écurie, un fournil, une bergerie et une laiterie. La terre de 10 arpents de Louis Bélanger étant un bien roturier, le droit d'aînesse ne s'appliquait pas et elle fut soumise au partage à part égale entre la veuve Lefrançois et ses 6 enfants.

Tout indique que le patrimoine soit demeuré partiellement indivis jusqu'au décès de Marguerite Lefrançois, veuve de Louis Bélanger. D'après les documents notariés, c'est seulement à ce moment que l'ensemble de l'exploitation aurait été fractionné entre les héritiers. Nous constatons en effet qu'après la mort de Marguerite, Pierre s'efforce de remembrer le patrimoine foncier de ses défunts parents.[28]

Entre-temps, Pierre rachète les parts seigneuriales que son père, Louis Bélanger, n'avait pu acquérir de l'une de ses soeurs cohéritières, Mathurine

Bélanger. Cette dernière avait transmis ses parts dans la seigneurie de Bonsecours à ses quatre gendres et à son troisième époux, tous demeurant à Neuville.[29] Bien qu'apparentés au réseau des Bélanger, ces héritiers contribuaient néanmoins à parcelliser à outrance le bien paternel et s'appropriaient une

TABLEAU 7

Bonsecours 1739: Patrimoine Foncier de fa famille Louis Bélanger.

fleuve Saint-Laurent

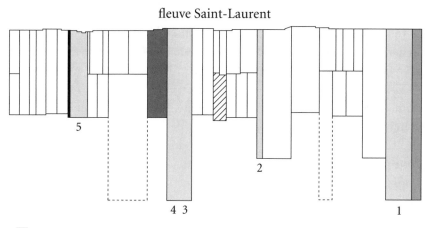

Terres feisant partie du patrimoine foncier de Louis Bélanger.

Terre détachée de l'habitation de feu Louis Bélanger, appartemant à Pierre par acte de donation de Marguerite Lefrançois, sa mère.

Terre que Pierre Bélanger a reçu par concession sous seing privé de sa mère en avril 1730. Il cède cette terre le 12/01/1736 à Joseph Bélanger, petit cousin.

Terre appartenant aux héritiers de feu Françoic Bélanger, fils aîné de feu Louis Bélanger.

Terre que Louis Langelier a reçu lors du partage de 1724.

Arpents non-concédés.

1 Terre appartemant aux héritiers de feu Louis Bélanger.

2 Terre détachée de la concession de Jacques Bélanger, appartenant aux héritiers de feu Louis Bélanger.

3 Une moitié du domaine appartenant aux enfants de feu Louis Bélanger.

4 Une moitié du domaine appartenant à la veuve et aux enfants de feu François Bélanger.

5 Terre apartenant aux héritiers de feu Louis Bélanger.

Échelle: front 1 cm pour 8,3 arpents
           profondeur 1 cm pour 28,38 arpents

Source: Aveux et dénombrements du Régime français

183

part du contrôle seigneurial du fief de Bonsecours. Marguerite Lefrançois se rendit elle-même à Québec effectuer la transaction pour le compte de son fils Pierre. Moyennant la somme de 78 livres 2 sols et 6 deniers, celui-ci devenait propriétaire de la huitième partie de la moitié de la seigneurie de Bonsecours, conservant ainsi le patrimoine au sein de la famille Bélanger, et exempt d'emprise «étrangère».

Entre la date où il acquiert les prétentions des «Neuvillois» et le 31 août 1735, date du décès de sa mère, l'activité de Pierre se limite à peu de choses selon la documentation. Ce n'est donc qu'après la mort de Marguerite Lefrançois que le patrimoine familial est vraisemblablement fragmenté entre les héritiers et que les efforts de Pierre afin de remembrer la terre principale où vivait ses défunts parents se font sentir.

Le 4 avril 1736, Pierre Bélanger et sa soeur, Françoise, concluent une vente et un échange de terres. Dans l'acte de vente, Pierre fait l'acquisition [pour 35 livres] d'une parcelle d'un demi-arpent de front sur 168 de profondeur, qui est une sixième portion appartenant à Françoise par droit de succession.[30] Cette parcelle fait partie d'une concession de 3 arpents de front située sur le Domaine [tableau 7, terre no. 3]. Pour ce qui est de l'échange, Pierre et Geneviève Lessard, sa femme, cèdent à Jean Fortin et à Françoise les terres qu'ils possédaient à l'Islet Saint-Jean.[31] En retour, ils obtiennent toutes les prétentions de Françoise dans la terre de Louis Bélanger [tableau 7, terre no. 1] soit, 14 perches et demie de front sur 168 de profondeur.

Le 24 juillet 1737, Pierre effectue un nouvel échange de terres, mais cette fois-ci, avec Jean Gaudreau et Geneviève Bélanger, fille de feu François Bélanger décédé en 1727. Aux termes de ce contrat, Pierre se départit de toutes les terres qu'il possédait dans le domaine seigneurial, tant par héritage que par achat, ce qui représente 14 perches et 6 pieds de front sur la profondeur de la seigneurie [en plus d'une grange et d'une étable]. Il se réserve toutefois les droits seigneuriaux qu'il possédait dans le domaine. En retour, Jean Gaudreau et Geneviève Bélanger cèdent une parcelle de 3 perches et 6 pieds de front sur 168 de profondeur sur la terre de Louis [tableau VII, terre no. 1], et une parcelle de 22 pieds de front sur 126 de profondeur sur la terre de Jacques[32] [tableau 7, terre no. 2].

Ensuite, Pierre fait l'achat, le 24 octobre 1741, des parts successorales[33] de Marguerite Lemieux, fille de sa soeur Élizabeth Bélanger et d'Alexis Lemieux. Étrangement, ses efforts de reconstitution semblent s'arrêter là. La logique entourant les transactions foncières effectuées par Pierre Bélanger est difficile à cerner. En y jetant un bref regard, nous constatons que Pierre semble céder davantage de terres qu'il n'en acquiert pour lui-même. Cependant, en analysant minutieusement la localisation des parcelles qu'il obtient, nous remarquons une concentration des efforts visant l'acquisition de parcelles situées sur la terre principale de feu son père au nord est de la seigneurie. Il est probable que la qualité des portions acquises par Pierre surpasse en valeur la quantité d'arpents qu'il cède en échange.

Selon notre analyse des documents, tout indique que l'objectif premier de Pierre fut de se constituer, peu importent les sacrifices consentis, un beau patrimoine dans la seigneurie de Bonsecours, près du réseau familial. De plus, les efforts de Pierre Bélanger ne furent pas étrangers au fait qu'il devait songer à établir convenablement ses enfants. Le 1er mai 1740, au moment de la rédaction du contrat de mariage de sa fille Marie-Geneviève, âgé de 14 ans, avec Charles Bernier, une des clauses du contrat stipule que Pierre et Geneviève Lessard marient leur fille avec ses droits, soit 2 arpents de terre de front sur une demi lieue de profondeur. Il est aussi mentionné que les futurs époux demeureront pendant neuf ans avec les sieur et dame Bélanger qui s'engagent à les nourrir et entretenir ainsi qu'à leur bâtir, suite à la période de cohabitation :

> une maison de 30 pieds de long sur 22 de large, cheminé de pierre, planché haut et bas de bois de pin, couverte de planche; une grange de 30 pieds d'assemblage couverte de paille bluterie de bois de pin; une étable de pièce sur pièce de 18 sur 20 au bout de la ditte grange et en fin des dites 9 années leurs donneront une paire de jeune boeufs de 2 ans et 3 ans, 1 cheval à son choix de l'élever s'il le souhaite ou en prendre un de ceux de la maison et leurs donneront aussi une mère vache et une torre pleine et 4 moutons mâle ou femelle et 2 cochons (. . .) et après le décès des dits sieur et dame ils auront et prendront un demi arpent sur la terre de feu Jacques Bélanger.[34]

En plus des biens fonciers, des bâtiments et du cheptel, Pierre Bélanger et sa femme promettent à la future épouse de lui donner tout l'assortiment nécessaire à la cuisine. Il semble que Pierre Bélanger se soucie grandement du destin de ses enfants[35] et n'épargne rien pour favoriser leur établissement.

APERÇU DE LA SITUATION FONCIÈRE ET SEIGNEURIALE EN 1741

Suite à des accidents démographiques répétés, le patrimoine foncier et seigneurial se voit fragmenté en 1741 [tableau 8]. La succession implique désormais, outre les enfants de Louis Bélanger, ceux du fils aîné, François Bélanger, décédé en 1727. La situation de 1741 diffère cependant de celle de 1730, alors que Marguerite Lefrançois vivait toujours et que les enfants de François et Geneviève Cloutier étaient trop jeunes encore pour assumer leur rôle. Au moment du partage de la seigneurie de Bonsecours, en date du 31 mars 1741, Marguerite Lefrançois est décédée depuis six ans et Jean-François Bélanger,[36] âgé de 15 ans au décès de son père François, est désormais en âge d'assumer le titre de seigneur primitif de Bonsecours.

TABLEAU 8

Proportion des rentes seigneuriales de chacun des héritiers
lors du partage du 31 mars 1741

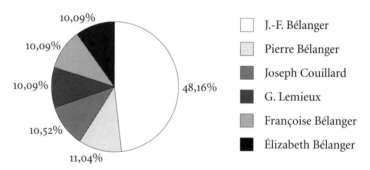

10,09%

10,09%

10,09%

10,52%

11,04%

48,16%

☐ J.-F. Bélanger

▨ Pierre Bélanger

▨ Joseph Couillard

▨ G. Lemieux

▨ Françoise Bélanger

▨ Élizabeth Bélanger

Lors de l'acte de partage, rédigé par le notaire Rousselot le 31 mars 1741,[37] la seigneurie de Bonsecours est divisée entre six seigneurs: Jean-François Bélanger, le fils aîné de François, considéré comme le seigneur primitif, Pierre Bélanger, Joseph Couillard, époux de Marthe Bélanger, Guillaume Lemieux, fils de Madeleine Bélanger, Élizabeth Bélanger et Françoise Bélanger épouse de Jean Fortin. Parmi eux, Jean-François, en tant que fils aîné de François, obtient la moitié de la seigneurie, l'autre moitié étant divisée également entre les cohéritiers.

Quant à Pierre, il ne peut participer au partage du côté de sa mère, car il est donataire de celle-ci. En effet, selon la Coutume de Paris, les qualités de donataire et d'héritier sont incompatibles.[38] Pierre a sûrement jugé préférable de demeurer éligible au douaire de sa mère plutôt que de participer au partage en tant qu'héritier de cette dernière.[39] Il devient quand même propriétaire de la huitième partie de la moitié de la seigneurie, en raison de son acquisition des prétentions des cinq Neuvillois en 1731. De plus, il conserve son statut d'héritier du côté de son père, comme le notaire Rousselot le mentionne dans l'acte de partage du 31 mars 1741:

> et comme le sieur Pierre Bélanger nous aurait proposez de luy adjoindre ce qui pourroit luy revenir du costé de feue son père dans la ditte seigneurie a ce qu'il a acheté cy devant attendu qu'il n'a pu partager du costé de madame sa mère dans la ditte seigneurie parce qu'il estoit donataire de la ditte dame et ce que les dittes parties [cohéritiers] luy ont accordé. . . .[40]

Donc, en plus de préserver son droit au douaire de sa mère, Pierre parvient également à s'approprier une bonne partie du contrôle seigneurial, grâce au rachat des parts seigneuriales des cinq Neuvillois et à ses parts d'héritage du côté de son père. En ce sens, le fait qu'il soit donataire de Marguerite Lefrançois n'a pas altéré outre mesure son statut d'héritier. Il importe donc de nuancer le concept d'héritier, car un enfant, s'il n'est pas éligible au partage du côté d'un de ses parents peut l'être de l'autre. La Coutume de Paris, comme l'ont démontré plusieurs autres exemples, permet une telle souplesse.

Nous constatons donc qu'au mois de mars 1741, la succession de Louis Bélanger était devenue des plus bouleversées. Seulement 17 années séparaient le moment où Louis transmettait à ses héritiers un patrimoine indivis et le jour où ce même bien était fragmenté par un partage. Louis Bélanger, grâce à plusieurs années d'efforts, avait réussi à transmettre à son fils François une seigneurie remembrée. Toutefois, en raison d'accidents démographiques, des années de labeur pouvaient être anéantis du jour au lendemain et, comme dans le cas du décès précoce de François Bélanger, provoquer l'éclatement tant du patrimoine familial que du contrôle seigneurial.

CONCLUSION

L'exemple de la famille Bélanger montre bien l'influence d'accidents démographiques sur les modalités de transmission des biens. Malgré l'absence de traces écrites résultant des ententes verbales et des lacunes dans les sources, tout un éventail d'informations d'appoint extraites des actes notariés et de quelques documents clés permettent de reconstituer adéquatement le processus successoral. En ce sens, l'âge au décès des parents revêt une grande importance. Quand le cycle familial subit une rupture brutale et inopinée, le devenir de chacun est remis en cause. Il faut trouver des solutions palliatives. Deux décès successifs ont remis en question l'intégrité du patrimoine foncier familial et abouti à un partage qui a eu pour effet, en plus d'atténuer le contrôle sur la seigneurie, d'inciter l'un des membres de la famille à entreprendre une autre phase de remembrement.

NOTES

1. Louis Lavallée, «La transmission du patrimoine selon le mode de partage dans la seigneurie de La Prairie sous le régime français», dans *Transmettre, hériter, succéder. La reproduction familiale en milieu rural France-Québec, XVIIIe–XXe siècle*, Actes du colloque franco-québécois sous la direction de Rolande Bonnain, Gérard Bouchard et Joseph Goy, ([Lyon/Paris]: Presses universitaires de Lyon/ École des Hautes Études en Sciences Sociales, 1992), 220.

2. Par ce concept, nous faisons référence au contrôle seigneurial exercé par un seul individu versus la fragmentation du contrôle au profit de différents cohéritiers. Selon Richard C. Harris, cette division du contrôle s'opère rarement du vivant du seigneur unique mais la plupart du temps au moment de sa mort. Richard C. Harris, *The Seigneurial System in Early Canada. A Geographical Study* (1966; Kingston and Montreal : McGill-Queen's University Press, 1984), 45 et 50.

3. Quelques historiens et historiennes se sont préoccupés des processus de transmission et des pratiques d'héritage dans le monde rural. Signalons quelques études: Louise Dechêne, *Habitants et marchands de Montréal au XVIIe siècle* (Montréal/Paris: Plon, 1979); P. Desjardins, «La coutume de Paris et la trans-

mission des terres. Le rang de la Beauce à Calixa-Lavallée de 1730 à 1975», dans *RHAF* 34, no. 3 (décembre 1980): 331–39; G. Bouchard, «Les systèmes des transmissions des avoirs familiaux et le cycle de la société rurale au Québec, du XVIIᵉ au XXᵉ siècle», dans *Histoire sociale* 16, no. 31 (mai 1983): 35–60; Lavallée, «La transmission du patrimoine . . . sous le régime français», 213–30; S. Dépatie, «La transmission du patrimoine dans les terroirs en expansion: un exemple canadien au XVIIIᵉ siècle», dans *RHAF* 44, no. 2 (automne 1990): 171–98; Harris, *The Seigneurial System in Early Canada*.

4. Il est nécessaire de préciser le cadre théorique, ou légale, qui régit les pratiques de successions à l'époque de la Nouvelle-France. Au XVIIIᵉ siècle, on se réfère à la Coutume de Paris pour déterminer la forme que va prendre la succession. Dans une étude comme la nôtre, il est de première importance de distinguer clairement les parties de l'héritage qui sont soumises au loi de successions nobles versus celles ayant la qualité des successions roturières. En ce sens, il est important de noter que selon la coutume, ce sont les biens qui détermine le type de succession, et non la qualité des personnes impliquées.

5. René Jetté, *Dictionnaire généalogique des familles du Québec des origines à 1730* (Montréal : PUM, 1983); ANQ-Q, Greffes des notaires du Régime français.

6. Ivanhoë Caron, «Aux origines d'une paroisse: Notre-Dame-de-Bonsecours-de-L'Islet (1677–1723)», *Mémoires et Comptes Rendus de la société Royale du Canada* (3e série, tome 34, 1940), 41.

7. Dépatie, «La transmission du patrimoine», 192.

8. Sur la Coutume de Paris et son cadre théorique, voir Claude de Ferrière, *Nouveau Commentaire sur la Coutume de la prévoté et vicomté de Paris* (Paris : Libraires associés, 1770), Tome 1; Harris, *The Seigneurial System in Early Canada*, 41–62; Yves Zoltvany, «Esquisse de la coutume de Paris», dans *RHAF* 25, no. 3 (décembre 1971): 365–84.

9. Caron, «Aux origines d'une paroisse», 41.

10. Deux enfants décédés en bas âge en 1685 et en 1689, Jean-François (1699), Barbe (1699), Jean-Baptiste (1702), Marguerite (1715) et Louis (1721). Marguerite, mariée depuis 1712 à Louis Couillard, sieur de l'Espinay, seigneur primitif de la Rivière-du-Sud et héritier d'un tiers de l'Islet Saint-Jean, est décédée à l'âge de 19 ans en 1715. Enfin, Louis Bélanger est décédé célibataire à l'âge de 30 ans, dans une expédition de chasse.

11. Louis Michel, «Varennes et Verchères des origines au milieu du XIXe siècle. État d'Une enquête», dans J. Goy et P. Wallot (dir.), *Évolution et éclatement du monde*

rural. Structures, fonctionnement et évolution différentielle des sociétés rurales françaises et québécoises, XVIIe–XXe siècle, Actes du Colloque franco-québécois d'histoire rurale comparée, tenu à Rochefort (France) en 1982, Paris et Montréal, 1986, 329.

12. Dépatie, «La transmission du patrimoine», 182.

13. François était âgé de 38 ans au décès de son père, Élizabeth 32 ans, Marie-Madeleine 30 ans, Pierre 24 ans, Françoise 20 ans et Marie-Marthe 18 ans.

14. À son mariage, le 29 octobre 1711, Louis Bélanger lui avait concédé une terre, voisine du Domaine de Bonsecours, côté sud-ouest, de 6 arpents de front sur 84 de profondeur, en bois debout, sans aucune terre défrichée, ni bâtiment. François n'occupa jamais cette terre. L'aveu et dénombrement de 1739 montre six arpents défrichés seulement et aucune habitation.

15. Le moment du mariage est remarquable si l'on considère que son père est décédé le 1er octobre 1724 et qu'environ un mois plus tard, soit le 11 novembre, il convole avec Geneviève Lessard. Le deuil est pratiquement inexistant et nous sommes en droit de nous questionner sur les raisons qui mènent à une union aussi pressante. La date du mariage avait-elle déjà été fixée avant la mort du seigneur Bélanger? Les époux ne font-ils que respecter cette échéance, ou Pierre ne veut-il sous aucun prétexte demeurer plus longtemps à la charge de son frère? Il est difficile d'apporter des réponses à de telles interrogations, mais le simple fait de les soulever demeure primordial à toute investigation sérieuse. En outre, ce questionnement permet une conscientisation des limites interprétatives auxquelles nous sommes confrontées.

16. Celui-ci consiste en deux arpents de terre de front sur 42 de profondeur, situés dans la seigneurie de l'Islet Saint-Jean, voisine de Bonsecours. ANQ, Greffe du notaire Abel Michon, 11 novembre 1724, Contrat de mariage de Pierre Bélanger et Geneviève Lessard; selon G. Postolec, il y a habituellement surmasculinité dans l'apport de biens fonciers au contrat de mariage, lorsqu'il s'agit de couples endogames, c'est-à-dire dont les deux conjoints habitent la même seigneurie. Chez les couples exogames toutefois, la proportion de femmes qui apportent une terre s'élève à 30%. Dans ces cas-là, le choix d'une conjointe semble s'accompagner de la recherche de terres. Geneviève Postolec, «La reproduction sociale à Neuville au XVIIIe siècle: l'apport foncier au mariage», dans Bonnain, Bouchard et Goy (dir.), *Transmettre, hériter, succéder*, 46.

17. En approfondissant la généalogie de Pierre Lessard, nous avons constaté qu'il existait des liens entre les deux familles, tissés depuis fort longtemps. En effet,

Pierre Lessard était marié avec Barbe Fortin, veuve en premières noces de Pierre Gagnon. Avec ce dernier, elle eut huit enfants, dont quatre se marièrent au sein du réseau familial des Bélanger: Marguerite avec Pierre Lefrançois, frère de Marguerite, femme de Louis Bélanger, Geneviève avec Charles Bélanger, neveu de Louis, Charles avec Anne Bélanger, nièce de Louis, Joseph avec Agathe Bélanger, nièce de Louis. Les deux familles n'étaient pas étrangères et le réseau de parenté, établi depuis l'époque où les familles demeuraient à Château-Richer, explique donc une part de cette alliance.

18. ANQ-Q, Greffe de Abel Michon, Mariage de Pierre Bélanger avec Geneviève Lessard, 11 novembre 1724. En considérant la quantité et la qualité des biens matériels que Geneviève Lessard reçoit de ses parents au contrat de mariage, nous pouvons observer une différence de richesse avec l'habitant. En plus de la terre citée plus haut, Geneviève reçoit à son mariage «[. . .] un fusil, lequel était à son défunt frère et aussi un lit garni, traversin et oreillers, couverte et courte-pointe, 3 paires de draps, 6 nappes, 2 douzaines de serviettes, une douzaine de chemises et quatre pièces d'habit d'étamine et crépon, et gilets et leur assortiment, 4 douzaines de coiffes tant fines que autres, 2 coiffes de taffetas, une robe de chambre d'indienne, 2 tabliers, un d'indienne et l'autre d'étamine et les hardes de tous les jours consistant en 2 rechanges, 4 paires de bas de france, 2 paires de souliers français, 2 paires de bas du pays, une vache mère, 2 moutons, 4 plats d'étain, une demi-douzaine d'assiettes d'étain, une demi-douzaine de cuillères, une demi-douzaine de fourchettes, une écuelle d'étain et un gobelet d'argent».

19. À cet effet, nous avons retrouvé, dans un échange de biens (24 juillet 1737) entre Pierre Bélanger et Geneviève Bélanger, fille de François, l'allusion au fait que Louis Bélanger et Marguerite Lefrançois avaient donné de leur vivant jouissance à François du Domaine seigneurial. ANQ, Greffe de Pierre Rousselot, 28 décembre 1741.

20. ANQ-Q, Greffe de Abel Michon, Partage des biens de Louis Bélanger, 12 novembre 1724.

21. Dans la reconstitution de la famille Langelier, nous avons trouvé 12 enfants. Toutefois, il semble peu probable que Charles, le fils aîné, et sa soeur Françoise, soient vivants au moment du partage car nous n'avons aucune mention les concernant. L'acte de partage de la famille Langelier, dressé en 1724, énumère les enfants issus de la communauté entre Charles Langelier et Françoise Destrois-maisons qui ne sont plus que 10 à ce moment. Les dates de décès de Charles et Françoise demeurent indéterminées car aucun acte de sépulture n'a été retrouvé.

ANQ-Q, Greffe de Abel Michon, Partage de la communauté entre Charles Langelier et Françoise Destroismaisons, 10 novembre 1724.

22. ANQ-Q, Greffe de Abel Michon, Échange entre Louis Langelier et Élizabeth Langelier, 10 novembre 1724.

23. ANQ-Q, Greffe de Abel Michon, Mariage entre Louis Langelier et Geneviève Fortin, 13 novembre 1724.

24. ANQ-Q, Greffe de Abel Michon, Partage des biens de Louis Bélanger, 18 avril 1730.

25. ANQ-Q, Greffe de Abel Michon, article 27, Billet sous seing privé de Marguerite Lefrançois à Pierre Bélanger, 15 avril 1730. Cette terre est située au deuxième rang dont l'ouverture est très récente en 1730 (tableau 7). Localisée dans la mouvance seigneuriale, son niveau de développement est donc peu appréciable. Pierre va finalement céder cette terre le 12 janvier 1736 à Joseph Bélanger, fils d'Ignace Bélanger son cousin germain. La cession, et non la vente de cette terre au fils de son cousin, nous laisse un peu perplexe quant à la logique de cette transaction. Cependant, tout indique que le geste de Pierre en est un de gratitude envers son cousin Ignace ou envers Joseph, le fils de ce dernier.

26. La terre principale est située à l'extrémité nord-est de la seigneurie et consiste en une censive de 10 arpents de front par 2 lieues de profondeur (tableau 7). Pierre et Geneviève, sa femme, vont y demeurer avec Marguerite.

27. Aucun acte de donation n'a été retrouvé. Cependant, dans l'acte de partage du 31 mars 1741, le notaire Rousselot mentionne que Pierre, étant donataire de Marguerite Lefrançois, ne pourra prendre part au partage du côté de celle-ci. ANQ-Q, Greffe de Pierre Rousselot, Acte de partage de la seigneurie de Bonsecours, 31 mars 1741.

28. Selon S. Dépatie, le dénouement le plus fréquent de la forme de transmission combinant partage et donation est le remembrement de l'ensemble de la terre par le donataire. Le cas de Pierre Bélanger vient donc appuyer les observations de l'auteur.

29. ANQ-Q, Greffe de J. N. Pinguet, Vente de parts de la seigneurie de Bonsecours à Pierre Bélanger, 5 mars 1731. Les vendeurs sont François Anger dit Lefèbvre, Léonard Fauché, François Grégoire et Charles Maufay, les quatre gendres de Mathurine Bélanger et Julien Grégoire, son troisième époux. Leurs prétentions consistaient dans la huitième partie de la moitié de la seigneurie, à la somme de 47 livres 3 sols et 9 deniers de rentes.

30. ANQ-Q, Greffe de Abel Michon, Vente de terrain par Jean Fortin et Françoise Bélanger à Pierre Bélanger, 4 avril 1736.

31. Au total, ils donnent trois terres: la première est de 2 arpents de front sur 42 de profondeur et leur avait été donnée lors du mariage par Pierre Lessard. La seconde est de la même dimension et la dernière mesure un arpent de front sur 42 de profondeur. Jean Fortin et Françoise Bélanger demeuraient déjà près de chez Pierre Lessard, car ils étaient donataires de Charles Fortin qui possédait la terre voisine. Par cet échange, Jean Fortin et Françoise Bélanger devenaient propriétaires d'un beau patrimoine à l'Islet Saint-Jean. Toutefois, dans le contrat, il était mentionné qu'ils ne pourraient en jouir qu'après le décès de Pierre Lessard et sa femme. Ils durent donc attendre jusqu'au 27 août 1737. ANQ-Q, Greffe de Abel Michon, Échange de terrain entre Jean Fortin et Françoise Bélanger et Pierre Bélanger, 4 avril 1736.

32. Jacques, décédé en 1699, est le frère de Louis Bélanger. Marguerite Lefrançois avait acheté, le 8 octobre 1728, une parcelle de un arpent et un tiers de front sur 126 de profondeur (tableau 6, terre no. 3) à François Bélanger, le fils héritier de Jacques. C'est pour cette raison que les héritiers de Louis avaient des prétentions sur cette terre. ANQ-Q, Greffe de François Rageot, Vente de terrain par François Bélanger à Marguerite Lefrançois, 8 octobre 1728.

33. Parts successorales consistant en 15 pieds de front sur 168 de profondeur sur la terre de Louis Bélanger, 5 pieds de front sur la profondeur dans le domaine et 2 pieds de front sur 126 de profondeur sur la concession détachée de la terre de Jacques Bélanger. ANQ-Q, Greffe de Abel Michon, Vente de J.-B. Michon et Marguerite Lemieux à Pierre Bélanger, 24 octobre 1741.

34. ANQ-Q, Greffe de Abel Michon, Contrat de mariage entre Charles Bernier et Marie-Geneviève Bélanger, 1er mai 1740.

35. En 1741, Pierre Bélanger avait encore quatre enfants d'âge mineur à la maison : Pierre (15 ans), Marie-Angélique (7 ans), Jean-Gabriel (5 ans) et Marie-Marguerite (3 ans).

36. Jean-François Bélanger épouse, le 8 janvier 1736 à l'âge de 23 ans, Marie-Louise Caron.

37. ANQ-Q, Greffe de Pierre Rousselot, Acte de partage de la seigneurie de Bonsecours, 31 mars 1741.

38. Ferrière, *Nouveau commentaire sur la Coutume de la prévoté et vicomté de Paris*, 1:846.

39. À ce sujet, voir Zoltvany, «Esquisse de la Coutume de Paris», 381.

40. ANQ-Q, Greffe de Pierre Rousselot, Acte de partage de la Seigneurie de Bonsecours, 31 mars 1741.

CHAPTER THIRTEEN

John Bourinot et la présence de la France au Canada atlantique au XIXe siècle

Robert Pichette

John George Bourinot (1814–1884) played an important role in Nova Scotia and Canadian politics in the nineteenth century. This enterprising ship chandler was one of the first two representatives of France in what was to become Canada. He was initially appointed in 1850 as the French consular agent in Sydney (Cape Breton), with a mandate to assist the French naval fleet charged with the protection of the fishery on Newfoundland's "French Shore." Bourinot expanded his role to include the promotion of trade and commerce and was so successful that the government of Napoleon III promoted him to the rank of honorary Vice Consul in 1854. Bourinot, who was appointed to the Canadian Senate at Confederation, continued to discharge his consular duties until his death, earning the praise of all who knew him. His undoubted diplomatic abilities contributed in no small way to the expansion on Canada's eastern coast of the climate of "Entente Cordiale" dear to the Emperor of the French.

L'île du Cap-Breton, l'ancienne île Royale, sise à l'entrée du golfe Saint-Laurent, aura été pendant des siècles l'une des principales colonies de la France en Amérique du Nord et l'enjeu constant des rivalités des empires français et anglais. Après que la France l'eut perdu définitivement en 1758, elle ne tarda pas à réapparaître et cette première manifestation française fut assez spectaculaire et pas du tout pacifique puisqu'en 1781, le célèbre La Pérouse lui-même, livra avec succès un combat naval contre quatre navires

John George Bourinot, vice-consul honoraire de France à Sydney, N.-É.,
Canada, photo prise vers 1857–1858. Photo Paul-Émile Miot. Collection
Fernand A. Lévi. Archives nationales du Canada. PA-188216.

britanniques dans le havre de Sydney.[1] Au milieu du XIXe siècle, la présence très active de la France sur le littoral atlantique des colonies britanniques, puis des provinces canadiennes, fut infiniment plus pacifique et dénuée de toute velléité de reconquête.

Cette communication tente d'esquisser les premiers développements de relations suivies entre la France et les colonies britanniques du littoral atlantique canadien durant la deuxième moitié du XIXe siècle. Peu de chercheurs ont étudié sérieusement cette question ce qui rend cet essai nécessairement incomplet et préliminaire. Il existe, cependant, une masse de documents importants aux Archives Nationales de France qui, éventuellement, éclairera davantage la question.

Trois facteurs sont à l'origine de la présence de la France dans ce qui avait été ses possessions: *primo*, les droits de pêche que la France avait conservés en vertu du traité de Paris de 1763 sur la côte de Terre-Neuve ainsi que sur l'archipel des îles de Saint-Pierre et Miquelon; *secundo*, l'empereur Napoléon III; et *tertio*, un Canadien tout à fait remarquable, John Bourinot, marchand, armateur, homme politique et agent consulaire de France à Sydney, principale ville du Cap-Breton. Celui-ci est le personnage central de cette communication car il a été sans contredit l'agent principal de la France au Canada atlantique durant plusieurs décennies.

Napoléon III n'est certes pas le chef d'État le plus admiré des Français, bien que le Second Empire ait apporté à la France une prospérité sans précédent. L'un de ses biographes dira de lui sans hésitation : «Napoléon III est à l'origine de la grande révolution des temps modernes».[2]

Quant à John Bourinot (1814–1884), il a vite été éclipsé par la brillante réputation de l'un de ses fils, sir John George Bourinot (1837–1902), constitutionnaliste et homme de lettres né à Sydney.[3] Même si John Bourinot père n'a pas encore eu les honneurs d'une biographie en bonne et due forme, il n'en reste pas moins que cet homme remarquable a joué un rôle majeur dans l'établissement harmonieux de relations françaises officielles dans les provinces du Canada de l'Atlantique.

Bourinot naquit à Grouville, dans l'île anglo-normande de Jersey, le 15 mars 1814, dans une famille d'origine huguenote qui, semble-t-il, s'y était réfugiée lors de la révocation de l'Édit de Nantes. Il mourut à Ottawa le 19 janvier 1884.[4] Il s'établit au Cap-Breton très jeune mais on ignore la date précise de son arrivée. Toutefois, il avait vingt et un ans lorsqu'il épousa à

Arichat, en septembre 1835, Margaret Jane Marshall, qui lui donna onze enfants. La présence d'un jersiais au Cap-Breton n'a pas de quoi surprendre car les grandes sociétés commerciales exportatrices de poisson, comme les Robin, les Janvrin et les LeBoutillier, sont des monopoles jersiais qui exerceront longtemps une emprise économique considérable, notamment en Gaspésie et au Cap-Breton, plus précisément à l'île Madame et à Chéticamp.[5]

Il est donc tout à fait probable que John Bourinot ait jeté son dévolu sur le Cap-Breton dans le sillage des grandes sociétés jersiaises qui ont si longtemps dominé la pêche commerciale. Cette probabilité s'appuie aussi sur le fait qu'il se soit marié à Arichat. Des navires de pêches venus des îles Jersey et Guernesey fréquentaient ce port de l'île Madame depuis 1766 et la société Robin, Pipon & Co. de Jersey y avait établi des agents permanents dès l'année suivante.[6] Plusieurs familles jersiaises s'y établirent au milieu d'Acadiens, d'Écossais et d'Irlandais.[7]

Chef-lieu du comté de Richmond, Arichat était une petite ville si prospère et un centre commercial si important qu'elle devint le siège d'un évêché catholique en 1844.[8]

En 1893, le commandant du *Magon*, du Service hydrographique de la marine française, ancré devant Arichat, notera dans un rapport que la population acadienne du Cap-Breton était de 12,426 âmes et que l'Île Madame était la partie la plus française du Cap-Breton.[9]

Par son mariage, John Bourinot s'alliait à une famille ancienne et considérable. Margaret Jane Marshall était la petite-fille d'un loyaliste qui avait obtenu une concession importante au Cap-Breton, avait été député puis juge. Son père, John George Marshall, avait été lui aussi député à l'Assemblée législative de la Nouvelle-Écosse, puis juge en chef de la Cour des plaidoyers communs pour l'île du Cap-Breton. Il semblerait que son père ait eu de sérieuses réserves au sujet de son nouveau gendre.

Quoi qu'il en soit, cette alliance ne nuisit certainement pas à la promotion sociale de Bourinot. D'abord juge de paix à Sydney, il devint surintendant du trafic maritime dans le port de Sydney. En 1859, il fut élu député du Cap-Breton à l'Assemblée législative de la Nouvelle-Écosse et réélu par acclamation en 1863. La même année, il devenait agent de la Lloyd's.

Initialement opposé à la Confédération canadienne, mais non à une union des provinces Maritimes, Bourinot se rallia au gouvernement Tupper en 1865. Son revirement le fit taxer d'opportunisme politique lorsqu'il fut nommé au

Sénat du Canada lors de l'avènement de la Confédération en 1867. Les opposants de la Confédération y virent le prix de sa défection. Il s'en défendit en arguant que le Cap-Breton trouverait mieux son profit au sein de la Confédération canadienne qu'en demeurant un insignifiant appendice de la Nouvelle-Écosse.[10] L'avenir devait lui donner raison.

Sa carrière politique, à Halifax ou à Ottawa, ne fut pas particulièrement éclatante et ne nous retiendra pas. Avant tout homme d'affaires et commerçant éclairé, ayant une vision précise et réaliste des possibilités économiques et commerciales que la nouvelle fédération offrait, Bourinot s'intéressa passionnément aux mines de charbon du Cap-Breton, au développement des ports de Sydney et de Louisbourg, ainsi qu'au projet de relier Sydney à Louisbourg par un chemin de fer.

Bourinot, qui avait fait ses études à Caen, en France, était si parfaitement bilingue qu'il parlait l'anglais avec un fort accent français. Tant et si bien qu'un journal d'Halifax, qui lui était hostile, écrivait en 1867 qu'il parlait français «and that was his sole excellence unless we add that he was cordially despised and hated by the members of the Administration».[11]

Sa qualité de fournisseur de navires, son sens des affaires et son bilinguisme allaient le désigner comme le candidat idéal au poste d'agent consulaire de France à Sydney. C'est d'ailleurs à la suite d'une suggestion d'un commandant de la station navale de Terre-Neuve, le capitaine de marine Thomas Ducos, que Bourinot fut nommé agent consulaire de France parce «qu'il serait utile que soit conféré à M. Bourinet [sic], notaire de cette ville [Sydney] le titre gratuit d'agent consulaire» puisqu'il parlait français et que cette nomination faciliterait «le service des lettres et aide aux achats qu'ont à faire les marins Français dans cette ville».[12]

La recommandation de Ducos indique que la marine française s'approvisionnait déjà à Sydney et qu'elle fréquentait Bourinot. À peine nommé, Bourinot adressa à l'ambassadeur de France à Londres un long rapport sur les relations commerciales de la France et de ses colonies avec l'ancienne Acadie et le Canada.[13] Il fit tant et si bien que le ministère des Affaires étrangères lui décerna un brevet de vice-consul honoraire en 1854 en récompense de son zèle.[14] Tous les témoignages de ses contemporains concordent : Bourinot remplissait ses fonctions non-rémunérées avec zèle et générosité.

Sydney servait de base de ravitaillement à diverses flottes mais elle était surtout le port de relâche de la marine française chargée des intérêts de la France sur le *French Shore* de Terre-Neuve, c'est-à-dire la côte ouest. Les navires français s'y approvisionnaient régulièrement en victuailles et en charbon. Les droits de pêche historiques de la France sur cette côte avaient été reconnus par le traité de Versailles, en 1784. Elle n'y renoncera qu'en 1904.[15]

La question des droits de la France sur cette partie de Terre-Neuve énerva longtemps les Terre-neuviens qui blâmèrent régulièrement le gouvernement impérial de Londres que l'on accusait, avec une vigoureuse férocité, de complaisance coupable avec le gouvernement français au détriment de leurs intérêts.[16]

Or, le prince Louis-Napoléon Bonaparte était devenu président de la République française en 1848. Il mit rapidement sur pied un vaste réseau d'agences consulaires qui furent l'ébauche d'une politique française de représentation auprès des colonies britanniques de l'Amérique du Nord. Chacune d'elle, Terre-Neuve en 1854, l'Île-du-Prince-Édouard en 1865, le Nouveau-Brunswick avec deux agences en 1856, et la Nouvelle-Écosse, en 1850, fut dotée d'au moins une agence consulaire.[17] Celle d'Halifax, envisagée en 1852, sera créée en 1854 avec, comme titulaire, le célèbre armateur et banquier, sir Samuel Cunard (1787–1865).

Les deux premières agences consulaires de France seront celles de Québec, confiée à Edward Ryan, et de Sydney, établies simultanément en 1850. Jusqu'en 1859, année de Magenta et de Solférino, alors que Napoléon lll instituera un consulat général de France à Québec, les agents consulaires relèveront de l'ambassade de France à Londres. Le choix de Sydney comme siège d'une agence consulaire de France s'explique par l'importance commerciale et géograpique que cette minuscule ville détenait à l'époque. Les abondantes houillières du Cap-Breton, sa vaste et commode rade, sa proximité de Saint-Pierre et Miquelon et de Terre-Neuve la désignait naturellement comme lieu de relâche et d'approvisionnement de la flotte française.

Les agents, tous sujets britanniques, donnaient à la France «une vision plus sérieuse et plus concrète du Canada; par eux elle y a des oreilles et des yeux mais se garde d'y vouloir une bouche».[18] Sans l'autorité d'un consul relevant de l'administration française, ces agents sont «peu voyants, peu spectaculaires, mais ils peuvent discrètement, trop peut-être, accroître la connaissance de la France sur le Canada, sans jamais inquiéter les autorités anglaises».[19]

Sous le Second Empire et au début de la IIIe République, la France n'accordera qu'une importance strictement utilitaire à ses agences consulaires au Canada atlantique, d'où son choix de ports maritimes pour y établir ses postes. Sauf à Québec et à Montréal, la France du Second Empire et de la IIIe République, du moins jusqu'au début du XXe siècle, n'entreprendra aucune action culturelle aux provinces atlantiques alors qu'elle mène de front une agressive politique culturelle, surtout à partir de 1883 avec la fondation de l'Alliance française, en Afrique, en Orient et en Extrême-Orient.[20]

Pour Napoléon III, devenu empereur des Français par le coup d'État de 1851, les possessions britanniques en Amérique du Nord ne feront jamais l'objet de convoitises coloniales. Cet homme éminemment pragmatique a été «profondément marqué par ses expériences britanniques. L'Angleterre lui a permis de comprendre ce qu'était une grande nation moderne et de mesurer la complexité des phénomènes économiques et sociaux. Il a aimé sincèrement ce pays, qui lui a beaucoup apporté et qui l'aura toujours dignement reçu».[21]

Bien plus : Napoléon III, disciple des saint-simoniens, avait profité de son incarcération au fort de Ham à la suite de sa tentative manquée de Boulogne, pour y rédiger plusieurs ouvrages. Dans l'un de ceux-ci, il projetait l'établissement de «comptoirs» en Amérique tout en estimant les «colonies onéreuses en temps de paix, désastreuses en temps de guerre».[22] Homme de vision, il entendait que la France rayonne culturellement dans le monde entier mais qu'elle profite également de la révolution industrielle. N'avait-il pas écrit : «La guerre et le commerce ont civilisé le monde. La guerre a fait son temps; le commerce poursuit aujourd'hui ses conquêtes. Donnons-lui une nouvelle route».[23] Cette nouvelle route passerait par l'Amérique du Nord et aurait son relais à Sydney comme autrefois Louisbourg avait été la plaque tournante du commerce nord-américain de la France de l'Ancien Régime.

Cette préoccupation essentiellement commerciale a pu se matérialiser de façon concrète grâce aux précautions que l'empereur prit pour ne jamais froisser la Grande-Bretagne. La guerre de Crimée, depuis 1854, avait fait de la France et de la Grande-Bretagne des alliés et, en 1860, les deux pays avaient conclu un traité de commerce, valable pour dix ans, mettant ainsi fin au protectionnisme douanier, sorte de libre-échange avant le mot. Un exemple anodin en soi montrera qu'il y réussit fort bien. Ainsi, en 1862, des marchands de la Nouvelle-Écosse, qui faisaient l'exportation du homard vers l'Europe depuis 1850, avaient expédié une caisse de crustacés vivants au couple impérial.[24]

Ces échanges commerciaux prendront une certaine ampleur lorsque le

Canada-Uni (l'Ontario et le Québec) participera à l'Exposition universelle de 1855, à Paris. La présence canadienne contribua à un regain d'intérêt de la part des Français pour leurs anciennes colonies du Canada.

Depuis 1849, les colonies britanniques de l'Amérique du Nord pouvaient commercer avec d'autres pays que la Grande-Bretagne et ses colonies. Les possibilités commerciales nouvelles qui s'offraient n'échappèrent pas au gouvernement français. En 1855, le gouvernement de l'empereur enverra la corvette *La Capricieuse* en mission au Canada pour s'enquérir des possibilités d'échanges commerciaux avec le Canada. C'était la première fois depuis la Conquête que la France retournait dans ses anciennes possessions.

La mission avait été confiée au commandant Pierre-Henri de Belvèze, commandant de la station navale de Terre-Neuve. Avant de remonter triomphalement le Saint-Laurent, Belvèze s'était rendu en visite officielle à Halifax, en mai 1854, juste à temps pour prendre part aux festivités qui marquaient la fête de la reine Victoria, ce qui fut l'occasion de célébrer aussi «l'alliance intime de la France et de l'Angleterre».[25] Belvèze notera que la présence d'un bâtiment français dans la rade d'Halifax donnait à la fête de la reine un caractère qu'elle n'avait jamais eu auparavant.

La question des pêches retiendra l'attention de Napoléon III. En 1859, un nouveau litige s'étant présenté entre la France et la Grande-Bretagne sur cette question de droits de pêche sur la côte ouest de Terre-Neuve, une commission bilatérale fut désignée par Paris et par Londres pour enquêter sur le différend. Le ministère des Affaires étrangères choisit Arthur de Gobineau comme commissaire impérial, et le ministère de la Marine fit choix pour le représenter du capitaine de vaisseau marquis de Montaignac de Chauvance, commandant de la station navale de Terre-Neuve.[26]

L'auteur, déjà célèbre, de l'*Essai sur l'inégalité des races humaines*, ancien chef de cabinet d'Alexis de Tocqueville à l'époque où celui-ci était ministre des Affaires étrangères, en tira un livre—*Voyage à Terre-Neuve*—publié en 1861.

Gobineau, fort perspicace il anticipera l'inéluctabilité de la Confédération canadienne entre autres anthropologue et sociologue avant la lettre, observateur minutieux, ne se contentera pas de décrire Terre-Neuve; il y ajoutera des chapitres sur Sydney et Halifax assaisonnés d'observations judicieuses et même savoureuses sur les mœurs coloniales anglaises, sur les Amérindiens du Cap-Breton et, bien entendu, sur les Acadiens du Cap-Breton qu'il rencontra grâce à John Bourinot.

En arrivant à Sydney, Gobineau, en compagnie du commandant du *Ténare*, alla présenter ses devoirs au vice-consul honoraire de France dont il dit que:

> Cet excellent homme est fort apprécié et aimé de nos états-majors. Il nous accueillit comme il est accoutumé à le faire pour tous les Français que la Division navale conduit chez lui depuis tant d'années. Il nous présenta à Mme B . . . et à sa famille.[27]

La marine française sur le littoral atlantique canadien ne faisait pas que de maintenir de vieilles traditions d'honneur, encore qu'elles aient eu leur importance; elle observait les événements politiques qui se déroulaient dans les colonies britanniques de l'Atlantique et, parfois même, les influençaient.

Un exemple suffira pour l'illustrer. En 1860, le prince de Galles, futur Édouard Vll, visitait le Canada et les États-Unis. Le commandant de la station navale de Terre-Neuve, le marquis de Montaignac de Chauvance, sur sa propre initiative, mais vivement encouragé par Bourinot, quitta Sydney sur le *Pomone* pour aller saluer le prince dans la rade de Charlottetown, à l'île-du-Prince-Édouard.[28] Le geste, qui avait le mérite de faciliter la tâche de la commission des pêches, n'a sans doute pas déplu au futur artisan de l'Entente cordiale qui devait être reçu officiellement à Fontainebleau par Napoléon III, en juin 1862.

Marchand cossu, Bourinot possédait une vaste maison sise directement sur le havre, à l'endroit où s'élève aujourd'hui le Royal Cape Breton Yacht Club. Elle était précédée d'un embarcadère que Gobineau décrit comme «fort beau et fort large qui servait de terrasse à une jolie maison à un étage, flanquée d'un mât de pavillon où flottaient les couleurs françaises».[29]

Un pasteur anglican, le révérend Richard John Uniacke, appartenant à l'une des plus anciennes et des plus influentes famille de la Nouvelle-Écosse, avait été lui aussi impressionné par la demeure de Bourinot. Il en donna la description suivante entre 1862 et 1865:

> Amongst the most conspicuous dwellings of the place is the house of the French Consul J. Bourinot, Esq also member of the Provincial Assembly. It is situated upon the border of the River. Several large trees shade it upon the land side; and a long and well constructed wharf with a commodious landing

place, runs out in front towards the water. A tri-coloured flag hoisted upon a staff near the gable regularly announces the arrival of a French ship. From the balcony of the river front of this house you may occasionally look out upon a gay scene. It not unfrequently happens during the summer months that two or three French men-of-war are anchored immediately abreast of the Consul's Residence at a very short distance from this wharf. Their bright flags, the bustling sounds from their decks and the morning and evening bugle quite enliven our otherwise tranquil harbour. Sometimes the band from the Admiral's ship is added to the other gay features of the scene.[30]

En 1895, dans un livre sur le Cap-Breton dédicacé à la mémoire de son père, John George Bourinot, devenu homme de lettres et greffier de la Chambre des Communes grâce d'ailleurs à l'intervention de son père laissera une description nostalgique de la maison paternelle en évoquant ses «quaint, low rooms, fitted with mementoes of French sailors, of many eminent men known in the naval history and in the official records of France, like Cloué[31] and La Roncière Le Noury,[31] have partaken of the hospitalities of the kindly owner, the late Senator Bourinot, long a vice-consul of France».[32]

De la ville de Sydney, à cette période, il y avait peu de chose à dire. Contentons-nous de citer Gobineau:

Sydney serait un peu abandonné du reste du monde, si la division navale française n'y venait pas chaque année. Presque jamais les navires de guerre de Sa Majesté Britannique n'y paraissent. Aussi, nos marins y sont ils accueillis avec d'autant plus d'empressement qu'ils n'ont pas de rivaux. La plupart des officiers avaient déjà visité plus ou moins fréquemment cette côte; c'étaient d'anciennes connaissances; ils étaient au fait de toutes les histoires du pays et ils présentaient les nouveaux venus qui, bientôt, n'étaient pas moins bien reçus qu'eux-mêmes.[33]

L'ouvrage de Gobineau avait fait du bruit, même à Sydney, où les dames n'avaient pas prisé certaine description peu flatteuse de leur appétit! On en parlait encore en 1861 lorsqu'un officier naval britannique, Nicholas Dennys, s'y rendit en mission. Celui-ci, dont on sait peu de chose à part la relation qu'il publia de sa visite, s'inquiétait de la présence française par trop voyante à son goût dans la paisible capitale du Cap-Breton et y voyait un danger possible pour l'hégémonie de l'Empire britannique:

> But certain it is, from the infrequency of a visit from an English vessel, and the fact of its being the headquarters of a French naval station, Sydney is becoming French in tone and feeling. I do not by any means mean to say that its loyalty is to be for a moment questioned; but I am sure that English naval officers are at a disadvantage when they visit the port, because their acquaintance with the people is that only of a day, whereas our Gallic neighbours have friends of long standing in the neighbourhood. Perhaps, as far as the society goes, it does not much matter, as there are but few families constituting it; but from the important position of the island in a geographical point of view, in relation to Canada and Nova Scotia, it may be worth while to bring the question under the notice of those with whom lies the remedy.[35]

Ces navires français mouillés dans la rade de Sydney constituaient une diversion sociale importante pour la gentry de Sydney mais aussi, comme le notait en 1868 le fils du vice-consul, John George, la flotte française contribuait d'une façon significative à l'économie locale. S'il faut en croire sir John George, la présence de la France en rade de Sydney n'affectait en rien la loyauté de ses citoyens.

Pour Bourinot fils, les citoyens de Sydney prenaient les rapports alarmistes de la présence française en leur milieu pour des chimères. Il écrivait:

> [. . .] for there are no fortifications whatever at St Pierre; nor are the good people of Sydney fearful that their loyalty is in peril because the tricolour waves so often, during the summer months, in their noble harbour, from His Imperial Majesty's ships. On the contrary, they would feel deeply disappointed if these ships were now to cease their periodical visits, which tend so much to enliven the town, and are so very profitable to the farmers of the surrounding country.[36]

La France ne se préoccupait nullement de fortifier Saint-Pierre mais Bourinot, Belvèze et Gobineau auraient bien aimé que le minuscule archipel devienne un vaste entrepôt et une plaque tournante du commerce franco-canadien. Belvèze proposait que les navires de pêches ayant chargé la morue auraient pu compléter leur chargement

avec des marchandises destinées aux marchés de l'Amérique du Nord et entreposées dans les magasins de St. Pierre, si ces mêmes magasins étaient en outre immédiatement approvisionnés de produits assortis, rien ne serait plus facile que de faire écouler ces produits dans les ports de la Nouvelle-Écosse et du Canada, soit par les transports qui perdent leur temps, soit par le cabotage, et de rapporter à St. Pierre des bois de construction, du blé, de la farine, etc. . . . qui s'entreposeraient également dans l'île et seraient ensuite dirigés avec opportunité sur les ports de France.[37]

Ni les rapports du commandant Belvèze, ni ceux de Bourinot ne trouveront d'écho à Paris.

À l'époque où Bourinot fils consignait ses observations [1868], deux navires français avaient jeté l'ancre devant la résidence du vice-consul. Il s'agissait du *Jean Bart*, un vaisseau de formation des cadets, et le *Sémiramis*, vaisseau amiral de l'amiral baron Megnet, commandant de la station navale de Terre-Neuve. Ces visites régulières étaient donc l'occasion de festivités et même, à l'occasion, de pompeuses civilités protocolaires qui ajoutaient un certain faste dans la vie plutôt terne d'une petite ville de province qui gardera longtemps la nostalgie de son rôle de capitale d'une éphémère colonie britannique autonome.

Le révérend Uniacke l'avait noté pour le compte de l'archevêque anglican de Dublin lorsqu'il écrivait:

[. . .] I have had the opportunity of seeing many distinguished officers of the French Navy as visitors in our harbour; and sometimes at the same moment when our own Frigates and Flagships have been anchored at no great distance from them. In the absence of Merchantmen, which at present carry on but a scanty trade in our harbour, such ships are always welcome visitors.[38]

Les visites protocolaires se faisaient avec toute la solennité voulue comme en témoigne la description suivante donnée par le *Cape Breton News*, dans son édition du 6 juillet 1861, et reprise a son compte par Nicholas Dennys :

Immediately after dropping anchor the band on board the *St George* played the French National Anthem. At eight o'clock next morning, the tri-colour of France was hoisted at the fore, and saluted; and ere the dying echo of the guns had ceased, the band of the *St George* struck up *Partant pour la Syrie*.[39] The effect of the whole was most pleasing. The French National Anthem concluded, up went the Ensign of Old England at the fore on board the French frigate *Pomone*, lying about three hundred yards from the *St George*, and which was likewise duly saluted. Again at twelve o'clock, noon, as J. Bourinot, Esq, who had been on board to pay his respects to the commander, left the side of the *St George*, her guns belched forth a salute due to the rank and dignity of a Consul of *la belle France*.[40]

Cette dignité consulaire comme représentant d'une puissance alliée, jadis tutélaire de l'île Royale, John Bourinot devait l'étaler avec éclat le 20 juillet 1861 à l'occasion de la visite du cousin germain de l'empereur, le prince Napoléon. Avant de se rendre à Halifax, le prince avait voulu visiter les ruines de Louisbourg. Il était accompagné d'un ami, Maurice, baron Dudevant, dit Maurice Sand, fils de George Sand. Il a laissé de cette visite une série d'articles, revus et corrigés par la célèbre écrivain. Ces articles furent d'abord publiés dans la *Revue des Deux Mondes*[41] en 1862, puis réunis en un volume, préfacé par George Sand, sous le titre *Six mille lieues à toute vapeur*.[42]

Maurice Sand, comme tant d'autres avant et après lui, n'échappera pas à l'envoûtement éxercé par les ruines de la forteresse de Louisbourg. De celles-ci, il écrira:

> Il ne reste de notre colonie canadienne que des ruines, où des pêcheurs ont installé leurs cabanes; c'est une poignée d'Irlandais catholiques et d'Écossais protestants qui se détestent cordialement les uns les autres. Le prince explore le théâtre des événements historiques, aujourd'hui recouverts d'herbage qui ne sont pas encore mûrs. Un bloc de fort écroulé, quelques pans de murailles, deux arches de pont perdues au milieu d'un marais, c'est là le Gibraltar du Saint-Laurent.[43]

Tous les visiteurs qui se rendront dans ce champ de ruines informes qui avait été aussi surnommé le Dunkerque de l'Amérique, en laisseront, sans exception, des descriptions peintes aux couleurs de la tristesse. Ainsi, même sir John George Bourinot écrira : «Louisbourg is in ruins, and the French flag is no longer seen in that lonely port, but floats only from the mastheads of ships of France in the very harbour which they neglected in the days when her king was master on his royal island».[44]

Le sénateur John Bourinot mourra en 1884, à Ottawa, loin de son île Royale. Quatre ans plus tard, un Canadien-français de haute volée, Henri-Edmond Faucher de Saint-Maurice (1844–1897), journaliste, publiciste, écrivain et même député, était un ancien soldat qui avait fait la guerre du Mexique dans le corps expéditionnaire français. Il avait connu le convivial vice-consul de France à Sydney, en 1879, et lui rendra l'hommage suivant qui servira d'élégante épitaphe à un homme à qui la France doit beaucoup :

> Ma seule visite à South Sydney a été pour l'honorable M. Bourinot. Ce sénateur a exercé, depuis trente ans, les fonctions de consul de France. Très estimé, honoré de la confiance de tous, il a été aimé de tous les amiraux, de tous les officiers qui sont entrés en relation avec lui. Sa maison était un musée où s'entassaient portraits de célébrités maritimes avec autographes, souvenirs de toutes espèces. Aujourd'hui ce brave homme dort son dernier sommeil tout près de l'endroit où il aimait tant à donner l'hospitalité.[45]

En dépit des appréhensions du juge Haliburton, reprises par Nicholas Dennys, Sydney ne fut jamais, pas plus hier qu'aujourd'hui, en danger de devenir ville de style et d'inspiration française, tant s'en faut! Sydney n'eut plus pour la France la même importance après la mort du sénateur Bourinot. Certes la personnalité hors du commun de ce premier agent consulaire de France, sa position officielle et sa longue expérience, faisaient de lui un interlocuteur exceptionnel qu'il eut été difficile de remplacer.

De plus, en 1904, la France, harcelée par le parlement colonial de Terre-Neuve, n'exerçant que peu ses droits de pêche, se retira avec autant d'élégance que possible du French Shore; cédant ses droits à la Grande-Bretagne en échange d'intérêts en Afrique, au large de la Gambie et du Niger.[46] Dès lors, les ports de Sydney et de Louisbourg ne serviraient plus que d'escales occasionnelles. Terre-Neuve avait été la cause de la présence prépondérante de la France au Cap-Breton durant le XVIIIᵉ siècle. Son abandon de ses droits résiduels à Terre-Neuve au XXᵉ siècle sera la cause du départ de sa flotte qui apportait annuellement une importante contribution à l'économie de l'île. À lui seul, pendant plus de trente ans, John Bourinot, aura maintenu dans la région atlantique du Canada, activement, généreusement, et noblement, l'honneur, les couleurs et le bon renom de la France. Les talents diplomatiques de ce premier représentant officiel de la France au Canada de l'Atlantique étaient fort appréciés de son vivant. Bourinot contribua habilement à établir un climat d'Entente cordiale avant la lettre entre la France et les colonies britanniques de l'Amérique du Nord.

NOTES

1. J. G. Bourinot, *Historical and Descriptive Account of the Island of Cape Breton* (Toronto, The Copp, Clark Co., 1895), 110.
2. Georges Roux, *Napoléon III* (Paris, Flammarion, 1969), 284.
3. Madge MacBeth, «Sir John Bourinot A Great Canadian», *The Atlantic Advocate* (août 1963): 73–76; et L. Le Jeune, *Dictionnaire biographique du Canada* (Ottawa, Université d'Ottawa, 1931), 1: 231–32.
4. A.A. MacKenzie, «Bourinot, John», *Dictionnaire biographique du Canada* (Québec et Toronto, Les Presses de l'Université Laval/University of Toronto Press, 1982), 11:105–6.
5. Marion G. Turk, *The Quiet Adventurers in Canada* (Detroit, Harlo Press, 1979). Lire aussi Rosemary E. Ommer, *From Outpost to Outport: A Structural Analysis of the Jersey-Gaspé* (Montréal et Kingston, McGill/Queen's University Press, 1991). Lire également Anselme Chiasson, *Chéticamp: histoire et traditions acadiennes* (Moncton, Éditions des Aboiteaux, 1969).
6. C.B. Fergusson, *Place-Names and Places of Nova Scotia* (1967; reprint Belleville, Ontario, Mika Publishing Co., 1974), 18.
7. Sally Ross, «Majorité ou minorité : le cas de l'Île Madame», La Société historique acadienne, *Les Cahiers* 23, nos. 3 et 4 (juillet 1992): 143–57, et Stephen A. White, «Les Fondateurs de la paroisse d'Arichat, Cap-Breton», *Les Cahiers* 23, no. 1 (janvier-mars 1992): 4–36.
8. Le siège épiscopal sera transféré à Antigonish en 1880.

9. Archives Nationales, MAR 3JJ 273, carton 65, 6 août 1893, le commandant du *Magon*, Service hydrographique de la marine, Service de l'Ingénieur en chef. Le rapport s'accompagne d'un joli dessin à l'encre d'Arichat.

10. Brian D. Tennyson, «Economic Nationalism and Confederation: A Case Study in Cape Breton», *Acadiensis* 11, no. 1 (automne 1972), 48.

11. Cité par Brian D. Tennyson, «Economic Nationalism . . .», 52.

12. Jacques Portes, *La France, quelques Français et le Canada 1850–1870—Relations politiques, commerciales et culturelles, thèse de doctorat de troisième cycle* (Université de Paris, juin 1974), 22.

13. Archives Nationales, archives du Ministère des Affaires Étrangères, correspondance consulaire et commerciale, Londres, vol. 37, fol. 124 et vol. 39, fol. 483.

14. La correspondance consulaire et commerciale en provenance de Londres conservée aux Archives Nationales de France comprend les volumes 10 à 48, de 1793 à 1858, et englobe les agences consulaires de Miramichi, Halifax et Sydney.

15. L. Labarère, *Éphémérides de la station navale de Terre-Neuve* (Paris, Bibliothèque historique de la marine, 1959).

16. Lire à ce sujet le chapitre que consacre à cette question D.W. Prowse, *A History of Newfoundland from the English Colonial and Foreign Records* (Londres et New York, MacMillan & Co., 1895; réimpression par Mika Studio, 1972), chap. 27, 539–63.

17. Portes, *La France, quelques Français et le Canada 1850-1870.* . . . Voir aussi Francis-J. Audet, «Les Représentants de la France au Canada au XIXᵉ siècle», *Les Cahiers des Dix*, no. 4, Montréal, 1939. Voir aussi *France et Canada 1855-1955*, Catalogue de l'Exposition, avant-propos de Charles Baibant, directeur des Archives de France, La Rochelle et Paris, 1955.

18. Portes, *La France, quelques Français* . . . , 41.

19. Ibid., 42.

20. François Roche et Bernard Pigniau, *Hisoire de la diplomatie culturelle des orgines à 1995*, Ministère des Affaires Étrangères, ADPF La Documentation française, Paris, avril 1995.

21. Philippe Séguin, *Louis-Napoléon le Grand* (Paris: Grasset, 1990), 74.

22. Cité par Louis Girard, *Napoléon III* (Paris: Fayard, 1986), 66.

23. Ibid., 74.

24. John Quinpool, *First Things in Acadia* (Halifax, N.-É., First Things Publishers Ltd., 1936), 252.

25. Cité par Jacques Portes, *La France*, 81–82.

26. Arthur de Gobineau, *Voyage à Terre-Neuve*. Introduction, chronologie, notes et index par Roland Le Huenen (Paris: Aux Amateurs de Livres, 1989).

27. Ibid., 58.

28. Portes, *La France*, 90.

29. Gobineau, *Voyage*, 57. Un tableau signé «J. Rallier», peint vraisemblablement vers 1850, et conservé à la galerie d'art de la University College of Cape Breton, à Sydney, confirme en tout point la description de Gobineau. La résidence originale ayant été détruite par un incendie, Bourinot se construira une autre vaste demeure mais moins impressionnante, qui existe toujours, aux numéros civiques 156–58 Esplanade, à Sydney. Voir Debra McNabb / Lewis Parker, *Old Sydney Town, Historic Building of the North End* (Sydney, N.-É., Old Sydney Society, 1986).

30. Cité par Brian Tennyson, ed., *Impressions of Cape Breton* (Sydney, University College of Cape Breton Press, 1986), 148–49.

31. Georges-Charles Cloué (1817–1889), vice-amiral et ministre de la marine dans le ministère Ferry.

32. Camille-Adalbert-Marie, baron Clément de la Roncière Le Noury (1813–1881), vice-amiral puis sénateur. Il avait commandé la station navale de Terre-Neuve en 1855.

33. J. G. Bourinot, *Historical and Descriptive Account*, 111.

34. Gobineau, *Voyage*, 77-78.

35. Nicholas Dennys, *An Account of the Cruise of the St George on the North American and West Indian Stations During the Years 1861–1862* (London: Saunders, Otley and Co., 1862), cité dans Tennyson, ed., *Impressions of Cape Breton*, 141.

36. John George Bourinot, «Notes of a Ramble Through Cape Breton», *New Dominion Monthly* (mai 1868), cité par Tennyson, ed., *Impressions of Cape Breton*, 157.

37. Portes, *La France*, 161–62.

38. Richard John Uniacke, cité dans Tennyson, ed., *Impressions*, 149.

39. Cette chanson composée par la reine Hortense, mère de l'empereur, était devenue l'hymne national officieux de la France du IIe Empire.

40. Nicholas Dennys, cité dans Tennyson, ed., *Impressions*, 139.

41. «Voyage du prince Napoléon aux États-Unis et au Canada», *Revue des Deux Mondes* (15 septembre 1933): 241–71, (1er octobre 1933): 549–87.

42. Maurice Sand, *Six mille lieues à toute vapeur*, préface de Geroge Sand (Paris: Michel Lévy, 1862). Sur le voyage au Canada de Maurice Sand, lire Robert Prévost, «Maurice Sand, l'un de nos premiers touristes», *La France des Québécois* (Montréal: Stanké, 1980), 255–58.

43. Cité par Robert Sylvain, «La visite du Prince Napoléon au Canada (1861)», *Mémoires de la Société royale du Canada*, tome ll : quatrième série : juin 1964, première section, 114–15.

44. Bourinot, *Historical and Descriptive Account*, 111.

45. Faucher de Saint-Maurice, *En Route . . . Sept Jours dans les Provinces Maritimes*, 1888 réédition par les Éditions du Grebbe, Saint-Pierre et Miquelon, s.d., 75.

46. Paul M. Charbonneau, collaboration de Louise Barrette, *Contre vents et marées, L'histoire des francophones de Terre-Neuve et du Labrador*, Moncton, N.-B., Éditions d'Acadie, 43.

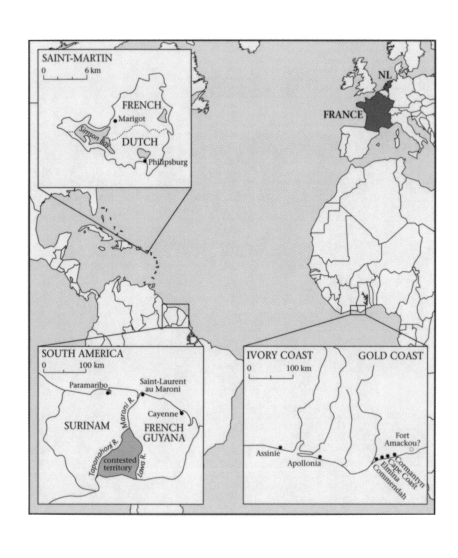

SAINT-MARTIN

0   6 km

FRENCH
•Marigot

Simson Bay

DUTCH

•Philipsburg

NL

FRANCE

SOUTH AMERICA

0   100 km

Paramaribo
•

Saint-Laurent
au Maroni
•

Maroni R.

Cayenne
•

SURINAM

FRENCH
GUYANA

Tapanahoni R.

contested
territory

Lawa R.

IVORY COAST   GOLD COAST

0   100 km

Fort
Amackou?

Assinie
•

Apollonia
•

Cormantyn
Cape Coast
Elmina
Commendah

Franco-Dutch Colonial Rivalry in the Nineteenth Century: Three Projects for French Contiguity

Louis Sicking

Dans l'historiographie des empires coloniaux au XIXe siècle, les relations entre les Français et les Hollandais ont été largement négligées. Le présent document vise à contribuer à l'étude de ces relations en analysant trois projets entrepris par des administrateurs coloniaux français dans l'intention d'étendre les possessions territoriales de la France en terre hollandaise, plus particulièrement à Saint-Martin, île située dans la mer des Antilles (1843–1853), au Ghana (1867–1871), et en Amérique du Sud, entre la Guyane française et le Suriname (1887–1891). Le document étudie les motivations des administrateurs français, et évalue dans quelle mesure ils ont réussi à faire endosser leurs projets par le gouvernement de la métropole. Il analyse le rôle des groupes de pression et les réactions des Hollandais, qui, en tant que puissance plus petite, ont trouvé particulièrement difficile de résister à la France. Les trois projets sont comparés selon le modèle de contiguïté établi par R. F. Betts.

In the historiography of the colonial empires in the nineteenth century, much attention has been paid to the large European powers of Great Britain and France. When the Dutch colonial empire is studied in an international context it is mostly in relation to the British empire. Little or no attention has been given by scholars to Franco-Dutch colonial relations. This gap is surprising given the fact that after Great-Britain, France and the Netherlands were the second and third largest colonial empires. In this paper nineteenth-century Franco-Dutch colonial relations will be discussed only as far as contiguous regions are concerned. The relations between the Dutch East Indies (Indonesia) and Indochina, although interesting, will be left aside. Three Franco-Dutch colonial frontiers existed: in South America between French Guyana and Surinam, in the Caribbean on the island of St. Martin, and in Africa for some years on the Gold Coast. In each of these regions French colonial administrators sought to extend French territory at the expense of the Dutch. Three cases or projects of Franco-Dutch rivalry arose from French pressure: on St. Martin from 1843 to 1853, on the Gold Coast from 1867 to 1871, and in South America from 1887 to 1891. What were the motives of the French administrators and how effectively did they exert pressure on the metropolitan government in order to effect their schemes? What was the role of interest groups? And finally how did the Netherlands react? Being a small European power, was it able to resist the French?

The three cases will be compared using the model of "contiguity," defined by R.F. Betts as the extension of power from existing positions to neighboring territories.[2] They will be compared in the general context of the transition from the so-called "reluctant" imperialism in the first two-thirds of the nineteenth century to the "New Imperialism" after 1880. This paper is largely based on research of archival materials deposited in the *Centre des Archives d'Outre-Mer*, at Aix-en-Provence, and on publications of Dutch sources containing most of the relevant information from the Dutch perspective. The consulted documents shed new and interesting light on the largely neglected relations between two major colonial empires in the nineteenth century.

ST. MARTIN, 1843–1853

The island of St. Martin, one of the Lesser Antilles, was discovered by Columbus in his second voyage to the Americas. By the 1630s the Dutch and the French had settled this island, so lucrative because of its salt deposits, and in 1648 concluded an agreement stipulating the division of the island. No further treaties seem to have been concluded to change the division. Nevertheless, in the middle of the nineteenth century, some French colonial administrators took a special interest in St. Martin when they recognized possibilities to alter the existing situation in favor of France. Why and under which circumstances did the interest for St. Martin increase?

In March 1842, Guizot, Minister of Foreign Affairs gave his famous speech in the Chamber of Deputies, where he renounced territorial acquisitions. Instead, he felt France should limit its ambitions to occupying strategic points (*points-d'appui*) across the world, thus protecting French maritime and commercial interests.[3] Guizot's speech was moderate and did not imply a complete abandonment of colonial expansion. A margin remained for projects to be initiated by passionate colonials. In this context the plan of Rear Admiral De Moges, commander of the French Antilles naval force in its attempt to annex the Dutch part of St. Martin must be understood. In a letter to the Ministry of Naval and Colonial Affairs dated 22 January 1843, De Moges laid out his ideas about St. Martin, which was an administrative dependency of Guadeloupe.[4] He stressed the strategic potential of St. Martin, from which several British islands could be controlled. In times of war the island could be used as a port of call, especially the port of Philipsburg, the capital of the Dutch part of the island, which was sufficient for military purposes. Its harbor allowed for large vessels and was defensible. The rear-admiral went on to present a few suggestions regarding the improvement of naval facilities and the defense of St. Martin as a key strategic point.

De Moges realized, however, that any strategic plan for the colony would be impossible to execute as long as St. Martin remained divided between France and the Netherlands. French defensive measures would be useless if the Dutch did not take similar action. In continuing the *status quo*, there was a risk of a surprise attack. In order to turn the strategic potential of St. Martin to its advantage, France had to become its sole proprietor. The French annexation of the Dutch part of the island, considered a *sine qua non* for development of a French naval base, is an example of a proposal for contiguity.

The minister of Naval and Colonial Affairs, Roussin, was pleased with the scheme. He asked his colleague in Foreign Affairs to gauge the disposition of the Dutch government on the matter of a Dutch cession of St. Martin.[5] The *Quai d'Orsay* did not believe the moment to be right. France had already caught the attention of foreign nations by its recent colonial acquisitions, and the French coffers had been emptied by these excursions.[6] Roussin's successor at Naval and Colonial Affairs acknowledged the situation and advanced yet another reason to abandon the annexation project: it would add a number of slaves to the colonial population. This change, in return, would increase the problems posed by the issue of the emancipation of slaves.[7] In this way, the plan to bring St. Martin under complete French sovereignty seemed to have run its course.

A few years later the same question led to a reappraisal of the original plan in the Ministry of Naval and Colonial Affairs. The establishment of the Second Republic in 1848 led to the complete and immediate abolition of slavery in all French colonies. St. Martin sugar planters complained about the consequences to their little colony of the abolition of slavery and claimed to have suffered more than planters in other colonies. The fact that the island was divided between two powers was the source of these complaints. The recently liberated slaves left for the Dutch part of the island to work in the rich salt mines, leaving the French planters of sugar without a labor force.[8] According to the planters there was but one remedy: the acquisition of the Dutch part, either by purchase or in exchange for a part of French Guyana. Beyond that, the proprietors of the sugar plantations stressed the economic importance of the salt deposits, which were mainly situated on the Dutch side. If France became the sole occupant of the entire island, the exploitation of the salt deposits would give St. Martin a new impetus. By presenting their plan in a petition, addressed to the French parliament, the planters sought to put pressure on the homeland government and arouse governmental interest.[9]

The abolition of slavery in the French part of St. Martin also affected the Dutch neighbors, for it encouraged slaves to escape.[10] A first escape, which occurred in June 1849, is indicative of the judicial friction of the two colonial powers. A French fisherman, John Tacklin, who was fishing with his two assistants in the jointly owned Simson Bay, was arrested by Dutch authorities. One of his two assistants was a Dutch maroon named Samuel, who was jailed.[11] The commander of French St. Martin considered Tacklin's boat as having been in French territory and thus considered the arrest of the *"citoyen"* Samuel as a violation of international law. When he protested to the Dutch governor of the island, The latter defended the arrest by pointing out that Samuel was a runaway slave and the property of an inhabitant of Dutch St. Martin.[12]

The matter became more thorny when the governor of Guadeloupe informed the Minister of the Naval and Colonial Affairs of the situation. The Minister replied that the principle of emancipation by the soil should be applied, a notion which implied that any slave touching French territory was to be automatically emancipated. Hence, there could be no question of granting claims for the restitution of slaves who fled from the Dutch part of St. Martin. The affair of Samuel must have been shelved by the French, as the Guadeloupe administration had not been able to prove that the maroon had either been on board or had in any way touched French territory. Apart from this case, the escape of slaves from the Dutch to the French side of St. Martin had essentially become a Dutch problem.[13]

The Dutch problems with the maroons seemed to offer the perfect opportunity for a French acquisition. A short column in the *Journal du Havre* of 3 November 1849 announced that there had been talk of a cession of the Dutch part of St. Martin to France. The Dutch had had great difficulties in keeping the slaves on their territory due to abolition in the French part of the island.[14] The governor of Guadeloupe, Aubry-Bailleul, was convinced of the economic opportunities of the island offered by its salt resources and considered the recent entanglements to be the perfect excuse for the acquisition of Dutch St. Martin. The Netherlands would be relieved of the problem only if they were to proclaim the liberty of their slaves. That move would in turn cause upheaval in other Dutch colonies. The French governor believed that the annexation could be realized in exchange for the cost of all the Dutch slaves. Finally, Aubry-Bailleul suggested that a company could be set up to exploit the salt deposits and pay the compensation to the Dutch slave owners.[15]

In April 1853, the French Minister of Naval and Colonial Affairs, Théodore Ducos, informed his colleague at the *Quai d'Orsay* that circumstances for the acquisition of Dutch St. Martin were favorable. In the following months, however, the potential viability of the proposal vanished as circumstances changed. Various newspapers announced the preparation of the emancipation of slaves in the Dutch colony of Surinam, and it was expected that slavery in Dutch St. Martin would be simultaneously abolished.[16] Therefore, Minister Ducos guessed, the Netherlands was unlikely to be in favor of ceding its colony.[17] Despite the rumors about abolition, slavery would exist in the Dutch colonies until 1863, but the Dutch inhabitants of St. Martin learned that the emancipation on the French side no longer encouraged slaves to flee. After 1853 there was no French hope for a cession of Dutch St. Martin.

Moreover, the possibilities for the exploitation of salt appeared to be less promising than Aubry-Bailleul had thought.[18] No company had been founded, and information coming from St. Pierre and Miquelon was even worse. The commander of the islands wrote to Ducos that salt from St. Martin was insignificant in volume and inferior in quality. It was therefore no surprise in December 1853, that circumstances no longer favored the development of plans for the acquisition of Dutch St. Martin. The subject was considered closed.[19]

To summarize, where originally the Ministry of Naval and Colonial Affairs was interested in the strategic and economic possibilities of the island of St. Martin, it turned out that unforeseen circumstances finally determined the end of the project for contiguity proposed in 1843. Neither in 1843 nor in 1853 did the Ministry of Foreign Affairs consider that the appropriate moment had arrived to approach the Dutch government about the cession of its part of St. Martin. The abolition of slavery on St. Martin played a major role since, among other reasons, the project was abandoned to avoid the addition of more slaves to the colonial population of France. Paradoxically, the project became current again after the abolition of slavery in 1848. France hoped to benefit from the problems of the Dutch administration on the island caused by the escape of its slaves to the French part. The rumor of the emancipation of Dutch slaves put an end to the project of contiguity at St. Martin. The partition of the island between France and the Netherlands persists until the present day and seems still to be satisfactory.

THE GOLD COAST, 1867–1871

Europeans established a large number of forts for the slave trade on the Gold Coast between the Assinie and Volta rivers. The forts helped create a complex territorial situation in the region during the nineteenth century. After the abolition of the slave trade, the Dutch and the British, who had erratic establishment patterns, felt the need to swap some of their forts and the surrounding areas to create more compact land holdings. After negotiations had dragged on for ten years, a treaty was finally concluded on 5 March 1867. It stipulated that the eastern part of the coast was to be allotted to Great Britain and the western part to the Netherlands.[20] As a consequence of the exchange of territories between the two powers, the Dutch became the neighbors of France, which held possessions on the Ivory Coast. During the ultimate negotiations for the Anglo-Dutch exchange, the French became interested and hoped to benefit from the fact that a weaker power, that is the Netherlands, was to become its neighbor in Apollonia, the western most territory to be exchanged. How did the French want to benefit from the Anglo-Dutch swap and what were its consequences?

The exchange treaty had implications for France, in that Britain and France ceased to be neighbors on the Gold Coast. As a consequence, a French plan proposed by Louis Faidherbe, governor of Senegal in 1864, became highly improbable. This plan entailed an exchange of the insignificant French possessions of Assinie and Grand-Bassam on the Ivory Coast for the rich British colony of Gambia, which was completely surrounded by the French colonies of Senegal and Casamance.[21] The British would never have exchanged Apollonia with the Dutch, had they been interested in the contiguous French territory of Assinie, as the French Minister of Naval and Colonial Affairs remarked in 1867.[22]

Realizing the negative consequences of the Anglo-Dutch exchange for the French plan, Rear Admiral Fleuriot de Langle, commander of the French Naval Forces along the West-African coast, understood the opportunities for expansion of French influence on the Gold Coast. According to the rear-admiral, France could lay claim to the old abandoned fort of Amackou, originally founded by the French in the eighteenth century, and situated between Cormantyn and Tamtamquerry, in a region which had become British, France could try to obtain Apollonia in exchange for Amackou. Thus Fleuriot de Langle hoped to intervene in the Anglo-Dutch exchange.[23]

The French Minister of Naval and Colonial Affairs was enthusiastic about the proposition and informed his colleague at Foreign Affairs, who was reticent as Apollonia had already been placed under Dutch sovereignty. The swap was unlikely to be accepted by the Dutch government in The Hague.[24] Fleuriot de Langle, however, was not discouraged and continued to plan the enhancement of French authority in the region. In December 1867, he presented to the Ministry of Naval and Colonial Affairs the results of an expedition to Amackou, where the memory of French presence was still vivid, and where the indigenous population in Amackou appeared to welcome the return of the French flag. The rear admiral developed several plans for the exchange of Amackou. If Britain could be asked to suspend the ratification of the Anglo-Dutch exchange treaty, it would then be possible to exchange Amackou for Apollonia. Another possibility envisaged by Fleuriot de Langle was the exchange of the French possessions on the Gold Coast, including Amackou, for Gambia. In spite of the doubts formulated by the *Quai d'Orsay*, Fleuriot de Langle suggested that, should British reactions to these propositions be negative, it might be possible to negotiate the Amackou-Apollonia exchange with the Dutch. The rear-admiral was optimistic about the economic developments in the region. He had, for example, heard that the Dutch company of Bouwman, Van Ryckevorssel and Co. in Assinie had sold merchandise worth up to 20,000 francs within two weeks. Accordingly, Fleuriot de Langle insisted that French trade in Apollonia should not be hindered.[25]

Paris, however, did not share his optimism and found the French claims to Amackou too vague. After 1868, no more mention was made of the exchange plans. When his projects were rejected, Fleuriot de Langle had to negotiate with the Dutch governor at Elmina, Nagtglas, in order to determine the border separating Assinie and Apollonia. The French rear-admiral was pleased to hear that the Dutch were willing to accept any French proposition. On 13 November 1869 an agreement on the frontier was concluded. Since no official ratification took place, the agreement was never registered in the form of a diplomatic protocol.[26] In any case, this European attempt at establishing a demarcation line became less important than the reaction of the indigenous peoples.

Since the African peoples on the Gold Coast had not been consulted about the Anglo-Dutch treaty of 1867, their first response is dated 1868, after the exchange of the forts had become official. The peoples concerned were the Fanti and the Asante.[27] The former were allies of the British, the latter of the Dutch. Four Dutch forts were ceded to the British without any problems, but difficulties arose when the Dutch authorities wanted to take possession of the four forts.

The inhabitants of Commendah refused to acknowledge Dutch authority and were prepared to fight. They ignored a Dutch ultimatum, and the Dutch then launched a bombardment that completely destroyed the fort and the town. After this violent attack, the Fanti organized a movement to assist the people of Commendah in their struggle against the Dutch. This so-called Fanti Confederation formed an army that from May, 1868 onwards blockaded Elmina, the main town of the Dutch possessions on the Gold Coast.[28] The inhabitants of Elmina supporting the Dutch were hoping for help from the

Asante, but the Asante leader, the Ashantehene Kofi Kakari, considered any concentration of military power by the Fanti Confederation, south of his own sphere of influence, as a threat. He therefore wanted to restrain Fanti expansion and decided to liberate Elmina. To this end he sent his relative Akyempon Yaw at the head of an expedition to the Dutch possessions.[29] When attempts by the British and the Dutch to broker peace failed, war between the Fanti and the Asante appeared to be inevitable.

Since the roads leading to the coast were closed by the Fanti, Akyempon was obliged to make a westward detour through the territory of Amatifu, king of the Sanwi and ally of France. France at first refused passage for it wanted to maintain strict neutrality and feared absorption of the Sanwi by the powerful Asante. Two weeks later the French changed their minds, realizing that a refusal could be interpreted as an offense to the Asante. The fact that the French rear-admiral in the region wanted to please his Dutch neighbors, who were awaiting Asante assistance, was of secondary importance.[30]

Although the Dutch arrival in Apollonia took place without problems, the situation remained unstable. Before, in 1866, the British governor at Cape Coast had stated that it would be a blessing to put the Apollonians under Dutch protection, for they had been disobedient to British rule. This attitude was one of the reasons for which the British agreed to the exchange in 1867.[31] The governor did not exaggerate. In 1869, a civil war broke out as a consequence of the rivalry between Amakye and Afou, the pretenders of the Apollonian throne. The former was supported by the Asante, the latter by the Fanti Confederation; Amakye was loyal to the Dutch and Afou to the English. The Dutch commandant of the ruined fort of Apollonia was unable to assert himself and was finally obliged to leave after the Fanti got the upper hand. Amakye fled to Sanwi where he waited for Asante assistance.[32] The situation became more and more problematic. Even after the death of Afou in 1870 the civil war in Apollonia continued. Neither Amakye nor the Dutch dared to penetrate Apollonia. Meanwhile the Asante alarmed Amatifu by trying constantly to extend their power to the coast. Fleuriot de Langle's successor, Rear Admiral Bourgois, feared sooner or later the Asante would invade Apollonia and the Sanwi region.

The French and Dutch presence on the Gold Coast became untenable. The French, whose influence in the region was based on the alliance with the Sanwi, were unable and unwilling to guarantee protection in case of an Asante or Apollonian attack. On the advice of Bourgois, Paris decided to evacuate the Gold Coast in 1870, a decision precipitated by the loss on the battlefield to Germany in September of the same year. Preserving its sovereign rights in Assinie and Grand-Bassam, France put Amatifu in charge of protecting the remaining French merchants. On 24 January 1871, the evacuation was completed and thus ended the Franco-Dutch proximity on the Gold Coast.[33]

The decision of the Dutch to leave their African possessions to Great Britain came a little later. The Dutch withdrawal from the Gold Coast in 1872, which was essentially precipitated by indigenous African rivalry,[34] may be understood in the broader context of Dutch colonial policy, which was concentrated on maintaining its empire in South East Asia. In return for the Dutch possessions on the Gold Coast, the British gave the Dutch a free hand in Sumatra.

The Anglo-Dutch exchange treaty of 1867 put an end to French projects to exchange its possessions on the Ivory Coast for the British colony of Gambia. For the French administrator, Fleuriot de Langle, the impossibility of acquiring Gambia justified a French reaffirmation on the Gold Coast. France could try to benefit from the fact that the Netherlands, a weaker power than Great Britain, had become its neighbor. This idea was the basis for the projects presented by Fleuriot de Langle to obtain Apollonia, contiguous to the French possession of Assinie. Although the Ministry of Naval and Colonial Affairs was interested, the Ministry of Foreign Affairs was not and the project was abandoned. The similarity between this case and the metropolitan response to the St. Martin question is remarkable.

If the Anglo-Dutch exchange treaty of 1867 was at the root of both the Franco-Dutch "neighborliness" on the Gold Coast and the French plan for the acquisition of Apollonia, the African reaction to the treaty led to the departure of both the French and the Dutch. The fact that France was a major European power and the Netherlands a small one was irrelevant in this case.

FRENCH GUYANA AND SURINAM, 1887–1891

Both French Guyana and Surinam (Dutch Guyana) were territories of long-standing but largely coastal colonization. Since the colonies were covered by forests, penetration into the hinterland was difficult. The Maroni River formed the border between the two colonies, but when the Lawa and the

Tapanahoni Rivers were discovered to be forks of the Maroni, the question became which one of the two should be considered the borderline. After the discovery of gold in the region between the two rivers, the question became even more crucial at the end of the 1880s. How did the French government respond to the pressure of the gold seekers? How did the Dutch government react? And finally, how was it possible that a major power like France accepted arbitration as a means to settle the question? The borderline dispute took place during the so-called New Imperialism, that is, the period from 1880 to 1914. The most apparent phenomenon of imperialism in these years was the partition of Africa, and the border dispute concerning the two Guyanas took place in the margin of this "Scramble for Africa".

Between 1886 and 1887, the government of French Guyana received the first demands from prospectors for gold mine concessions in the disputed region. Disregarding a governmental refusal, gold seekers continued to explore the region. This activity drew the attention of the Surinam governor, who complained to his French colleague in Cayenne. Meanwhile, French gold seekers demanded that the Ministry of Naval and Colonial Affairs protect their interests and the delimitation of the region. This form of pressure succeeded: after the French Ministry of Foreign Affairs was informed of the matter, the latter approached the Dutch government in October 1887.[35]

In addition to the gold seekers, pressure on the French government came from the Boni, escaped slaves from Surinam who had lived independently in the disputed region since the eighteenth century. Although they were willing to accept French authority, they found themselves adversaries of the gold seekers. Their pleas addressed to the governor of French Guyana for protection against the gold seekers were in vain, for Paris made it clear that absolute priority be given to the French gold seekers.[36]

A French proposal to accept provisional exploitation of the auriferous regions was turned down by the Dutch, who argued that the region was not a disputed one, for a joint Franco-Dutch commission had reported in 1861 that the Lawa was the upper course of the Maroni. Hence, it formed the border separating Surinam from French Guyana.[37] The French government, constantly pressed by gold seekers, announced that this commission did not have any authority in the matter. France thus stood by its claims in regard to the disputed territory. The *Quai d'Orsay* pursued a division of the region upon further assurances from the governor of French Guyana, Gerville-

Réache. These assurances entailed that most of the auriferous formations were situated near the Lawa, that is, on the "French side" of the disputed region.[38] After the Dutch had refused to negotiate a partition, France claimed the entire region in June 1888. This move strongly embarrassed the Dutch government in The Hague. The Netherlands, unwilling to submit to "une telle décision autocratique", stood by its earlier position that the Lawa River was the border separating the two colonies. The deadlock was complete.[39]

As time favored the French, who permitted their gold seekers to penetrate the contested territory, the Dutch knew but one way out of the deadlock: submitting the dispute to arbitration. The proposition was to involve the czar of Russia as the arbitrator, because the czar was immensely popular in France at the time. In that way the Dutch showed their good intentions. The czar was in fact the only feasible candidate acceptable to France, which had no objection in principle to arbitration, but preferred a bilateral solution. The shrewd Dutch ambassador in Paris, De Stuers, then managed, in November 1888, to connect the pending question of the Suez Convention ratification with that of the Guyana border dispute. After all, France had broken its promise to the Netherlands regarding support for the latter's demand to be informed in case of exceptional circumstances in the Suez. The French then risked to be compromised by a Dutch refusal to ratify the convention. In exchange for ratification, France accepted arbitration in the boundary dispute.[40]

An agreement about the arbitration was reached between the two nations on 29 November 1888. This promise led to new problems. The Dutch parliament demanded that the power of the arbitrator be limited to the choice between the Lawa or the Tapanahoni as the colonial border, in order to exclude any possibility of a partition. For Paris, however, the Dutch pressure fell away upon the ratification of the Suez Convention. Therefore, there could be no question of any restriction that excluded the desired partition. France subsequently delayed the ratification of the arbitration convention, until it was unconditionally accepted by the Dutch government. Finally, Czar Alexander III was separately approached by the two states.[41]

The czar initially refused to arbitrate because he desired unlimited authority to solve the dispute in a way that he judged fair. This refusal was advantageous to France, which now could take steps to protect its interests in the region between the Lawa and the Tapanahoni. The Dutch, however, were desperate. The Dutch minister of Foreign Affairs, Hartsen, feared an annexation of the disputed territory if arbitration should fail. When France put pressure on the Netherlands to accept the arbitration without further restrictions, the Dutch government saw no other course than to accept the proposition. However, the Dutch realized that acceptance established "an extremely dangerous precedent" for the country with its vast colonial possessions. On 28 April 1890, the two powers concluded a new agreement about the arbitration without any limitation of competence for the arbitrator. This time the czar accepted.[42]

On 25 May 1891, Alexander, in clear terms, assigned the Lawa as the border between Surinam and French Guyana, thus the affair was decided to the advantage of the Netherlands. The Dutch were nevertheless obliged to respect the "bona fide" mining concessions thus far granted by the French government. The Dutch Minister of Colonial Affairs (to whom the affair had been transferred) stated that, although the Netherlands was not obliged to recognize French concessions given on a provisional basis, he desired that the czar's decision be wholly executed and that the French interests be protected.[43]

To realize this decision, a conference was organized in August 1891, in Saint-Laurent au Maroni. The governors of the two colonies agreed that the provisional concessions delivered by French Guyana would be recognized by Surinam. Before the agreement of Saint-Laurent could take effect, it needed to be approved by the colonial states of Surinam and the French government. The latter was satisfied, but opinions in The Hague and Paramaribo varied. Surinam feared that the French would obtain the lion's share of the gold mines. Only after the Surinam governor declared that concessions had been given to the French for approximately 115,000 hectares and that any other solution postponed exploitation of the gold, did the Colonial States accept the agreement. The metropolitan government, however, was glad to be released from the affair.[44]

The attitude of the Netherlands concerning the disputed region in the years 1887–1891 can be understood by the disproportion between the small, politically and militarily insignificant mother country and its immense and prosperous colonial empire. This contradiction completely determined Dutch political and diplomatic conduct. In the era of New Imperialism, support for its most important colony, the Dutch East Indies had first priority. The colonial possessions in the West Indies were considered to be of lesser importance.[45] This attitude did not imply indifference on the part of the Dutch government with regard to colonial Surinam. On the contrary, the tenacity of The Hague during the affair over the Lawa region is remarkable. From the beginning the Netherlands demanded maintenance of the *status quo.* The Dutch refusal to divide the region can not be explained merely by the concentration of gold near the border of French Guyana. The Hague was not interested in gold, as was demonstrated by its broad interpretation of the clause concerning the French concessions in the arbitrated decision. For the Netherlands, its position as a colonial power was at stake. To secure its empire, the small country needed to stand by its terms, or risk losing its importance under pressure from stronger European powers. Therefore, any precedent such as automatic recognition of foreign pretensions needed to be prevented. An acceptance of the French proposition to divide the disputed region would have created this sort of precedent.

Besides, the Dutch government was strongly embarrassed by the French attitude. The Netherlands felt it had been treated as a second-rate power. In colonial matters, the Dutch sought to be recognized as a major power, but they did not have the political or military means to enforce that recognition. That weakness is the reason why the Dutch insisted on arbitration in the border dispute. As only small countries have an interest in seeing the principle of arbitration executed, the Netherlands paradoxically recognized its own position as a second-rate power.[45]

Gold fever was the source of French interest in the Lawa region in the end of the 1880s. For the Ministry of Naval and Colonial Affairs the gold offered an economic justification for expansion in the contiguous region between French Guyana and Surinam. Paris proposed to divide the disputed territory only after it had become clear that the gold-bearing strata were located on the side of French Guyana. The Netherlands refused to negotiate on the basis of a partition. For a small country with such an immense empire, the acceptance of a compromise could create a dangerous precedent that would lead to the loss of colonial possessions. The Dutch avoided a French occupation of the Lawa region because of the diplomatic inventiveness of the Dutch ambassador in France, De Stuers. Thanks to his efforts, France accepted arbitration of the dispute. Nevertheless, the Dutch lost a large part of their advantage when the Dutch parliament hesitated to accept the unlimited competence of the arbitrator. The initial refusal of the czar to accept the role of arbitrator was to the advantage of the French gold seekers, who received provisional concessions from the Governor of French Guyana. In this way, the Dutch government was pressed to accept the arbitration without conditions.

After the czar assigned the Lawa as the border between the two colonies in 1891, the determination of the validity of the provisional French concessions remained the central question for the execution of the arbitrator's decision. In spite of the opposition in Surinam, the attitude of The Hague was characterized by benevolence. In principle, all French concessions were recognized. This satisfied each party. The French gold seekers had access to the auriferous territory, the government in Paris had preserved the economic interests of its subjects, the Dutch government had ended a border dispute with a major European power, and, finally, the gold seekers of Surinam still had enough territory for their activities.

Of the twenty-five concessions obtained by French subjects in 1891 from the government in Paramaribo, only six were renewed in 1892. This renewal was not due to the interpretation of the arbitrator's decision, which had been entirely satisfactory to the French. Gold fever did not lead to the expected gold rush in the formerly disputed region, because the area was difficult, and therefore costly, to reach.[47] As was often the case in the history of imperialism, myth exceeded reality.

COMPARISON AND CONCLUSION

Projects for contiguity were put forward in the three regions considered above. Significantly, in each case the impetus came from the colonies. In the case of St. Martin and the Gold Coast, the initiative was that of the French colonial administrators. In French Guyana, the governor played an important role in attracting the attention of Paris to the importance of extending the colonial territory. The colonial administrators were sometimes supported and stimulated in these projects by interest groups. On St. Martin, French planters forced to abandon sugar cultivation pleaded for the annexation of the Dutch part of the island to develop the production of salt as an alternative means of subsistence. French gold seekers pressed the government in Cayenne and Paris to claim the Lawa region.

In each of the three cases, the Minister of Naval and Colonial Affairs became interested from the start. Each time, contact was established with the Ministry of Foreign Affairs to gauge the attitude of the Dutch government concerning the French ambitions. It was at the *Quai d'Orsay* where the projects for St. Martin and the Gold Coast were rejected. Only in the case of Guyana were French interests considered to be of sufficient importance to provoke a diplomatic question with the Netherlands. Thereafter, it was the Minister of Foreign Affairs who decided the stand that France would adopt during the succeeding phases of the conflict. He accepted arbitration because there arose a more important issue than that of the Guyana border dispute. The interests in the Lawa region were considered to be of secondary importance compared to the interests of France in the Suez convention. From the metropolitan side, it was always the Minister of Foreign Affairs who determined the French position concerning the projects of acquiring contiguous territory coming from overseas. In general, he was less enthusiastic than his colleague at Naval and Colonial Affairs because he had to take into account the diplomatic implications.

Beyond the administrators, interest groups, and the metropolitan government, other parties were involved in these cases. On St. Martin, the maroons escaping from the Dutch part of the island gave the impetus for the second instance for the annexation project. After the Anglo-Dutch exchange treaty, the African peoples on the Gold Coast determined all the subsequent developments which led to the French and Dutch departure. In contrast, in French Guyana gold fever trumped any influence the Boni possessed in the disputed region. Nevertheless, in general, Europeans could not ignore the influence of the indigenous peoples.

French ambitions with regard to Dutch colonial territory brought a reaction from the Netherlands only in the case of Guyana. The projects for contiguity at St. Martin and the Gold Coast were rejected by Paris before the Dutch would have had to make objections. That the authorities in France were not more forceful can be explained by the lack of strong interests in the two regions, for it was not so much the interests of France that generated the enthusiasm of the administrators and the Ministry of Naval and Colonial Affairs as it was the likelihood of achieving the projects at St. Martin and the Gold Coast. The absence of a fixed colonial policy before 1870 also helps explain the negative attitude of Paris. In this regard, the perspective expressed in Guizot's speech about strategic points must be seen as a confirmation of existing colonial practice.

In contrast, the interests of France and the Netherlands that were at stake in Latin America caused a serious diplomatic conflict. Although the interests of the two countries were completely different, their attitudes fit well within the period of the New Imperialism during which the border dispute took place. The French willingness for expansion into the contiguous territory of Guyana was motivated quite simply by the presence of gold. This attitude may be called a classic motivation for imperialism. France was one of the major powers that played an important role in the race for colonies in the period 1880-1914, during which years its empire was vigorously extended. Although the country did not succeed in the case of the Lawa region, the efforts to enhance French Guyana were typical of those during the New Imperialism.

The Dutch attitude in the case of the Lawa region was completely determined by its interest in securing its empire in Asia. For the Dutch there was no question of an active policy to extend their empire. They were aware that they already had to protect more than they could realistically defend, and that they already possessed more than they could exploit. In the Guyana border dispute the Netherlands wanted only to avoid a precedent which could affect its position as one of the major colonial powers in the world. For France, the New Imperialism led to an active colonial policy seeking to extend its empire, where, for the Netherlands the goal was to maintain what it already possessed. One could therefore say that Dutch imperialism in the nineteenth century was motivated only by the imperialism of others.[48] That the question of the boundary dispute between French Guyana and Surinam was settled by arbitration reflects the real balance of power between France and the Netherlands. Arbitration was the only way for the little kingdom to be put in the right. In general, Franco-Dutch colonial relations in the nineteenth century were determined by the imbalance between the two countries in Europe itself. It is for this reason that the Dutch were to do better when following their old principle: *Amicus Galli sed non vicinus.*[49]

NOTES

1. This paper is based on a thesis written under the guidance of Professor Marc Michel for the D.E.A. "*Histoire d'Outre-Mer*" at the University of Provence (Aix-Marseille I). It has been financially supported by the Faculty of Arts of the University of Leiden and the Netherlands Organization for Scientific Research (NWO). I wish to thank Robert Hössen and Frans Koks for correcting the English text.

2. R.F. Betts, *The False Dawn. European Imperialism in the Nineteenth Century. Europe and the World in the Age of Expansion VI* (Minneapolis: University of Minnesota Press, 1975), 81–83. The importance and usefulness of the concept of contiguity has recently been stressed by M. Kuitenbrouwer in "KPM: Macht, markt en ruimte," *Bijdragen en Mededelingen betreffende de Geschiedenis der Nederlanden* 109 (1994): 264.

3. J. Martin, *L'empire renaissant, 1789–1871. L'aventure coloniale de la France* (Paris: Denoël, 1987), 87–88, 291. X. Yacono, *Histoire de la colonisation française. Que sais-je?*, no. 452 (Paris: Presses universitaires de France, 1988), 35. J. Meyer, J. Tarrade, A. Rey-Goldzeiguer, J. Thobie, *Histoire de la France coloniale. I. Des origines à 1914* (Paris: Armand Colin, 1991), 349–50.

4. De Moges to Naval and Colonial Affairs (22 January 1843), Archives Nationales. Centre des Archives d'Outre-Mer, Aix-en-Provence (CAOM), Section d'Outre-Mer (SOM), série Géographique Guadeloupe c88 d617.

5. Naval Affairs to Foreign Affairs (9 June 1843); Naval Affairs to De Moges (29 July 1843) CAOM, SOM, Guadeloupe c88 d617.

6. Recent French acquisitions were Gabon, Grand-Bassam, Assinie, Tahiti, the Marquises and Mayotte. Foreign Affairs to Naval Affairs (10 August 1843), CAOM, SOM, Guadeloupe c88 d617.

7. Naval Affairs to Foreign Affairs (26 September 1843), CAOM, SOM, Guadeloupe c88 d617.

8. In 1844 there were 2,445 slaves on French St. Martin. Guadeloupe and its dependencies in total counted 92,322 slaves that year. Report of the attorney-general on Guadeloupe (15 November 1844) CAOM, SOM, Guadeloupe c259 d1555. For the sugar culture and slavery on Guadeloupe and its dependencies see C. Schnakenbourg, *Histoire de l'industrie sucrière en Guadeloupe aux XIXᵉ et XXᵉ siècles I. La crise du système esclavagiste (1835–1847)* (Paris: L'Harmattan, 1980).

9. Petition of the sugar planters of French St. Martin to the Assemblée nationale législative (1 August 1849), CAOM, SOM, Guadeloupe c88 d617.

10. One can even say that the developments on St. Martin formed an impetus for the abolition movement on the Netherlands Antilles. C. Goslinga, *A Short History on the Netherlands Antilles and Surinam* (The Hague, Boston, London: Martinus Nijhoff, 1979), 135. For the slavery and its abolition on Dutch St. Martin see A.F. Paula, *"Vrije" slaven. Een sociaal-historische studie over de dualistische slavene-mancipatie op Nederlands Sint Maarten 1816–1863* (Zutphen: Walburg Pers, 1993)

11. Tacklin to the commander of French St. Martin (30 June 1849) CAOM, SOM, Guadeloupe c88 d619.

12. The commander of French St. Martin to the governor of Dutch St. Martin (30 June and 3 July 1849); The Dutch governor to the French commander (2 July 1849), CAOM, SOM, Guadeloupe c88 d619.

13. The governor of Guadeloupe to Naval Affairs (25 July and 26 August 1849); Naval Affairs to the governor Guadeloupe (Paris, 13 July 1849); Naval Affairs to Foreign Affairs (Paris, 28 March 1850), CAOM, SOM, Guadeloupe c88 d619.

14. On the consequences of the abolition on French St. Martin for the Dutch Paula, "Vrije" slaven, 95–98.

15. The governor of Guadeloupe to Naval Affairs (25 February 1850), CAOM, SOM, Guadeloupe, c88 d617.

16. These rumors were a consequence of the establishment in 1853 of a Dutch commission that had to do proposals on the preparation of the abolition in the Dutch West Indies. C. Fasseur, "Suriname en de Nederlandse Antillen, 1795–1914," *Overzee. Nederlandse koloniale geschiedenis, 1590–1975* (Haarlem and Bussum: Fibula-Van Dishoeck, 1982), 196. Paula, "Vrije" slaven, 137–41.

17. Naval Affairs to Foreign Affairs (30 April 1853) and to the governor of Guade-loupe (Paris, 10 October 1853) CAOM, SOM, Guadeloupe c88 d617.

18. On the production of salt on French St. Martin: Y. Monnier, *"L'immuable et le changeant," étude de la partie française de Saint-Martin. Iles et archipels I* (Bordeaux: Talence 1983), 42–45. A. F. Perrinon, partisan of Victor Schoelcher, played an important role in the development of the salt exploitation on French St. Martin. J. Adelaide-Merlande, "Perrinon: La Guadeloupe et Saint-Martin," *Cahiers de la fondation Schoelcher* II (without date), 4–11. A.F. Perrinon, "Résultats d'expériences sur le travail des esclaves," *Annales maritimes et coloniales* 32, 3rd serie, vol. III, IInd section: *Revue Coloniale* (1847), 477–490. CAOM, SOM, Guadeloupe c4 d45.

19. The governor of Guadeloupe to Naval Affairs (19 November and 27 December 1853); The commander of St. Pierre and Miquelon to Naval Affairs (8 July 1853), CAOM, SOM, Guadeloupe c88 d617.

20. A. van Dantzig, "Le traité d'échange de territoires sur la Côte de l'Or entre la Grande Bretagne et les Pays-Bas en 1867," *Cahiers d'études africaines* 13, vol. 4 (1963) first cahier, 69–97.

21. B. Schnapper, *La politique et le commerce français dans le Golfe de Guinée, de 1838 à 1871*. Le monde d'outre-mer passé et présent, 1st serie Études XI (Paris and The Hague: Mouton, 1961), 241.

22. Naval Affairs to Foreign Affairs (5 August 1867) and to Rear-admiral Dauriac (19 December 1867), CAOM, SOM, Ministère des Colonies, Gabon I/7a.

23. Fleuriot de Langle to the Minister of Naval Affairs (4 May 1867), CAOM, SOM, Afrique IV/15b. J. N. Matson, "The French at Amoku," Transactions of the Gold Coast and Togoland Historical Society I section II (1953), 47–61.

24. Naval Affairs to Fleuriot de Langle (20 June 1867), CAOM, SOM, Gabon I/6a. Foreign Affairs to Naval Affairs (6 July 1867), CAOM, SOM, Afrique IV/15b.

25. Fleuriot de Langle to Naval Affairs (10 and 27 September, and 30 December 1867) CAOM, SOM, Gabon I/6b. Schnapper, *Politique*, 212.

26. Fleuriot de Langle to Naval Affairs (28/30 November 1869) CAOM, SOM, Gabon I/7c. Naval Affairs to Foreign Affairs (16 January 1874) Gabon XV/4.

27. W. E. F. Ward, *A History of the Gold Coast* (London: Allen & Unwin, 1948), 231. The most recent study of the Asante in the nineteenth century is R.B. Edgerton, *The Fall of the Asante Empire* (New York: The Free Press, 1995).

28. Van Dantzig, "Traité," 96. Ward, *Gold Coast*, 232–34. Rear-admiral Dauriac to Naval Affairs (22 July 1868), CAOM, SOM, Gabon I/7c.

29. H. M. Feinberg, "Who are the Elmina?," *Ghana Notes and Queries* 11 (1970/71): 20–26. R. Baesjou, ed., *An Asante Embassy on the Gold Coast. The Mission of Ak-yempon Yaw to Elmina, 1869–1872*. African social research documents 11 (Leiden and Cambridge: African Studies Centre, 1979), 16, 28. Ward, *Gold Coast*, 236.

30. Dauriac to Naval Affairs (22 July and 22 September 1869); Dauriac to the commander of Assinie (October 7, 1869), CAOM, SOM, Gabon I/7c.

31. D. Coombs, *The Gold Coast, Britain and the Netherlands, 1850–1874* (London: Oxford University Press, 1963), 42.

32. Van Dantzig, "Traité," 95. Baesjou, *Asante Embassy*, 15–16, 33–35. Rear-admiral Bourgois to Naval Affairs (29 June 1870 and 20 February 1871) CAOM, SOM, Gabon I/9b.

33. Rear-admiral Bourgois to Naval Affairs (20 February 1871) CAOM, SOM, Gabon I/9b. Schnapper, *Politique*, 253. P. Atger, *La France en Côte d'Ivoire de 1843 à 1893. Cinquante ans d'hésitations politiques et commerciales* (Dakar: Université de Dakar, 1962), 61.

34. M. Kuitenbrouwer, *Nederland en de opkomst van het moderne imperialisme. Koloniën en buitenlandse politiek 1870–1902* (Amsterdam and Dieren: De Bataafsche Leeuw, 1985), 43–47, 54.

35. The governor of French Guyana to Naval Affairs (21 October 1887), CAOM, SOM, série géographique Guyane c39 d3(03); the governor of Surinam to the governor of French Guyana (30 June 1886) Guyane c39 d3(04); A. Vitalo to Naval Affairs (2 July 1887); Naval Affairs to the governor of French Guyana (9 July 1887), Guyane c171/6. Kuitenbrouwer, *Nederland*, 95.

36. Grand Man Anato to the governor of French Guyana (2 January 1887, 25 April 1888, 14 January 1889), CAOM, SOM, Guyane c39 d3(04–06); Naval Affairs to the governor of French Guyana (9 July 1887); Foreign Affairs to Naval Affairs (22 January 1889), Guyane c171/6. R. Price, *The Guiana Maroons. A Historical and Bibliographical Introduction* (Baltimore and London: Johns Hopkins University Press, 1976)

37. The governor of French Guyana to the governor of Surinam (16 August 1886), CAOM, SOM, Guyane c39 d3(04). Foreign Affairs Netherlands (NL) to French ambassador in The Hague (15 October 1887), Guyane c39 d3(05). J. Woltring, ed., *Bescheiden betreffende de buitenlandse politiek van Nederland, 1848–1919. Tweede periode, 1871–1898*, vol. 4, 1886-1890. Rijks Geschiedkundige Publicatiën (RGP) Grote Serie 126 (The Hague: Martinus Nijhoff, 1968), 202–4.

38. French ambassador in The Hague to Foreign Affairs (NL) (29 February 1868); Foreign Affairs to Naval Affairs (30 March 1888); the governor of French Guyana to Naval Affairs (31 May and 2 June 1888), CAOM, SOM, Guyane c39 d3(05).

39. Woltring, *Bescheiden*, 307, 331–36.

40. Ibid., 307, 311, 321–24, 381–83, 388–90, 392–94, 403–6.

41. Foreign Affairs to Naval Affairs (6 December 1888 and 13 March 1889), CAOM, SOM, Guyane c39 d3 (05) and (06). Woltring, *Bescheiden*, 382, 395–96, 415, 560–61, 607–09.

42. Foreign Affairs to Naval Affairs (30 January 1890 and February 1890), CAOM, SOM, Guyane c39 d3(07). Woltring, *Bescheiden*, 603–4, 624, 631–32. Kuitenbrouwer, *Nederland*, 96.

43. Woltring, *Bescheiden*, vol. 5 (1891-1919). RGP 132 (The Hague 1970), 158–60.

44. Protocol of the conference at Saint-Laurent (23 August 1891); The governor of French Guyana to Naval Affairs (31 August 1891); Naval Affairs to the governor of French Guyana (12 October 1891); French ambassador in The Hague to Foreign Affairs (8 October 1891), CAOM, SOM, Guyane c40 d3(11). Woltring, *Bescheiden,* 5:188–91.

45. H.L. Wesseling, "Le modèle colonial hollandais dans la théorie coloniale française, 1880–1914," *Revue française d'histoire d'Outre-Mer* 63 (1976): 235. Wesseling, "Les Pays-Bas et le partage de l'Afrique noir: à propos de la conférence de Berlin, 1884–1885," *Études africaines offertes à Henri Brunschwig* (Paris: Éditions de l'École des Hautes Études en Sciences Sociales, 1982), 146. Kuitenbrouwer, *Nederland,* 205–6.

46. Woltring, *Bescheiden,* 4:382.

47. Foreign Affairs to Colonial Affairs (24 December 1894), CAOM, SOM, Guyane c40 d3(11).

48. Wesseling, *Indië verloren, rampspoed geboren* (Amsterdam: Uitgeverij Bert Bakker, 1988), 188–89.

49. Translation: "Friends with the Frenchman [Gaul], but no neighbor."

CHAPTER FIFTEEN

Faidherbe, Lugard, and Africa

Bruce Vandervort

La comparaison des carrières de Louis Faidherbe, conquérant français et gouverneur du Sénégal sous le Second Empire, et de Frederick Lugard, conquérant anglais et gouverneur du Nigéria du Nord au tournant du siècle, révèle que leur choix de servir en Afrique a été dicté par un intérêt personnel semblable. Les deux hommes ont en effet presque la même attitude à l'égard des sociétés africaines qu'ils gouvernent, plus particulièrement en ce qui concerne la traite des esclaves et l'esclavage. Cette comparaison vient appuyer l'école de pensée soutenant que la différence entre les administrateurs anglais et français en Afrique, en ce qui concerne la motivation professionnelle, l'attitude à l'égard des questions raciales et le souci du bien-être des Africains dont ils avaient la responsabilité, est moins importante que certains l'imaginent.

This essay is a by-product of efforts to answer a broad question I have posed to myself in the opening stages of writing a biography of Louis Léon César Faidherbe, governor of the French West African colony of Sénégal from 1854 to 1861 and 1863 to 1865. The purpose of the essay is to compare and contrast the African project of Faidherbe with that of another European proconsul of the imperial age, in this case a well-known Englishman, Frederick Dealtry Lugard. Through a process of comparison we can hope to learn some of the reasons why Europeans like Faidherbe, who were able to choose, decided to devote their energies to Africa rather than to some other corner of empire or, indeed, to affairs at home. I also hope that this undertaking can offer insights into how well the professed idealism of these European proconsuls with respect to, for example, the slave trade and domestic slavery, stood up in the face of their changing perceptions of the African societies over which they ruled.

For purposes of this exercise comparisons will be drawn between Louis Faidherbe and Frederick Lugard, veteran of British campaigns to open up Nyasaland in 1888–89 and Uganda in 1890–92, but best known as the conqueror of Northern Nigeria in 1898–1903 and the governor-general of united Nigeria from 1912 to 1919. Faidherbe has been credited with drawing up the blueprint for the eventual French conquest of the Western Sudan in the 1880s and 1890s, and was the founder in the 1850s of the legendary West African fighting force, the *Tirailleurs sénégalais*.[1] Lugard, meanwhile, quite literally established the style of British imperial governance known as Indirect Rule, with the publication in 1922 of his *Dual Mandate in Tropical Africa*. Lugard's name is also linked with that of a famous West African military unit, the West African Frontier Force of Nigeria.[2]

On the face of it, the comparison being undertaken may strike some observers as pointless. To begin with, there is a generational problem. When Lugard was born in 1858, Faidherbe had in some ways already reached the summit of his powers as governor of Senegal. And 1889, the year of Lugard's first independent command in Africa, in what was to be Nyasaland, was the year of Faidherbe's death. The two men were therefore products of vastly different epochs, or so it would seem. Thus, one of Faidherbe's biographers, Georges Hardy, has made an interesting but in the end not very convincing attempt to portray the young Faidherbe as a Romantic, a utopian dreamer along the lines of Dussardier in Flaubert's *Sentimental Education*.[3] Lugard, on the other hand, is unmistakably, quintessentially, a product of the English Victorian age. His youth was imbued in the sticky religiosity common to that time. Faidherbe's religious background, on the other hand, is probably best described as Voltairean.

The two men also came from very different social backgrounds. Louis Faidherbe's rise is a typical saga of the French provincial middling bourgeoisie. His father, a former sergeant-major in Napoleon's army, died when Louis was young, leaving the family's modest dry goods business in Lille in the care of his wife. Although he was the youngest of five children, Louis happened to be the only boy. Thus, it was decided that the family's hopes for the future would be pinned on him. A period of scrimping and saving and begging favors from influential men ensued, with the result that young Faidherbe, who had shown some aptitude for math and drawing, managed to receive a *demi-bourse* to the prestigious *École Polytechnique* in Paris.[4]

Lugard came of much more genteel stock. Both sides of his family boasted solid roots in the English landed gentry. The Lugards were a soldierly clan, Frederick's grandfather having been an officer in the army of the "Grand Old Duke of York" during the French revolutionary wars, while his father's brother, Gen. Sir Edward Lugard, served as Permanent Under-Secretary of War from 1861 to 1871. Sir Edward had won his spurs during the Indian Mutiny of 1857. Lugard's mother had also been in India during the time of the Mutiny, working as an Anglican missionary. There she met Lugard's father, a missionary clergyman with a pronounced evangelical bent, and there Frederick Lugard was born the year after the Mutiny was crushed.[5]

Some years ago, in an essay entitled "Africa in Britain," Robert O. Collins, a U.S. historian of the Anglo-Egyptian Sudan, drew a particularly pointed contrast between Faidherbe and Lugard and, by extension, between the attitudes of French and British colonial rulers toward their African charges.

> The British were always in Africa, not of it. Inoculated with the values of the English public school and the squirearchy, the class from which they came, their role was to govern, not to mingle, to rule by the fewest means possible by maintaining an aloofness commensurate with their arrogance. By mingling with the "natives" or adopting their culture and life-styles, one destroyed the aura of august authority. The idea of a Sir Reginald Wingate or Sir Frederick Lugard walking down the main street of the colonial capital as did Louis Faidherbe to register and legitimize his African sons, boggles the imagination.[6]

After contemplating this crop of bloodless English Victorians, Collins seemed to be saying what a relief it is to turn to passionate, warmhearted Louis Faidherbe! Faidherbe, the black man's (and black woman's) friend; Faidherbe, who encouraged "Liaisons between European men and full-blooded African women . . . as a means of increasing the links between Europeans and Africans";[7] Faidherbe, the renowned student of African languages and cultures; Faidherbe, the man of "boundless faith in the future of Africa," in the words of Robert Delavignette, the great French colonial administrator and writer on colonial affairs.[8]

There may be, however, less here than meets the eye. The closer look I propose to take at key aspects of the two men's African careers will demonstrate, I think, that Collins's dramatic contrast between Louis Faidherbe and Frederick Lugard, while possessing some validity, is nonetheless misleading. In assessing the two men's motives for undertaking an African commitment, for example, it is Lugard who comes off as the more passionate, although for reasons that at bottom have little to do with Africa or Africans. And a closer examination of their careers also may show that in their evolving attitudes toward their African subjects, the differences between Faidherbe, who served France in the era of the Napoleon III and the Second Empire, and Lugard, who served Victorian Britain during the high noon of its power, were more apparent than real.

Part of the legend of Louis Faidherbe is the claim that he went out of his way to secure a post in Senegal because he liked being among black people and because he wanted to free the people of Senegal from the curse of slavery. The evidence to support this claim comes in the first place from Faidherbe's alleged experiences as a young captain of engineers in Guadeloupe in 1848-49. He appears to have witnessed with great satisfaction the emancipation of the island's slaves and to have participated with much fervor in the successful campaign of the abolitionist leader, Victor Schoelcher, for a seat in the Chamber of Deputies. Legend has it that Faidherbe's behavior so outraged Guadeloupe's planters that they conspired to have him recalled to France.[9] Leland Conley Barrows has convincingly demonstrated that this blacklisting never occurred, although he does concede that the Guadeloupe experience did turn Faidherbe into something of a negrophile.[10] Certainly, Faidherbe never ceased to proclaim himself a disciple of Schoelcher; his last and most ambitious book, *Le Sénégal*, completed just before his death, is dedicated to the great emancipationist. The real story of Faidherbe's choice of a Senegal posting, however, is somewhat more complex.

While a student at the *École Polytechnique*, Faidherbe proved to be fonder of good times than of hard work. He would be remembered best by classmates for his satirical drawings, some of which can still be seen, and for the smutty songs he composed for guitar.[11] The commandant of the *École*, Gen. Vaillant, wrote of Faidherbe: "His bearing is quite good, but his behavior is very dissipated." Faidherbe graduated near the bottom of his class in 1840. The good times continued during Faidherbe's two-year stint at the *École d'Application* for engineers at Metz, where he appears to have accumulated sizable gambling debts.[12] The situation in which the young man found himself in the early 1840s—undistinguished, heavily in debt, and a disgrace to the family that had sacrificed to give him an education—virtually dictated that he seek a colonial posting. Promotions came much more rapidly in the colonies, even for undistinguished officers of modest background. Even more important, officers assigned to the colonies received double pay and extra allowances to compensate for the hardships of colonial service and for the risk of death by combat or, more commonly, by disease.[13] These were bonuses that Faidherbe desperately needed to pay off his gambling debts and to buy his way back into the good graces of his mother. Thus, while one cannot discount entirely Faidherbe's claims of an abolitionist vocation, it seems clear that his request to be assigned to Senegal was largely dictated—as earlier service in Algeria and Guadeloupe had been—by pressing financial need.

The story of Frederick Lugard's choice of an African field of endeavor is just as interesting. Despite his genteel background, Lugard's educational opportunities proved to be much more limited than those of his French *moyen bourgeois* counterpart. To some extent, this difference seems to underscore the salutary aspects of the French Revolution of 1789 in opening up careers to talent. But it may have more to do with the fact that the early death of Lugard's mother proved to be a greater disaster for him than the early loss of Faidherbe's father had been for him. While Madame Faidherbe managed to keep the family business afloat, Lugard's father, the otherworldly clergyman, Frederick Lugard Sr., floundered from one meager living to another, with the result that he could only afford to send his son to a succession of third-rate public schools. It is a tribute to Lugard's basic intelligence that despite this travesty of an education, he managed to place sixth among one thousand candidates taking army officer exams in 1877.

In 1878 Lugard was posted to India with an infantry regiment, the Royal Norfolks. There, he fell madly in love with a spirited young divorcee known to history only as "Celia." On detached assignment in Burma, the young man learned that his beloved had been involved in an accident back in Lucknow. Fearing for her life, he convinced his commanding officer to allow him to return to Lucknow to be with her. When he arrived back in India Lugard discovered that his loved one had taken ship back to England. Those readers who have recognized this story for the Victorian melodrama it is will not be surprised to learn that Lugard, at the risk of his career, sailed for England in search of his "Celia." Unfortunately, in the discreet words of Lugard's biographer, when "upon landing he went straight to her address in London [Lugard] found a different woman, at that very moment engaged in bestowing her affections elsewhere." To make a long story short, Lugard, devastated by the infidelity of the one who would be the one true love of his life, decided to end it all. Being a Victorian officer and gentleman, however, he did not jump into the Thames. Instead, he decided to go to Africa, which, explains Margery Perham,

> had the two main qualifications—it was unknown and dangerous. . . .
> Moreover [Lugard] had not forgotten [Dr. David] Livingstone [his youthful
> hero] and he had an idea, not perhaps yet very clearly defined, that, even if
> he did mean to end his life, he might at least do this in some useful way and
> what could be at once more dangerous and more valuable than some service
> against the slave-trade?[14]

Thus did two of the greatest of Europe's proconsuls march off to their assignments in Africa, one to earn the money to pay off his gambling debts; the other to commit ritual suicide. It was precisely cases such as these which prompted the Nigerian historian A. E. Afigbo to make the harsh judgment that "The conclusion is thus in some respects inescapable that most of the colonial governors needed Africa more than Africa needed them."[15] But what did these two proconsuls, one a product of the early nineteenth century, of the July Monarchy and Second Empire of France, the other of late Victorian England, make of sub-Saharan Africa and its people, the people both had vowed to rescue from slave traders and liberate from domestic bondage? Their mature observations differ surprisingly little, sharing as they do a basic paternalism and poorly disguised contempt for the perceived passiveness and resignation of their African subjects.

First, Lugard. In 1888, he embarked on his first African campaign, an expedition against Arab slave traders on the shores of Lake Nyasa. As he set out, Lugard wrote to his brother, his closest confidant through the years, that "I can think of no juster cause in which a soldier can draw his sword. My chief idea in coming out here was to do my little to aid in stopping the Slave Trade and *this* would be a blow at its very roots."[16] In 1890, in the course of a mission to claim Uganda for a British chartered company, Lugard created an enormous furor by attempting to free the country's many domestic slaves.[17] By the time of his Nigerian campaigns in the late 1890s and early 1900s, however, Lugard's attitude toward African domestic slavery and toward the slave-owners he had battled in the early days had come almost full circle. The reasons for this changed attitude were actually evident as early as 1893, however, as the following quote will demonstrate.

... if we are earnest in our efforts to benefit the slaves, we must be content to accept, as a part of the task the natural apathy of the people, and their indifference to a yoke, which to us would be terribly galling. We must realize that the ties between husband and wife are often of the loosest kind; that a greater affection is said to exist between the sexes (as is often seen among the lower animals); that mothers, and more especially fathers, do not feel so intense a love for their children as Europeans generally do, and hence ruthless separation from relatives or family, though it may involve some grief, cannot be said to be so terrible an ordeal as we should imagine by analogy with our own feelings. . . . [The slave's] apathetic and submissive nature adapts itself to his surroundings, and he often ceases to desire to be free. We must recollect, moreover, that some of those acquired by purchase in the interior are probably the scum of the villages—criminals or loafers, sold to the slavers by their tribesmen for the good of the community.[18]

Although relatively free of the Social Darwinism rampant later in the nineteenth century and evident in some of Lugard's writings, Faidherbe's observations on these matters are no less negative in their racial stereotyping. His biographer, Georges Hardy, wrote that at the outset of his nine-year governorship of Senegal, Faidherbe

proposed very sincerely to free the blacks of Africa from a long past of servitude and to make them not only free men, but men worthy of freedom. He fought stubbornly against slaving practices, so deeply rooted in the life of the country that in spite of the most severe laws against them, they constantly kept cropping up.[19]

Although Hardy and other French writers have drawn a generally laudatory picture of Faidherbe's anti-slavery efforts, it seems clear that he was never as assiduous in fighting domestic slavery or even the slave trade as he liked to claim. Writing in 1875, just a decade after completion of his last term as governor of Senegal, Faidherbe revealed that his declining emancipatory fervor had been prompted by the gradual development of a pessimistic view of African human nature. Africans, he said, were weak-willed and lacking in initiative, "which is why they can be enslaved. One would never think of enslaving Arabs, for they would assassinate their masters." Faidherbe found the cause of this passiveness among blacks in "the relatively weak volume of their brains."[20]

Given this pessimistic judgment of the African character, it may not have been a radical departure for Faidherbe to conclude that perhaps slavery was not such a dire fate for such feckless people after all. By the last years of his life, it must have been evident to Faidherbe that, far from dying out, domestic slavery and even the slave trade were alive and well in the Western Sudan, in the context of the French campaigns of colonial conquest he had done so much to promote.[21] Thus, in the pages of the book that was to be his last will and testament, the book dedicated to the great abolitionist Victor Schoelcher, Louis Faidherbe offered this observation:

> The African blacks, slaves or freemen, in spite of the Moors, slave traders, and the excesses of their own chiefs, are in general happy people. . . . You cannot really compare the lot of the domestic slave in Africa to that of the blacks in the Antilles, even so-called free laborers on the plantations. In Africa, their black masters demand very little of their slaves . . . ; the slaves are treated like members of the family; they speak the language of their masters; they dress almost the same way as they do; and they eat from the same vessel.[22]

In conclusion, it would appear that, whatever may have been their original intentions, the two proconsuls profiled here (and, one suspects, many other European governors in Africa) found it less agreeable to take action against domestic slavery than against the slave trade. The reasons for this may vary, but surely one of them was the concentration on suppressing a commerce in human beings that had done much to compromise the claims of Western civilization to moral superiority. For the same reason, the ownership of slaves by white planters or householders had to be ended as well. But black on black slavery, it seems, was another matter altogether. Its continuance, while distasteful, did not jeopardize white claims of moral hegemony. Rather, it served to underscore growing beliefs in the moral and intellectual inferiority of the black race. Besides, as the careers of Faidherbe and especially Lugard would amply demonstrate, when it was politically expedient to wink at the continuation of African domestic slavery, scruples quickly gave way.

NOTES

1. There is to date no really satisfactory biography of Louis Faidherbe. In French, the standard account remains Georges Hardy, *Faidherbe* (Paris: Editions de l'Encyclopédie de l'Empire Français, 1947). Hardy's biography is marred by its indiscriminate reliance on Faidherbe's autobiographical *Le Sénégal: La France dans l'Afrique occidentale* (Paris: Hachette, 1889). Joseph Emile Froelicher, *Trois colonisateurs: Bugeaud, Faidherbe, Galliéni* (Paris: H. Charles-Lavauzelle, 1903), an attempt to assign Faidherbe a place in the constellation of nineteenth-century French imperial proconsuls, is now hopelessly dated. So is André Demaison, *Faidherbe* (Paris: Plon, 1932). Robert Delavignette, "Faidherbe," in Delavignette and Charles-André Julien, eds., *Les techniciens de la colonisation (XIXᵉ–XXᵉ siècles)* (Paris: Presses Universitaires de France, 1946), 75–92, is only a sketch, although an intelligent one. The closest equivalent to a biography of Faidherbe in English is Leland Barrows' unpublished Ph.D. dissertation, "General Faidherbe, the Maurel and Prom Company, and French Expansion in Senegal" (University of California, Los Angeles, 1974). See also Barrows, "Louis Léon César Faidherbe (1818–1889)," in L.H. Gann and P. Duignan, eds., *African Proconsuls: European Governors in Africa* (New York: Free Press, 1978). The more purely military side of Faidherbe's governorship in Senegal is covered with authority in A.S. Kanya-Forstner's *The Conquest of the Western Sudan: A Study in French Military Imperialism* (Cambridge: Cambridge University Press, 1969).
2. The standard biography of Lugard is Margery Perham, *Lugard*, 2 vols. (London: Collins, 1956–60): volume 1 is subtitled *The Years of Adventure, 1858–1898*; volume 2, *The Years of Authority, 1898–1945*.

3. Hardy, *Faidherbe*, 15–16.

4. Ibid., 9–11.

5. Perham, *Lugard*, l:4–5.

6. Collins, "Africa in Britain," in G. Wesley Johnson, ed., *Double Impact: France and Africa in the Age of Imperialism* (Westport, Conn.: Greenwood Press, 1985), 368. Collins probably exaggerated the number of Faidherbe's Senegalese offspring. Leland Barrows believes that Faidherbe fathered "one and possibly two children by his Sarakholé mistress [actually, common-law wife], Dionkounda Siadibi." Barrows, "Louis Léon César Faidherbe," 68.

7. Barrows, "Louis Léon César Faidherbe," 68.

8. Delavignette, "Faidherbe," 90.

9. Hardy, *Faidherbe*, 19–22.

10. Barrows, "Louis Léon César Faidherbe," 53–54.

11. Ibid., 52.

12. Hardy, *Faidherbe*, 11.

13. Barrows, "Louis Léon César Faidherbe," 52.

14. Perham, *Lugard*, 1:36–42; 39–64.

15. Afigbo, "Men of Two Continents: An Interpretation," in *African Proconsuls*, 530.

16. Quoted in Perham, *Lugard*, 1:104. Lugard's emphasis.

17. Lugard's Uganda foray is described in detail in his own largely autobiographical account, *The Rise of our East African Empire: Early Efforts in Nyasaland and Uganda*, vol. 2 (1893; reprint London: Cass, 1968).

18. Lugard, *The Rise of our East African Empire*, 1:190–91. Lord Lugard's acceptance of the continuation of domestic slavery in restive Northern Nigeria at the turn of the century is documented in Paul E. Lovejoy and J. S. Hogendorn, "Revolutionary Mahdism and Resistance to Colonial Rule in the Sokoto Caliphate, 1905–6," *Journal of African History* 31 (1990): 217–44.

19. Hardy, *Faidherbe*, 75.

20. Faidherbe, *Essai sur la langue peul* (Paris: Société de Géographie de Paris, 1875), 14. Quoted in William B. Cohen, *The French Encounter with Africans: White Response to Blacks, 1530–1880* (Bloomington, Indiana: Indiana University Press, 1980), 231.

21. For a concise account of the difficulties French civilian administrators faced in the late nineteenth century in trying to impose emancipationist codes upon a military which condoned and even profited from slavery, see Martin Klein,

"Slavery and Emancipation in West Africa," in Klein, ed., *Breaking the Chains: Slavery, Bondage, and Emancipation in Modern Africa and Asia* (Madison, Wisconsin: University of Wisconsin Press, 1993), 171–96.

22. Faidherbe, *Le Sénégal,* 385.

CHAPTER SIXTEEN

Cyprian Clamorgan and The Colored Aristocracy of St. Louis

Julie Winch

En 1858, Cyprian Clamorgan, petit-fils né libre d'un voyageur français et d'une esclave antillaise, a écrit un petit ouvrage dans lequel il fait une description de ses amis, de ses ennemis, de ses voisins et de lui-même. The Colored Aristocracy of St. Louis *est un livre remarquable portant sur un groupe de personnes elles-mêmes remarquables. «L'aristocratie colorée», comme on l'appelait, de Saint Louis se composait d'autres descendants de voyageurs comme Clamorgan. Certains avaient gardé leur nom français, tandis que d'autres avaient anglicisé le leur. Leurs ancêtres étaient arrivés plusieurs décennies avant l'achat de la Louisiane. Selon Clamorgan, les «aristocrates colorés» en tant que groupe se considéraient comme différents des immigrants noirs installés à Saint Louis et venus de la Virginie, du Tennessee, de la Caroline du Nord et du Sud et du Kentucky, ainsi également que supérieurs à eux. Certains Anglo-africains, qui sont arrivés plus tard, ont parfois réussi à entrer par mariage dans de vielles familles «françaises». L'attrait de la culture française a toujours été tres grand. Francophones ou anglophones, catholiques ou protestants, enfants de voyageurs français ou de planteurs anglo-americains, les «aristocrates colorés» possédaient un trait en commun : ils savaient que le sang africain qui coulait dans leurs veines les différenciait des Blancs de Saint Louis.*

By 1830 the French colonial outpost of St. Louis had undergone a profound cultural and demographic change. Travelers who had known the city in the days before and immediately after the Louisiana Purchase could see the difference. The old residents were painfully aware of it. The change began slowly after the transfer of Louisiana to the United States, then accelerated after 1821, when statehood brought a flood of migrants from Virginia and Kentucky into Missouri. For many, St. Louis was only a stopping-off point as they registered land purchases or replenished supplies before settling on farms in distant counties of Missouri. For others, the motivation was to trade. Trade had always been the life-blood of St. Louis—in furs with the Native peoples of Upper Louisiana, or down the Mississippi with New Orleans, or with the Spanish Southwest—but the patterns of trade were changing. St. Louis was on its way to becoming a major entrepôt. With rapid commercial growth, ties with the East, and trade, not in furs but in the agricultural produce of the rural hinterland, the end of French cultural dominance arrived.

One could hear the change as well as see it. In 1818, one observer recalled: "The prevailing language of white persons on the streets was French."[1] Such was not the case a decade later. French was still spoken by those who tried "in some degree [to] keep up [the] manners of their native country," but they were fighting a losing battle. The first city directory listed fewer than one-third of households headed by someone with a French name.[2] The French Creoles accepted the inevitable. Some cast their lot with the newcomers, others retreated.

> Many old French families who were fond of a rural life retir[ed] . . . into the country, as facilities for their obtaining a subsistence were daily diminished in the city. The hunters, trappers, bargemen and voyageurs also gradually disappeared as new comers of other occupations acquired their places of residence.[2]

The white Creoles, however, had never accounted for the entire population of the city. From its earliest days St. Louis had numbered among its residents free black men and women, whose numbers rose steadily. The transition from Spanish and French to American rule did not halt their increase, despite the passage of laws designed to prevent the migration of free people from other states and restrict the freedom of those men and women born in Missouri. From 42 *gens de couleur* in 1796 the black population of St. Louis rose to 296 free black inhabitants in 1832, 673 in 1844, 1398 in 1850, and over 1700 by the time of the Civil War. By 1861 the free people of color outnumbered the slaves in the city.[4]

Who were these men and women? Where did they come from? How did they secure their freedom? How did they maintain it in a city where the laws were designed to protect the institution of slavery? Most important, with regard to the present discussion, how did *their* lives change as St. Louis underwent a cultural and economic transformation? How did they weather the change from *gens de couleur* to "free people of color"? How many considered themselves "French," and how many regarded themselves as "Americans," even if they were denied the full enjoyment of the rights of American citizens? Was ethnicity as important to them as it was to their white contemporaries, or did the factor of race unify them more effectively than any other consideration? We will try to answer these questions by analyzing *The Colored Aristocracy of St. Louis*, a remarkable little book written in 1858 by a member of one of the oldest colored Creole families in the city.

The author of *The Colored Aristocracy* was Cyprian Clamorgan, who hinted he had secrets to tell if he chose.

> The free colored people of St. Louis are surrounded by peculiar circumstances.
> Many of them are separated from the white race by a line of division so faint
> that it can be traced only by the keen eye of prejudice—a line so dim indeed
> that, in many instances that might be named, the stream of African blood
> has been so diluted by mixture with Caucasian, that the most critical observer
> cannot detect it.[5]

However, it was not Clamorgan's intention to reveal the African ancestry of "the scions of some of our 'first families'. . . Our business is with those who have the mark unmistakably fixed upon their brows." He waxed lyrical about the origins of what he called the "colored aristocracy."

> When Upper Louisiana was settled by the French and Spaniards, the emigrants
> were necessarily nearly all of the sterner sex. Stem[m]ing the current of the
> Father of the Waters in their light canoes and pirogues, and taking up their
> abode in the wild wilderness, where beasts of prey and prowling savages beset
> them on all sides, they could not bring with them the soft partners of their

bosoms, but left their families in peaceful security at home, while they undertook the task of exploring a continent. But man without woman, even in the wildest state of society, becomes a savage, morose and discontented being. He longs for the endearments of a wife, and sighs for the prattle of children in the solitude of his forest home.[6]

Some "sought wives among the sylvan maids of the forest." Others looked elsewhere.

At that time the blood of Africa had crossed the Atlantic, and the colored race had found a foothold in the West Indies. It was there that many of the *voyageurs* . . . obtained wives to share their fortunes in the wilderness; and from this union have sprung up many of those whom we designate the "colored aristocracy."[7]

Clamorgan cast a rosy glow over the unions of voyageurs and women of color. In truth, many of the unions were the result of coercion and the exercise of the power that the *Code Noir*, no less than the laws of the thirteen English colonies, gave a master over his "chattel personal."[8] Few of the women were accorded the legal status of wives. When their lovers took white wives, as most eventually did, the women of color were generally relegated to the position of concubines. As for their children, they might remain slaves, bound to their white siblings for life. Some did, nonetheless, secure their freedom, and a few amassed wealth, either through inheritance or through their own industry. *They* constituted, as far as Clamorgan was concerned, the "colored aristocracy" of St. Louis.

Not surprisingly, Cyprian Clamorgan placed himself and his relatives firmly in this aristocracy. His grandfather, Jacques Clamorgan, syndic of the Company of the Discoverers and Explorers of the Mississippi, had been a redoubtable presence in St. Louis for decades before his death, at age 80, in 1814. He had struggled to open trade with Santa Fe and dreamed of reaching the Pacific. He had amassed vast land holdings, and made and lost two fortunes. The various administrators charged with the task of governing Upper Louisiana had learned he was a force to be reckoned with. And yet Jacques Clamorgan had never quite been accepted by the "great ones" of St. Louis, the Chouteaus and the Gratiots, the Labbadies and the Laclèdes. This slight occurred because he had flouted the conventions. Instead of taking a white wife, he had chosen to live exclusively with women of color, all of them at one time or another his slaves.[9] He did what he could for his mulatto children, the youngest of whom he fathered at age 73. He had them baptized at the Cathedral of St. Louis, and manumitted them. Given the confused state of his finances at the time of his death, that action was an important consideration. Had Jacques Clamorgan not formally freed his children, his creditors could have sold them as slaves.[10]

Jacques Clamorgan's four children, the offspring of three different women, clung together after their father's death. The eldest, St. Eutrope, went into business as a barber and married Pelagie Baptiste, a young ex-slave who had bought her freedom for $3. When St. Eutrope died, the widowed Pelagie married again. Her second husband was Louis Rutgers, the son of Dutch merchant Arend Rutgers by one of his slaves.[11] The older Rutgers made generous provision for his son, but his generosity was challenged after his death by his two legitimate daughters. According to Cyprian Clamorgan, it was his own half-brother, Louis, who came to the rescue of Pelagie and Louis Rutgers. Thanks to Louis Clamorgan, they retained title to their estate, but they never repaid him. Cyprian Clamorgan did not forgive or forget. In *The Colored Aristocracy* he wrote of Pelagie Rutgers, now a widow for the second time: "Mrs. R. is a member of the Catholic church, but is not noted for her piety; she worships the almighty dollar more than Almighty God."[12]

The author, Cyprian Freyor Clamorgan, was the son of Jacques Clamorgan's only daughter, Apoline.[13] Orphaned, and with limited resources, Apoline Clamorgan had made the best of her situation. In 1818, when she was 15, she bore her first child, fathered by Theodore Papin, a young Creole from a socially prominent family. That child died. Her second son, Louis, was the child of Louis Langon, another white Creole. Henry, born in 1822, was fathered by Irish-American trader Henry Ford. It is not clear who fathered Apoline's youngest son, Cyprian. Like her father before her, Apoline presented each of her children for baptism at the Cathedral of St. Louis and declared to the priest their paternity, but she did not live long enough to arrange for Cyprian's baptism. She died eight days after his birth, in April 1830, and the child's guardian, businessman Charles Collins, kept silent about the identity of Cyprian's father. Perhaps he himself was the child's father.[14]

Apoline left money to educate her sons. Since the schooling of children of color was technically illegal in Missouri, Collins sent Henry, Louis and Cyprian to the nominally free state of Illinois for their education. One by one, they returned and went into one of the few trades available to them, barbering. Perhaps it was with a certain degree of bitterness that Cyprian Clamorgan wrote: "It will doubtless be observed by the reader, that a majority of our colored aristocracy belong to the tonsorial profession; a mulatto takes to razor and soap as naturally as a young duck to a pool of water."[15] But he acknowledged that barbering could bring a steady income. He and his half-brothers did well, as did other free men of color who chose the "tonsorial profession."

Cyprian Clamorgan wrote of his pride in belonging to the colored aristocracy. The achievements of its members were considerable, especially in the face of legislation intended to keep them firmly in "their place." They worked hard to make money, they struggled to educate their children, and they took a lively interest in politics. They might not be able to vote, but those who owned rental properties could lean heavily on their white tenants, and those in business could "suggest" to white tradesmen how *they* should vote.[16] The rise of the Republican Party in Missouri was

> the result of the unwearied and combined action of the wealthy free colored men of St. Louis, who know that the abolition of slavery . . . would remove a stigma from their race, and elevate them in the scale of society. . . . When slavery is abolished, where will be found the power of excluding the colored man from an equal participation in the fruits of human progressional and mutual development? What political party will . . . dare . . . erect a platform on which the black man cannot stand side by side with his white brother? . . . Wealth is power, and there is not a colored man in our midst who would not cheerfully part with his last dollar to effect the elevation of his race.[17]

Even as Clamorgan praised the "aristocrats" for their energy and their achievements, he revealed his personal prejudices and acknowledged that the "aristocracy" did not constitute a completely unified class. He knew there had been a time when "the [N]egroes of the town all spoke French," and when a name like Labbadie or Charleville or Clamorgan had meant something.[18] Now, the old families were being challenged by newcomers from the East, for the flood of settlers from Kentucky and Virginia had included not only white farmers and their slaves but also enterprising free people of color. These newcomers were eager to try their luck on the frontier and ready to endure the restrictive legislation passed in Missouri even before statehood because, for all its harshness, it was less onerous than the legal codes of their native states.[19] Frankly, Clamorgan preferred natives of St. Louis, especially those of French stock, to anyone else. Southerners in general he could tolerate, especially those who had the good sense to marry into the old "French" families. Northern migrants he generally disliked.

> As a general remark it may be said that the colored people who have come here, especially from the free States, bring with them more faults and vices than they find among those who have been reared upon the soil. We . . . assert it as a fact, that but few of the free colored men among us, who have been raised in those States where the laws make all men literally equal, possess the same amount of honesty, virtue and intelligence belonging to those who have always lived among those whom they have been taught to regard as belonging to a superior race.[20]

One wonders whether Clamorgan was aware of the contradictory nature of his position. He wanted to see an end to slavery, insisting that it would improve the lot of all people of color, free and slave. Yet he did not care to associate with those who had grown up in states where slavery had been abolished. Was it that he saw some peculiar quality in free people of French origin? Were they, in his thinking, able to make better use of their freedom than those of Anglo-African stock?

The old French families of St. Louis were certainly striving hard to keep their identity. Often they married among themselves. For example, there was nurse Mary Aubuchon, praised by Clamorgan for her "patience, gentleness and watchfulness." She had been born Marie Beaugenoux, the granddaughter of a farmer from Canada, and a free woman of color. In 1829, she married François Aubuchon, the son of a white settler from Ste. Geneviève, Antoine Aubuchon, and an ex-slave, Elizabeth Datchurst. (On Antoine's death, Elizabeth successfully sued for a share of his estate for herself and the ten children she had borne him).[21]

There was Pelagie Nash, whose "great ambition," according to Clamorgan, "is to have her daughter marry a man as nearly white as possible." She had been born Pelagie Papiche, the daughter of Joseph Papiche and Marie Gross Louis. Her first husband had been a steward on the river.[22] In 1857 she wed Antoine Morin, the son of two free people of color. Antoine's first wife had been Josephine Labadie, a scion of the influential mulatto Labadie and Charleville clans.[23]

Then there was barber Antoine Crevier, born in 1809, who married another Creole, Helène Tayon.[24] Crevier was hard-working and did well for himself, but his fortune could not compare with that of enterprising Creole Pelagie Foreman. This handsome ex-slave was, in Clamorgan's words, a "Delilah" who had "shorn the locks of more than one Samson." Like Apoline Clamorgan, she had capitalized on the one asset available to her in an environment where men far outnumbered women—her body. Her white lovers provided handsomely for her. In 1858, retired from her profession, she lived quietly on her farm just outside St. Louis, although she could occasionally be seen driving about the city in her carriage to visit her married daughter and her friends.[25]

Cattle dealer Antoine Joseph Labadie was, in Clamorgan's words, "nearly white, and looks more like a Mexican than anything else." He was in partnership with his brother, Pierre, who lived across the river in Illinois. The precise racial identity of the Labadie brothers baffled census-takers. They were wealthy and they were obviously kin to the white Labbadies, and related through them to the Chouteaus and the Gratiots. Antoine Labadie wed another Creole from a prominent family, Julie, the daughter of merchant Jonathan Baptiste Mathurin Irbour and a free woman of color, Susanne Jeanette.[26]

Like the Labadie brothers, Louis Charleville was a cattle dealer. Born in St. Louis, he was "a strict member of the Catholic church." When he suffered a reversal of fortune, the Catholic prelate of St. Louis, came to his aid. Charleville had more permanent plans to recoup his losses: he intended to marry one of his sons to Creole heiress Antoinette Rutgers, the daughter of Louis and Pelagie Rutgers, "but the young lady does not appear to smile upon his suit; the courtship is like the wooing of Mistress Ann Page by Master Slender—the old man doing most of the 'soft talk' himself."[27]

Antoinette Rutgers preferred a migrant from Tennessee to either of Charleville's two sons. James Thomas was the son of a justice of the Tennessee Supreme Court and a slave woman. His father did nothing for him. It was his mother who scraped together the money to buy his freedom. While still a slave, James Thomas embarked on a remarkable career. He traveled in the North as the valet of a wealthy white Southerner, built up an extensive barbering business in his native Nashville, and made several trips up and down the Mississippi. Once free, he went filibustering in Nicaragua with William Walker. In the mid-1850s he visited St. Louis and was offered work by Henry Clamorgan, Cyprian's brother, in his "Italian Salon," the finest barbershop in the city. He was working at Clamorgan's when "a gentleman occupying the front rank of the statesmen of the West" paid him a compliment "of which he may justly feel proud on account of the source . . . The gentleman remarked to Thomas, that all that prevented him from becoming one of the greatest men of the age was his color."[28]

In St. Louis, James Thomas met Antoinette Rutgers. Theirs was a protracted courtship. He did everything to forward his suit, even converting to Catholicism and joining the Church of St. Vincent de Paul, where Pelagie Rutgers and her daughter worshipped. Antoinette found the Tennessean much more to her liking than either of M. Charleville's sons, but Mme Rutgers was appalled. Although an ex-slave herself, she declared her daughter would marry a freeborn man, and not a former bondsman. As a result, Antoinette and James could not marry until the redoubtable old lady died.[29]

Other newcomers besides James Thomas chose to marry into old "French" families. Gabriel Helms, a former slave from South Carolina took a Creole wife from the old colored aristocracy of St. Louis. One of Henry Clamorgan's business partners, William Moses, wed Eliza Papiche, a free woman of color. Albert White of Ohio married Charlotte, a thrifty and enterprising St. Louis native who accompanied him to California during the Gold Rush, helped him make his fortune there, and returned with him to St. Louis, where the couple opened a fashionable barbershop.[30] Kentucky native Charles Lyons, the son of a free man of color and a Seneca woman, married a Creole. Nancy Lyons, a woman of white, African and American Indian ancestry, had been born not in St. Louis but in nearby Cahokia. "Living among the French inhabitants she, of course, learned their language, and was educated in the tenets of the Catholic church." She spoke French and enjoyed a reputation as a devout Catholic. She had also visited France as a nurse in the service of a prominent white family. In 1844 she married Kentuckian Charles Lyons, the son of a free man of color and a Seneca woman. Nancy Lyons died, aged 107, in 1922, the last of the colored aristocrats of St. Louis.[31]

Samuel Mordecai's wife, Mary Eagleson, was the younger sister of Henry Clamorgan's first wife, Harriet. Mary and Harriet were the daughters of a Creole couple, William Eagleson and Catherine Fillicit.[32] Samuel Mordecai, a barber and professional gambler, was the son of plasterer Harry Mordecai, one of the richest free men of color in Kentucky. He had the good taste (in Clamorgan's opinion) to admire all things French and consider making his home in France.

> He is a man of general information, and has traveled a great deal; he talks seriously of taking up his abode in Paris. . . . In France a colored man is more respected than in any other part of the world; some of the most talented men in that country can trace their origin to the shores of Africa, and their blood is no reproach to them. .·. . In Paris Mordecai would be received into the first circles, and has the ability and address to maintain his position in any society in which he may be thrown.[33]

As it turned out, Mordecai did not leave. He stayed in St. Louis through the Civil War and prospered as a barber. He and his wife raised young Louis Clamorgan, Mary's nephew—and Cyprian Clamorgan's—when Henry Clamorgan's wife died. Samuel and Mary Mordecai and their children remained prominent members of the colored aristocracy.[34]

Of business rival Robert Jerome Wilkinson, Clamorgan wrote: "I am sorry to say his character is not such a one as should be recommended to the young as a model of excellence." Wilkinson allegedly fled Cincinnati to escape the gun-toting relatives of a young woman he had seduced. He eventually married "a native of St. Louis, whose connections enabled him to obtain admission into society." In fact, he married a kinswoman of Clamorgan's. Julia Spears or St. Pierre was the daughter of George St. Pierre and Theresa Denys. Theresa's grandmother, Esther, had been one of Jacques Clamorgan's "Negro wives."[35]

Many of Clamorgan's "French" aristocrats of color reached out to befriend others of French and African ancestry. St. Louis native Rosalie Jacquet found a home with Antoine and Julie Labadie. She lived with them for two decades, although she was neither a kinswoman nor a servant. Mary Papin lived with Pelagie Nash and her family. Alexander Pellerin, a cook on a steamboat, moved into the widowed Mary Aubuchon's home with his nephew and nieces after Mary's daughter married and moved away. When her husband died, Mary Lyons opened a boarding house. Three rivermen, all mulattoes of French extraction, were boarding with her when the census-taker called in 1860. The Vanderlines, free people from Louisiana, lived with Henry Clamorgan. Louis Charleville stood surety for William Narcissé and Pierre Alfred Mauhaud when, as required by the Black Codes of Missouri, the two men applied for licenses to live and work in St. Louis.[36]

The network of marriages, friendships, and business relationships that linked the Creole families to one another was a complex one, but by 1858, when Cyprian Clamorgan wrote *The Colored Aristocracy of St. Louis*, he and the other "French" aristocrats were struggling with their sense of identity. In many ways they were clannish. They helped one another, they socialized together, they kept alive their knowledge of the French language, they gave their children French names, and, most importantly, they remained true to the Catholic faith. And yet, with all the external pressures on them, they could not afford to remain an isolated group, refusing to interact with non-Creoles. They knew the penalties for such exclusiveness would far outweigh the rewards. One might *feel* French, *speak* French, and *know* one was different in many subtle ways from a free black migrant from Virginia or Kentucky, who had an English name and was a Baptist or a Methodist, but the white citizens of St. Louis saw no differences, and neither did those who wrote and enforced Missouri's Black Codes. Whether Clamorgan cared to admit it or not, the hostility, or, at best, the indifference, of the white community forced the French aristocrats of color to embrace the Anglophone, Protestant new-comers. Racial proscription obliged the Labadies, the Charlevilles, the Aubuchons and the St. Pierres to join forces with the Wilkinsons, the McGees, and the Reynoldses. Not to show a united front was to court disaster. By the time of the Civil War French identity still mattered, but race mattered far more. In yet another way external pressures had undermined the distinctive French character of old St. Louis.

And what of Cyprian Clamorgan? He finished *The Colored Aristocracy of St. Louis* with a promise. "Our next attempt will be to give a true account of the *second class* of colored people. The number is large, and the developments we shall make will startle many of our white friends. The romantic incidents connected with this subject surpass the wildest dreams of fiction."[37] The promise was not fulfilled. With the Civil War over, Clamorgan and his family "passed" into the majority society.[38] They evoked the memory of the venerable "Jacques Clamorgan," or "Don Yago Clamorgan," and launched a series of lawsuits against various individuals, the State of Missouri, and eventually against the United States government, to secure compensation for land which had been taken away at the time of the Louisiana Purchase.[39] They made much of their Creole heritage at a time when the citizens of St. Louis, Creole and non-Creole, were romanticizing their city's glorious past. When racial violence intensified in the aftermath of Reconstruction, the Clamorgans avoided mentioning *all* the details of their family background. Like his grandfather before him, Cyprian Clamorgan traveled the length of the Mississippi time and again over the years. When he wrote *The Colored Aristocracy* he already had a wife and daughter in New Iberia, Louisiana.[40] During the Civil War he moved to New Orleans and was accused by his enemies back home of disloyalty to the Union cause. Eventually he returned to his native city. In 1900, a good Catholic to the last, he was admitted to the Alexian Brothers' Hospital in St. Louis. The Brothers described him as a white man of French and Spanish descent.[41] He died soon after.

By 1911, less than a decade after St. Louis had celebrated the centenary of the Louisiana Purchase, the rest of the Clamorgan family became embroiled in a scandal that rocked the city and exposed the complex nature of Creole society. Passing as white, two great-nieces of Cyprian Clamorgan married into white families. It transpired that the husband of one of the young women was also "passing." The child born to the couple was unmistakably of African ancestry - a living reminder, to those who had chosen to ignore it, that there had been many men and women of color among the French Creoles of St. Louis.[42] If St. Louis had had its Gratiots, its Chouteaus, and its Laclèdes, it had also had its Creviers and Charlevilles, its Papins and its Clamorgans. If it had had its white Creole grandees, it had also had its aristocrats of color.

NOTES

1. John F. Darby, *Personal Recollections of Many Prominent People Whom I Have Known, and of Events—Especially of Those Relating to the History of St. Louis—*

During the First Half of the Present Century (St. Louis, 1880), 5, quoted in Glen E. Holt, "St. Louis's Transition Decade, 1819–1830," *Missouri Historical Review* 76 (July 1982): 380.

2. Holt, "St. Louis' Transition Decade," 379–80.

3. Elihu H. Shepard, *The Early History of St. Louis and Missouri from Its First Exploration by White Men in 1673 to 1843* (St. Louis, 1870), 95, quoted in Holt, "Transition Decade," 380.

4. Charles Van Ravenswaay, *St. Louis: An Informal History of the City and Its People, 1764–1865* (Urbana: University of Illinois Press for the Missouri Historical Society, 1991), 63, 264; W.D. Skillman, *The Western Metropolis of St. Louis in 1846* (St. Louis: The Author, 1846), 118; William Hyde and Howard L. Conrad, *Encyclopedia of the History of St. Louis* (New York, Louisville and St. Louis: Southern History Company, 1899), 4:2082.

5. Cyprian Clamorgan, *The Colored Aristocracy of St. Louis* (St. Louis, 1858), 3–4.

6. Ibid., 4.

7. Ibid.

8. On the *Code Noir* and relationships between French and Spanish settlers and black and mulatto women, see Lorenzo J. Greene, Gary R. Kremer and Antonio F. Holland, *Missouri's Black Heritage*, rev. ed. (Columbia: University of Missouri Press, 1993), 13–14; and Ira Berlin, *Slaves Without Masters: The Free Negro in the Antebellum South* (New York: The New Press, 1974), 108–11.

9. Little is known about Jacques Clamorgan's ancestry or origins. He has been variously described as Welsh, Spanish, Scottish, and French. There are indications that he might have been a mulatto, and that that accounted for the attitude of the white creoles towards him. For a brief account of his remarkable career, see A. P. Nasatir, "Jacques Clamorgan: Colonial Promoter of the Northern Border of New Spain," *New Mexico Historical Review* 17 (April 1942): 101–12.

10. Oscar W. Collet, *Index to St. Louis Cathedral and Carondelet Church Baptisms* (St. Louis, 1918), 53. Details of Jacques Clamorgan's will and his manumission of his children are to be found in three cases heard by the Missouri Supreme Court, *Charles Collins v. Adm'r of Pauline Clamorgan*, 5 Mo 161; *Clamorgan, et al. v. Lane*, 9 Mo 263; and *Landes, et al. v. Perkins*, 12 Mo 151.

11. *St. Louis City Directory . . . 1821*; Collet, *Index . . . Baptisms*, 53; Oscar W. Collet, *Index to St. Louis Cathedral and Carondelet Church Marriages* (St. Louis, 1918), 14, 90.

12. Clamorgan, *The Colored Aristocracy*, 7.

13. I am grateful to Mr. Anton J. Pregaldin of St. Louis for tracking down Cyprian Clamorgan's full name.

14. Oscar W. Collet, *Index to St. Louis Cathedral and Carondelet Church Burials* (St. Louis, 1918), 21, 86; Collet, *Index . . . Baptisms*, 53, 93, 146. On Theodore Papin's family connections see Collet, *Index . . . Marriages*, 64. For the birthdates of Apoline Clamorgan's children and the appointment of Charles Collins as their guardian see *Clamorgan, et al. v. Landes*, 9 Mo 263, and *Clamorgan v. O'Fallon & Lindell*, 10 Mo 77.

15. Clamorgan, *The Colored Aristocracy*, 10.

16. Ibid., 4–5.

17. Clamorgan, *The Colored Aristocracy*, 5; Clamorgan's "aristocrats of color," unlike their counterparts in New Orleans and Charleston, South Carolina, did not own slaves.

18. Darby, *Personal Recollections*, 5, quoted in Holt, "Transition Decade," 5.

19. On the deteriorating legal status of free people of color in Missouri in general, and in St. Louis in particular, see Greene, et al., *Missouri's Black Heritage*, especially 21, 64–65; Maximilian Reichard, "Black and White on the Urban Frontier: The St. Louis Community in Transition, 1800–1830," *Bulletin of the Missouri Historical Society* 33 (October 1976): 4, 11–12, 15; Donnie D. Bellamy, "Free Blacks in Antebellum Missouri, 1820-1860," *Missouri Historical Review* 67 (January 1973): especially 199, 204–5, 222–23.

20. Clamorgan, *The Colored Aristocracy*, 18.

21. Ibid., 8. Collet, *Marriages*, 2; Collet, *Burials*, 4; Carl J. Ekberg, *Colonial Ste. Geneviève: An Adventure on the Mississippi Frontier* (Gerald, Mo.: The Patrice Press, 1985), 226–27.

22. Clamorgan, *The Colored Aristocracy*, 7. Collet, *Marriages*, 61.

23. Collet, *Baptisms*, 155. St. Louis Genealogical Society, *Index of St. Louis Marriages* (St. Louis Genealogical Society, n.d.), vol. 1.

24. Clamorgan, *The Colored Aristocracy*, 14. Collet, *Marriages*, 16. St. Louis Genealogical Society, *Index of St. Louis Baptisms* (St. Louis Genealogical Society, n.d.).

25. Clamorgan, *The Colored Aristocracy*, 7.

26. Ibid., 13; U.S. Census (1850), St. Louis, Ward 2, 213, and Ward 3, 319; (1860), St. Louis, Ward 4, 46, and St. Clair County, Illinois, 327; *St. Louis City Directories*, 1838–42, 1845, 1847–48, 1851–52, 1854, 1859–60; Collet, *Marriages*, 42, 45; Collet, *Baptisms*, 138; William E. Foley and C. David Rice, *The First Chouteaus: River Barons of Early St. Louis* (Urbana and Chicago: University of Illinois Press, 1983), 211–12.

27. Clamorgan, *The Colored Aristocracy*, 16–17; Collet, *Baptisms*, 44; Collet, *Marriages*, 17; *St. Louis City Directories*, 1836–37, 1842, 1848, 1851, 1852, 1854, 1857, 1859–60. In some directories he is listed as white; in others as "colored." U.S. Census (1830), St. Louis, 359 (where he is listed as white) and (1860), St. Louis, Ward 4, 46 (where he is mulatto). By 1870 he had moved his family out of the city of St. Louis to Central Township and had purchased a farm there. Away from the city where they had been born, and where their ancestry was known, the Charlevilles became "white." U.S. Census (1870), Central Township, St. Louis County, Mo., 190.

28. Clamorgan, *The Colored Aristocracy*, 19; Loren Schweninger, ed., *From Tennessee Slave to St. Louis Entrepreneur: The Autobiography of James Thomas* (Columbia: University of Missouri Press, 1984), introduction.

29. Schweninger, *From Tennessee Slave*, introduction; St. Louis Genealogical Society, *St. Louis and St. Louis County, Missouri Probate Records* (St. Louis Genealogical Society, 1989), 3:48; St. Louis Genealogical Society, *Index of Marriages*, vol. 2. An article on the wealthy free people of color in St. Louis noted that James Thomas was married to the "heiress to the Rutger [sic] property, her parents being of the French creole stock." *New York Daily Tribune*, 6 July 1871.

30. Clamorgan, *The Colored Aristocracy*, 12, 17; *St. Louis City Directories*, 1836–42, 1845, 1847, 1851, 1859–60, 1870; U.S. Census (1850), St. Louis, Ward 4, 55; (1860), St. Louis, Ward 4, 42, 201; Church of Jesus Christ of Latter-Day Saints, *International Genealogical Index*.

31. Clamorgan, *The Colored Aristocracy*, 11. St. Louis Necrology Scrapbooks, Missouri Historical Society; *Opinion in the Case of Charles Lyons, A Free Negro, Determined in the St. Louis Circuit Court, November Term, 1846* (St. Louis, 1846).

32. St. Louis Marriages, 2:401, and 3:30, St. Louis Archives; Collet, *Baptisms*, 86.

33. Clamorgan, *The Colored Aristocracy*, 10; For information on Harry Mordecai see U.S. Census (1850), District 1, Franklin County, Kentucky, 39.

34. Tiffany Papers, Box 61, Missouri Historical Society; William B. Gatewood, *Aristocrats of Color: The Black Elite, 1880–1920* (Bloomington and Indianapolis: Indiana University Press, 1990), 16, 117; U.S. Census (1860), St. Louis, Ward 4, 74; (1870), Ward 4, 30; *St. Louis City Directories*, 1854, 1857, 1859-60, 1872, 1881.

35. Esther's daughter, Celée, may or may not have been Jacques Clamorgan's child. She had five children. Her eldest was born while she was still a slave. His father, a visiting English nobleman, paid Jacques Clamorgan to set the child free. Only later did Celée secure her freedom. Van Ravenswaay, *St. Louis: An Informal History*,

70; Collet, *Baptisms*, 245; St. Louis Genealogical Society, *Index of Marriages*, vol. 1; U.S. Census (1860), St. Louis, Ward 4, 47; "Documents relating to the Esther Claim," Hamilton R. Gamble Papers, and Tiffany Papers, Box 63, Missouri Historical Society.

36. U.S. Census, St. Louis, Mo., 1850 and 1860; Tiffany Papers, Box 61, folders 13 and 14, Missouri Historical Society.

37. Clamorgan, *The Colored Aristocracy*, 21.

38. See U.S. Census (1870), St. Louis, Ward 3, subdivision 7, 209 (Julia Clamorgan); (1880), St. Louis, 36:17 (Henry Clamorgan); (1900), St. Louis, 91:8 (Amanda Clamorgan); (1910), St. Louis, enumeration district 459, 98 (Louis Clamorgan or Morgan).

39. See *Henry Clamorgan, et al., Defendants in Error, v. Isaac T. Greene, Plaintiff in Error*, 32 Mo 285; *Clamorgan v. The Baden and St. Louis Railway Company*, 72 Mo 139; *Clamorgan et al., Plaintiffs in Error, v. Hornsby, et al.*, 94 Mo 83; *United States v. Clamorgan*, U.S. Reports 101, 822; *Claim of Heirs of Jacques Clamorgan* (Congressional Hearing, 1910, Y4. P93/5: C52/2).

40. Cyprian Clamorgan's daughter, Mary Bell Bellanger Morgan, settled in Massachusetts in the 1880s. See *Marriages*, 397:167; Massachusetts State Archives, Boston, and *New Bedford City Directory*, 1911.

41. U.S. Census (1900), St. Louis, vol. 91, enumeration district 436, 1; Patient Register Book (1900), Alexian Brothers' Hospital, St. Louis. I am grateful to Ms. Donna Carl Dahl, the archivist of the Alexian Brothers' Order, for supplying the information on Cyprian Clamorgan's admission to the hospital.

42. On the resulting scandal, see *St. Louis Republic*, 9, 10, 18 June and 17 August 1911; *Crisis*, August 1911, 144.

CHAPTER SEVENTEEN

The Historical Atlas of Quebec

Serge Courville

Cette note d'information donne un aperçu du Projet d'Atlas historique du Québec, réalisé par le Centre interuniversitaire d'Études québécoises. A partir d'un exemple concret, consacré à la croissance démographique de la vallée du Saint-Laurent au XIXᵉ siècle, elle veut montrer l'intérêt d'introduire une approche spatiale en histoire, comme moyen d'expliciter les processus sociaux du passé.

As an old colonial society, Quebec is an excellent subject for an historical atlas. Several atlases have already been published, with their focus being on the major events and structures in the history of the region. Few, however, have dealt with people's territoriality seen in historical depth and in terms of evolutionary processes. To accomplish that, new perspectives are essential if one is to raise more clearly the issue of socio-cultural changes over time. Such an atlas would need to integrate and harmonize both a range of knowledge and the latest *problématiques*. Well under way, and nearing publication, is a project entitled *The Historical Atlas of Quebec*, which sets out to produce the required combination of text and images. The *Atlas* project is managed by a research center known as the Centre interuniversitaire d'études québécoises[1], which is jointly based at the Université Laval and at the Université du Québec à Trois-Rivières. The research is carried out in collaboration with the extended scientific community.

THE PROJECT

The recent pattern of research on Quebec has furthered the grouping of researchers oriented towards an integrated approach to their subject. The *Atlas* project follows the same direction. It aims to study Quebec society from the French Regime to the present day, drawing upon collaborators from several disciplines, all interested in the analysis of socio-cultural changes and spatio-temporal dynamics. The goal is to make apparent the processes and consistencies which have been significant—both in the long-run and in their various specific contexts—to the making of the present society. As social facts are never simple, they are addressed from various angles and in a relational perspective which enhances the principle of the fundamental unity of human sciences.

Produced entirely by computer,[2] the *Atlas* benefits from similar recent experiences elsewhere in Canada, in Europe, and in the United States. Like most of the other works, the Quebec atlas offers an assessment *and* a perspective. Yet it cannot be described as a synthesis presented in one or two volumes. Rather, it comes in the shape of a collection of thematic books, each devoted to a particular aspect of the history of Quebec and presented in a form combining the qualities of both a book and an atlas.

The decision to resort to two different but complementary forms of presentation follows from the very nature of the project, which is to give an account of complex phenomena. To be adequately stated, and understood, the phenomena need to be presented in their full temporal, spatial, social, and cultural dimensions. And as the perspective is transhistorical, the double support is required: the picture making up for the shortcomings of the writing and vice-versa.

More precisely, each of the books of *The Historical Atlas of Quebec* consists of two parts:
- a *written part* which reads like a standard book, but with more abundant illustrations,
- and a *graphic part*, which takes the form of integrated color plates, set at the end of each chapter, where the main part of the message is presented in the form of texts, maps, tables, charts, and old illustrations. Complete by itself, this section will eventually fill out a more didactic edition, intended for pre-university teachers and for the general public. Steps are also being taken to place databanks and maps on CD-ROM.

Applied to the interpretation of Quebec history, the combination of text and illustrations should offer a more complete as well as a more "relational" vision of the past. The approach aims to make apparent the ideas, the actors, the representations, and the actions, regulations or decisions of a period. It should also help demonstrate that geographical space is an essential category in the understanding of human societies, something which has impact on the *rapports* and processes which set the pace and pattern for so many relationships. As such, the *Atlas* offers to all disciplines a new mode of exploration, understanding and interpretation of the past, thereby contributing to our collective efforts of analysis and synthesis.

AN EXAMPLE

The example presented here forms the first chapter of volume 3 of the collection. It deals with population growth in the St. Lawrence valley in the nineteenth century.

The chapter, which seeks to illustrate the relationship between population, territory and habitat, is divided in two parts. The first, seen in figure 1, is a book-like presentation of the population increase from 1831 to 1871, depicted as a process and as a spatial expression.

FIGURE 1

Croissance démographique du XIXᵉ siècle

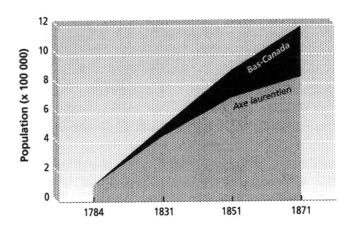

Along with the text describing the demographic growth, we find tables, charts, maps, and old paintings illustrating the many dimensions of the problem, and the ways chosen by the authors to approach it. The mapping of the demographic data from the nineteenth-century censuses reveal that while there was a major increase of population in the St. Lawrence valley during the period, the increase did not necessarily bring about excessive pressures on the resources. Various mechanisms existed—detailed in the text—which allowed for a local relief of the population pressures.

Immediately following the written part of the chapter is the visual presentation of the problem. A series of illustrated plates (see figure 2), similar to those found in recent historical atlases, summarize the substance of the observations made in the written part. These plates are built around an integrated and a consistent ensemble of messages, leading readers to a better understanding of the processes by which the Quebec society not only territorialized its space, but also solved its demographic difficulties.

The plate reproduced in figure 2 presents a extended view of the demographic growth of the nineteenth century. From approximately 335,000 inhabitants in 1815, the population rose to over one million by the end of the period, three quarters of which still lived in the St. Lawrence valley.

As shown in the first section of the plate, the growth was not steady. It varied from census to census, according to the different geographical sectors of the axis (figure 3). As it grew, the population diversified. Thousands of immigrants arrived, establishing themselves in the towns and countryside of Lower Canada (figure 4).

Just as important as the scale of the population increase was the migration of the population in space, following movements which prolonged and emphasized those of the French Regime. The first movement went from east to west and from the Quebec City area to the eastern portions of the territory. The second went from the shores of the river towards the interior, even towards the exterior limits of the axis, beyond which it finally extended in several places (see figure 5). It was the centrifugal movement which progressively relieved the old riverside localities of their demographic surplus. This was well demonstrated in old paintings of Quebec landscapes, where the full lands of the north-east were contrasted with the new countries to the south-west (figure 6).

The first important message of the plate is that there was a *strong increase in the population* during the 19th century in the St. Lawrence Valley. To that fundamental message are added two others: that of *a growing social diversification* and of *movements in space, or territory.*

The second plate (figure 7), an extension of the first, raises the question of demographic densities. Indeed, with such an increase in population, much higher demographic pressures could have been expected than those observed on the basis of census data, when these are mapped by locality. Yet what happened is exactly the opposite: not only do the pressures remain low, but they actually decrease over the century. How can we explain that phenomenon? First, by the migrations towards the interior lands which, as already seen, decreased the demographic pressure in the riverside localities. Second, by another, much subtler movement that drove a portion of the local population toward the towns and villages, which were in full growth at the time.

The balance of the two movements (centrifugal and centripetal) left net densities that were not only low, but that varied in time and space according to the advance of the pioneer settlements. The result was differentiated human contexts, whose human load seemed much less important than was believed before this study was undertaken for the *Historical Atlas of Quebec.*

The third plate (figure 8) is an exploration of the factors accounting for the demographic growth and the impact which that growth had on the space in Quebec, in terms of the structure and size of households.

The main component of the plate is the population growth percentage at the level of the Laurentian axis. Here, two lateral inset maps attempt to explain the changes on the basis of a study devoted to two specific groups: people younger than 14 or 15, and the adult population.

A significant finding of this work lay in discovering a crucial difference between the first half of the nineteenth century and the second. From 1830 to 1850, population growth is relatively high. Subsequently, it becomes much lower and even negative in some places; for instance, in the Montreal region. The relative decrease touches all age groups, whose relative numbers decrease during the second half of the century.

All these variations had impacts on the size and structure of households, which fluctuated over the century. The average number of persons per household attests to this. The number is almost always higher in pioneer communities than in the old riverside parishes.

Another finding relates to the distribution of widowers and bachelors, a distribution which varies according to gender. It shows that single men were attracted to pioneering frontiers and to zones of river transportation. Widowed or unmarried women, on the other hand, were drawn to towns and villages.

The above, in summary form, presents the basic messages of the first chapter of volume 3 of the *Historical Atlas of Quebec*. By reconstituting movements in space, the text and illustrations attempt to go deep into the subject of Laurentian population changes. It is by way of the movements in space (migrations) that the inevitable tensions caused by the demographic growth of the nineteenth century were relieved. It was also through these movements that the St. Lawrence valley was territorialized and transformed into a cultural area.

Such is the meaning given to the *Historical Atlas of Quebec*. More than a mere reconstitution of former geographies, this project seeks connections essential to the delivery of a more unified vision of the past. In addition to assessing and synthesizing the best research conducted in the field, it aims to further the research, turning space into an historical category available not only to geographers and historians, but to all disciplines interested by historical problems. In doing so, it remains conscious of its limits, considering itself more like the testimony of a whole generation of researchers marked by their time and ways of knowledge, than like a "true and authentic picture" of the Quebec of days gone by.

NOTES

1. The research center was created in 1993. It encompasses the *Laboratoire de géographie historique* de l'Université Laval and the *Centre d'études québécoises* (CÉDEQ) of the Université du Québec à Trois-Rivières, and groups more than twenty researchers from various disciplines (geography, history, litterature, philosophy, sociology, ethnology, religious sciences . . .). The Atlas project is under the responsability of the two directers, the historian Normand Séguin and myself. Financial support is granted by the Fonds FCAR and the two founding universities.

2. We use both IBM and Macintosh environments in our work. The final presentation, however, is done with Macintosh.

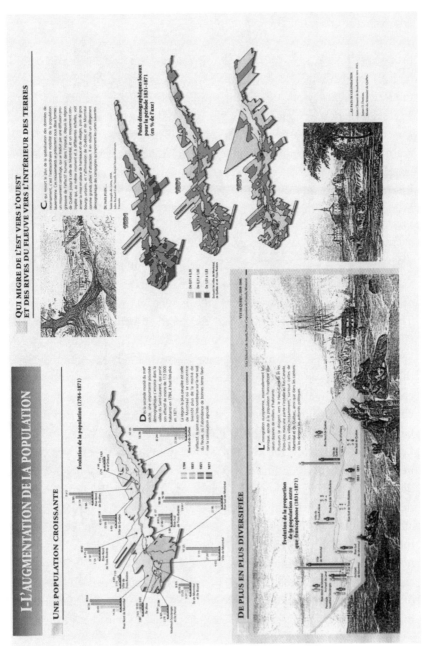

FIGURE 2

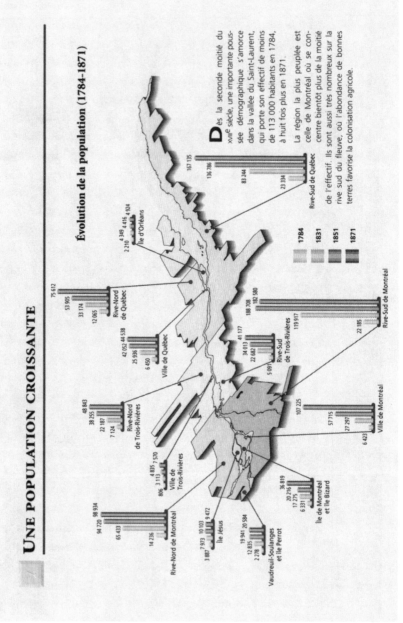

UNE POPULATION CROISSANTE

Évolution de la population (1784-1871)

Dès la seconde moitié du XVIIIe siècle, une importante poussée démographique s'amorce dans la vallée du Saint-Laurent, qui porte son effectif de moins de 113 000 habitants en 1784, à huit fois plus en 1871.

La région la plus peuplée est celle de Montréal où se concentre bientôt plus de la moitié de l'effectif. Ils sont aussi très nombreux sur la rive sud du fleuve, où l'abondance de bonnes terres favorise la colonisation agricole.

FIGURE 3

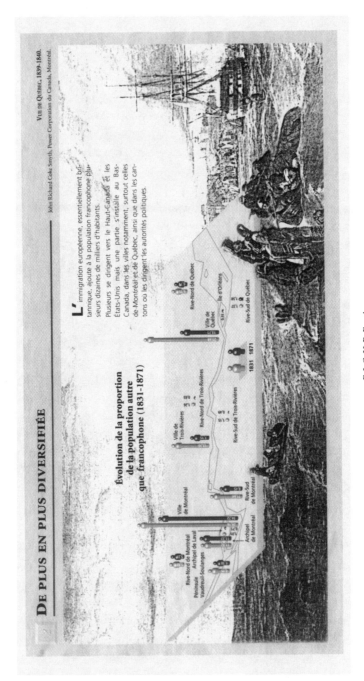

DE PLUS EN PLUS DIVERSIFIÉE

VUE DE QUÉBEC, 1839-1840.
John Richard Coke Smyth, Power Corporation du Canada, Montréal.

L'immigration européenne, essentiellement britannique, ajoute à la population francophone plusieurs dizaines de milliers d'habitants.
Plusieurs se dirigent vers le Haut-Canada et les États-Unis mais une partie s'installe au Bas-Canada, dans les villes notamment, surtout celles de Montréal et de Québec, ainsi que dans les cantons ou ils dirigent les autorités politiques.

Évolution de la proportion
de la population autre
que francophone (1831-1871)

FIGURE 4

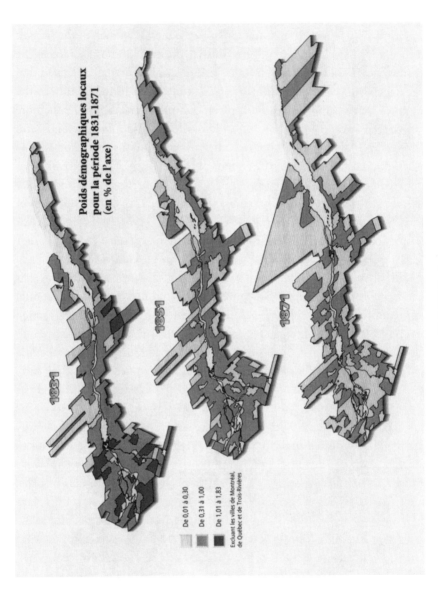

Poids démographiques locaux
pour la période 1831-1871
(en % de l'axe)

1831

1851

1871

De 0,01 à 0,30

De 0,31 à 1,00

De 1,01 à 1,83

Excluant les villes de Montréal,
de Québec et de Trois-Rivières

FIGURE 5

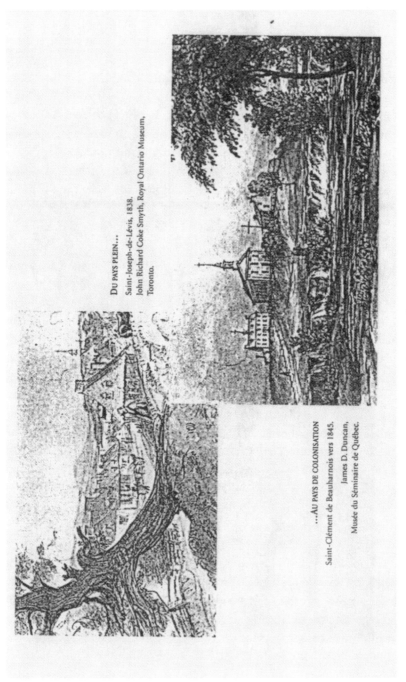

Du pays plein...

Saint-Joseph-de-Lévis, 1838.
John Richard Coke Smyth, Royal Ontario Museum,
Toronto.

...Au pays de colonisation

Saint-Clément de Beauharnois vers 1845.
James D. Duncan,
Musée du Séminaire de Québec.

FIGURE 6

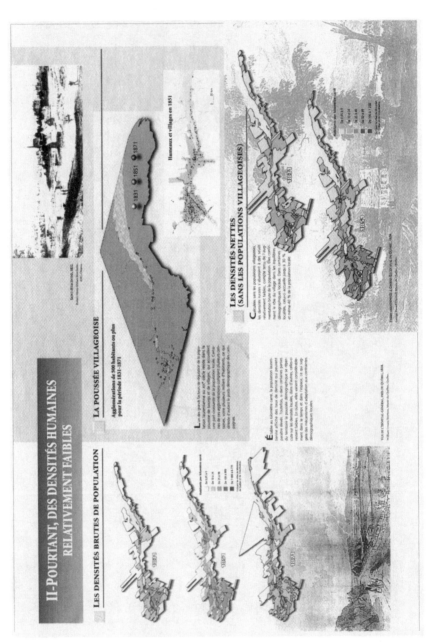

FIGURE 7

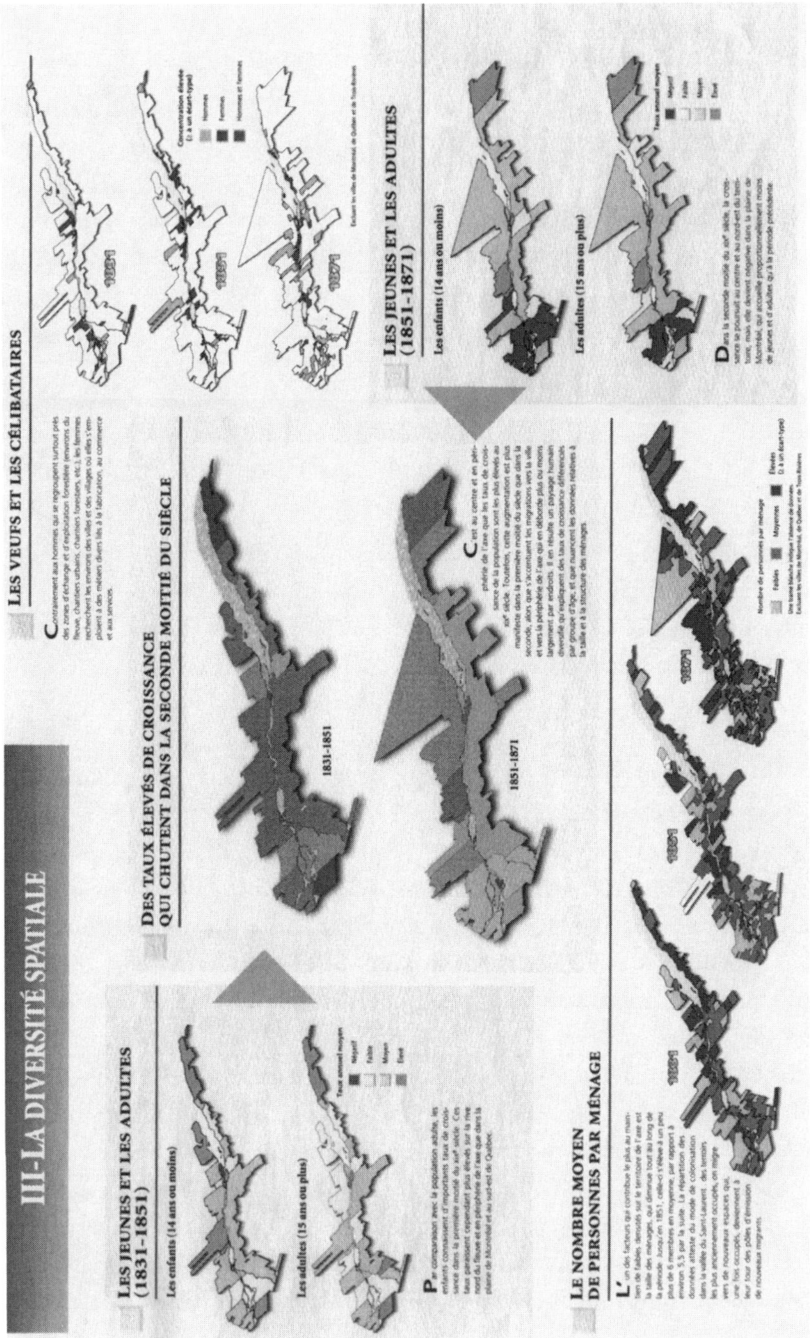
III-LA DIVERSITÉ SPATIALE
LES JEUNES ET LES ADULTES (1831-1851)
Les enfants (14 ans ou moins)
Les adultes (15 ans ou plus)
DES TAUX ÉLEVÉS DE CROISSANCE QUI CHUTENT DANS LA SECONDE MOITIÉ DU SIÈCLE
1831-1851
1851-1871
LES VEUFS ET LES CÉLIBATAIRES
LE NOMBRE MOYEN DE PERSONNES PAR MÉNAGE
LES JEUNES ET LES ADULTES (1851-1871)
Les enfants (14 ans ou moins)
Les adultes (15 ans ou plus)

FIGURE 8